THE WELSH
IN THE
UNITED STATES

by

ELWYN T. ASHTON

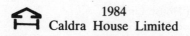

1984
Caldra House Limited

First published in Great Britain 1984.
Copyright © Elwyn T. Ashton.

Printed by Caldra House Limited,
23 Coleridge Street, Hove, Sussex.

DON   SHA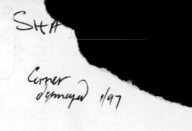

Corner
damaged 1/97

This book is to be returned on or before
the last date stamped below.

SUTTON LEISURE SERVICES

To Professor Edward G. Hartmann, Ph.D. of Suffolk University, Boston, Massachusetts, whose scholarly work first inspired me, then led me to paths of research I might not have discovered from this side of the Atlantic.

The Welsh in the United States

TABLE OF CONTENTS

Chapter 1

INTRODUCTION
People and places

THIS is a book not only for those who are Welsh with an interest in the United States, and Americans of Welsh extraction, but for all those in Britain and America who care about our relationships with each other. Similar, and very interesting, books have already been written about the Scots and the Irish in the States, not to mention the many other ethnic groups. Not so much has been written about the Welsh, probably because they were fewer in numbers, say, than the Irish or the Germans. Yet there was very helpful material in Professor David Williams' *Wales and America* (1941). Alan Conway's *The Welsh in America* is a most readable account of letters back home by Welsh immigrants in the States, mainly in the nineteenth century. Professor Hartmann's *Americans from Wales* was valuable, especially on the part played in Welsh-American life by the religious denominations, not only in catering to spiritual needs, but in their contribution to the social life of the Welsh immigrants.

Much information can be obtained from Welsh-American Societies (I would like here to express my gratitude for his help to Mr. Daniel E. Williams, Secretary of the Philadelphia Welsh Society) and also, of course, from travel in the United States, which for me was as useful as it was enjoyable. Friendly encounters with Welsh-Americans helped a lot, especially in the opportunities for asking questions, making comparisons, and guidance on where to proceed next. Surprises sometimes occurred, such as finding a Swansea district in Denver, Colorado, and a Cardiff in Southern California. Since then, Americans who have come over for the National Eisteddfod have proved good sources of information.

George R. Stewart has said, "Names had grown out of the life,

7

and the life-blood of all those who have gone before." (George S. Stewart, *American Place-names,* 1945.) In Southern California, for instance, one is impressed by the number of Spanish place-names such as Santa Barbara and San Luis Obispo, from the days when the Catholics built their lovely Missions. In Louisiana one notes the number of French names. In New England and the East Coast generally, occasional Welsh names appear from early days, among the Indian, English, Scottish, and later, Irish. As exploration, followed by settlement, moved westwards, the Welsh, like others, started to move out from the early settlements, such as eastern Pennsylvania. Thus Meriwether Lewis, one of the leaders of the famous Lewis-Clark Expedition across America to the Pacific, came from a Welsh family settled in Tennessee for generations.

A few warnings are necessary here, before going on to survey the scatter of Welsh names throughout the United States. One difficulty for the researcher is that in statistical tables the Welsh were often 'lumped in' with the English. Even today, for instance, R. Morris, in his otherwise excellent *Encyclopedia of American History,* does not specify Welsh immigrant numbers separately. In his Table of National or Linguistic Stock in the United States in 1790, he gives Scots and Irish figures separately, but includes Welsh under 'English'. This may well be because no distinction was made between the two in available early figures. Yet Mr Jock Whitney, former U.S. Ambassador to the United Kingdom, stated that there were over six million persons of Welsh descent in the United States; the population of Wales itself today is about two and a half million, with perhaps another million in London and the rest of England. Note that, though many Welsh place-names survived, many earlier Welsh place-names disappeared from the map, owing to subsequent developments. Although this sometimes happened in the United States, the best examples come from further North. In *The Discovery of North America* (Cumming, Skelton and Quinn, 1971), there is reproduced a map of Newfoundland by John Mason. It appeared first in William Vaughan's *Cambrensium Caroleia* (1625). At top left of that map can be seen the names, Glamorgan and Cardiff, and slightly to the east Carmarthen, Pembroke, Cardigan and Brecon. The whole area, on the map, was called Cambriola. The map of Newfoundland today shows no sign of these names. Another map, in the same excellent book, is of the Hudson Bay area (map 276). On it are New South Wales and New North Wales, long since disappeared from the map.

Another difficulty arises from this latter map. James Bay was on the map then, and is still on the map. But is James Bay named after the Captain James who sailed round that coast, or after King James I, who was on the throne during the same period (early 17th century)? This difficulty arises at several points in this study. Sometimes it is quite clear which is meant — the royal or the non-royal. Lewiston, Idaho, for instance, is clearly named after Lewis of the famous expedition; there was no English king called Louis or Lewis. A Lewisville in Louisiana might derive from a Louisville of French days.

Another difficulty arises from this name, Lewis, and other names such as Morgan, and even Jones. To a Welshman they all sound thoroughly Welsh, as Evans, Williams and so on. A study of Welsh Nonconformist ministers (or Welsh International Rugby teams) would abound with such names. Yet there are Morgans in Ireland, Lewises in Scotland (and many such as Morris are often Jewish). John Paul Jones, renowned in American naval history, as the scourge of the British, was born in Scotland; Cadwalader Colden, with the very Welsh Christian name, was a famous New York Scotsman. As with James, so with Williams. Some Williamstowns in the United States may have been named after some historic Williams, but just as many, particularly in 'the Colonies', may have been named after William III. I have tried to leave out names where there might be too much ambiguity, unless the context makes it clear. The numerous Jonesboros and Evansvilles seem more certain, but even here John Paul Jones should serve as a warning.

One of the fascinating things about studying American place-names is their great variety, including ethnic variations. George R. Stewart illustrates this neatly, "Within the limits of a single Pennsylvania county bearing the English name 'Lancaster', are townships named Caernarvon and Brecknock for the Welsh, Manheim and Lititz for the Germans, Colerain and Donegal for the Irish and New Holland for some wandering home-sick Dutchman."

Welsh place-names in the United States, as well as being named after Welsh home-towns and villages, were often named after prominent Welsh families, as in several Jonestowns. This is often pointed out in biographical studies, such as those in the very useful Dictionary of American Biography. Many Welsh surnames derive from English Christian names, due to obvious social class factors. "Some thirty-nine surnames," states Professor Hartmann, "include about 95% of the Welsh, wherever they are found." (p.58.) He puts them in four categories, the first being that already mentioned, Welsh surnames from English Christian names. His second category includes names deriving from 'Ap' meaning 'son of', like the Scottish 'Mac'. So, Ap Owen becomes Bowen, with the 'p' hardened to 'b'; other Welsh names in this class are Bevan and Bryce. In Pritchard, Pugh, Powell, Price and Probert, the 'p' remains as first letter. An important third category would be those

9

names derived from pure Celtic sources — Lloyd, Morgan, Gwynn, Vaughan, Meredith and Llewellyn. A fourth category would be surnames from English sources which have long become well known in some parts of Wales, generally either north or south, but not both. e.g. Easton or Cutts.

I do not know whether any Welsh place-names in the United States derive from a nick-name. If not, there ought to be one or two, to conform to a national pastime. Professor Hartmann declares that the Welsh took their skill in nicknames to America with them. "Virtually every Welsh colony," he said, "had its John Jones the Shop, John Jones the Deacon, John Jones Peg-leg and the like." He gives the amusing case of Powell township in South Dakota, which had three Hugh Roberts. They were called Hugh Roberts Religious, Hugh Roberts Ungodly and Hugh Roberts In-between (E. G. Hartmann, *Americans from Wales*, 1967).

Many books have been written about names, names of places, Christian names, nicknames, surnames. The Pelican Book of Surnames has one fascinating entry (among many). Under the heading 'Meyrick', it claims this to be a Welsh surname, and adds moreover that this is the name from which 'America' is derived. The name was apparently common in Wales and in London at the time of the Tudors. It was often preceded, as a surname, it is said, by 'Ap', 'son of' in English. When Cabot returned to Bristol after his second trans-Atlantic voyage (1498), the king's pension was handed to him by a collector of taxes named Richard Ameryk (corrupted from Ap Meryk); he had probably been the heaviest investor in Cabot's voyage. The Pelican excerpt on 'Meyrick' concludes, "His title to be the eponym of the continent is surely stronger than the frivolous claim of the Italian Amerigo Vespucci".

It may be said that this book would have been easier to write, and probably to read, if there had been a greater variety of Welsh surnames. Thus, 'John Evans' can refer to the immature young man who was sent by Penn to help govern his new State, to the much more admirable John Evans who explored the Missouri Valley, and prepared the map to help Lewis and Clark in their expedition, or to the John Evans, last century, who was Governor of Colorado.

The limited number of Welsh surnames makes it more difficult to trace Welsh-Americans back to their ancestors, as can be illustrated by the Lewis family. Thus, Ellis Lewis (1798-1871), Pennsylvanian judge and attorney-general, was descended from another Ellis Lewis, a successful Welsh immigrant who became a magnate in Philadelphia insurance companies and a trustee of Pennsylvania University. Also descended from the latter Ellis Lewis was Edmund Darch Lewis (1835-1910), a landscape-painter

10

and rich art collector, born in Philadelphia where his family had lived since 1708. In the South, however, there were the other Lewises, of whom Meriwether Lewis was a member, descended originally from Robert Lewis of Brecon, mid-Wales, who settled in Gloucester County, Virginia, in 1635. Another of his descendants was Dixon Hall Lewis of Alabama, congressman, then Senator. Other Lewises were in descent from Evan Lewis who came from Pembroke, West Wales. In other words, because Lewis families lived in different parts of Wales originally, they settled in different parts of the United States. This became even more complicated as members of various Lewis families moved west as 'the Frontier' moved West.

Such 'geographical' difficulties were not helped by the fact that spellings of Welsh names varied anyway. Perhaps the best example is 'Cadwallader' used as a Christian name or a surname; in either case it could be spelt with one 'l' or two.

Chapter 2

Welsh Place-names in the United States

BEFORE going on to discuss the distribution of Welsh place-names State by State, it will be interesting as well as helpful to note one or two general points. One is that the earlier Welsh settlements in the East gave their names to new settlements in the West, as the Welsh, like so many other ethnic groups, headed towards the Rockies and then to the Pacific. For example, Utica and Oneida in New York State were names adopted by the Welsh who settled in Illinois. 'Wales' itself as a place-name moved west from Massachusetts to North Dakota, Tennessee, Utah and Alaska. Sometimes it retained the Latin form, Cambria.

Another point is that some Welsh-Americans, often Welsh-speaking but having an English surname, gave their names to places in the United States. One example is that of Isaac Shelby, a very interesting Welsh character who will be discussed at several points later. His name was adopted in Shelby County, Alabama, and at Shelbyville in Kentucky. Also to be found are frequent variations in the spelling of some names. In several States, Rees or Rhys may be spelt Reese, as in Reese Air Force Base in Texas. The alternative forms of Stevens or Stephens may be found in several States, and indeed both of them sometimes in the same State.

ALASKA, at first glance seems to have decidedly fewer place-names than most American States, despite its large area. These place-names are mostly English or Eskimo. Yet, oddly enough, to the west of Alaska, in fact its most westerly point, on Cape Prince of Wales, with a population of 131, is little Wales. It is the nearest point, on the American mainland, to Russia. Across the Bering Strait, it faces Uelen in Siberia. Tin-Town a few miles south of Wales, is a reminder of the Welsh tin-workers who went there at the

12

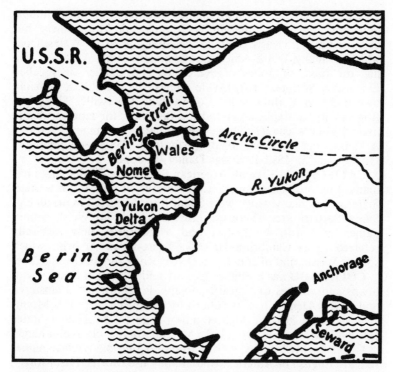

end of last century, some of them living in Wales (Alaska), now an Indian Reservation.

In Alaska there are also a Cape Denbigh, Jones Islands, and, back on the mainland, the small villages of Hughes and Stevens.

ALABAMA has counties named Morgan and Montgomery. The city of Montgomery has a population of over 200,000. A large town in Alabama is called Prichard, with a population of over 40,000. Rogersville has a population of about a thousand, but Cardiff in 1979 had only 127 inhabitants, a village in fact, like Jones (140), Rehoboth (300), and Morris (1979). We British hear far more about the big cities of the United States; one thing this study revealed was the enormous number of small towns and villages throughout America.

ARIZONA has no county names with a Welsh sound about them, but it does have a small town called Saint David (1250) and another called Williams (2386). Additionally it has a Powell Lake. From now on, some States have place-names recognisably Welsh, but varying a bit from the original spelling e.g. Swanzey for Swansea. After these I shall put the customary 'sic', meaning 'as spelt'.

13

ARKANSAS has counties named Montgomery and Phillips. Sometimes the Montgomery refers to a Captain Montgomery, but at other times it clearly refers to the county in North Wales, from which so many Welsh-Americans originally came. Arkansas also has the town of Jonesboro (27,050), and smaller ones called Evansville, Wynne, Griffithsville, Jones Mill (he almost certainly owned the local flour mill), Conway and Lewisville. There is a Rogers City, a Stephens, and also a Bethesda, the latter probably named after a chapel. There cannot have been many Welsh in Arkansas, but the Governor of the State in 1885-89 was Simon P. Hughes, and in 1897-1901 was Daniel W. Jones.

CALIFORNIA. Like all American States, the Golden State has many English place-names. Like several of the south-western States, it has many which were Spanish (or Mexican) in origin e.g. Santa Barbara etc. There are however, while no Welsh county names, a Cardiff-by-the-Sea and a Cambria, now generally referred to as Cambrian Heights. There is an Angwin, which sounds Welsh, and of course, an Owens River and an Owens Lake.

COLORADO has a Phillips County and a Morgan County with towns and villages of Edwards, Evans, Fort Morgan, Johnstown and Lewis. Denver has its suburb of Swansea. There is a Mount Evans, which has the highest motor-road in the United States (11,264 feet); there is also a Lake Meredith, a fine old Welsh name.

CONNECTICUT has, as one would expect, many place-names that are English or American-Indian, but also Morris, East Morris, Bethel, quite a large town with a population of over ten thousand, Milford with over fifty thousand and Thomaston with over six thousand.

DELAWARE has no counties with Welsh names, but it has a Saint Jones River. It has towns of Milford and Owen, also a Newport. There was some hesitation in including Newport, as there are several other Newports in Britain, e.g. on the Isle of Wight. One can assume that some of them in U.S.A. will have Welsh connections, especially when there are several other Welsh place-names in the particular State.

FLORIDA has a fair share of both English and Spanish place-names, but no Welsh county names. It does have, however, a place called Lake Wales with a population of 8240. (Other small towns and villages in Florida seem to have taken the name of the local lake, which must have been given a name before there was a settlement there.) The only other Welsh names are Pembroke Park, with three thousand population, Pembroke Pines with five times this number of people, and Conway with over eight thousand.

GEORGIA, despite being named after an English king, has the following among its county names: Evans, Montgomery, Jones,

14

Floyd, Morgan, Thomas, Glynn (sic) and Jenkins. There are a Thomaston and a Thomasville, both being large towns with a population well over ten thousand. Then there are smaller towns and villages named Davisboro, Evans, Jenkinsburg, Jonesboro, Morris, Morgan, Morganton, Pembroke. It also has a river called Flint. One of my favourite names in Georgia is Ty Ty. In Welsh that would mean 'house house'. Or is it an Indian name? Georgia had Governors Henry Ellis in 1756-60 and Myrick Davies 1781.

IDAHO. Far away from Florida, a very beautiful, but to Britishers a rather unknown State. Yet it has a county called Lewis, a large town Lewiston (26,068) and a much smaller Lewisville. It also has a Samuels village and one called Roberts. Leaving the Welsh for a moment, it has two lovely river names — Little Lost River and Saint Joe River.

ILLINOIS has to me a surprising number of Welsh place-names. There are Counties of Morgan, Jo Daviess, Edwards and Montgomery; cities and towns starting with Berwyn (52,502) and Evanstown (79,808), Morris (8194), Swansea (5432) and Monmouth (11,022). If all these inhabitants were really Welsh, they would together fill another Glamorgan. This being America, the truth is very different. The Welsh names are mainly of historical interest. These populations are now an exotic mixture of many ethnic or national groups, with Irish, Italians, Poles, German origins etc., not to mention the numerous black population. Nevertheless there are still many Jones, Evans, Williams, etc., families in the large urban communities, some dating back a generation or two to Welsh origins, others going back several generations, coming first in many cases from New England or Pennsylvania, then, before that, from old Cymru; this has been established in several cases. As well as the Welsh place-names mentioned above, there are in this State, Saint David, Cambria, Barry, Evansville, Jonesboro, Lewistown, Montgomery, Morristown and Milford. There is also a River Edwards in the State.

INDIANA has counties of Montgomery, Morgan, Owen, Floyd, and Davies. It has the big city of Evansville with its centre-city population of over 139 thousand (in 1979) and total metropolitan population of nearly a quarter of a million. Griffith is quite a big town, with over eighteen thousand population. Smaller places with 'Welsh' names include Edwardsville, Edwardsport, Gwynville (sic), Jonesboro, Jonesville, Newport, Williams, Walesboro, Matthews, Morgantown, Morris, Morristown, Owensburg, Owensville, Montgomery, and Williamsport.

IOWA has counties of Floyd, Jones and Montgomery. It has the small towns or villages of Evansdale, Floyd, Lewis, Williams, Monmouth and Milford, in all, a poor showing of Welsh names

15

compared with Illinois, or even Indiana. Yet many older Welsh and Welsh-Americans, and no doubt many other English and Americans, will remember the name of one of Iowa's most famous citizens, John Llewellyn Lewis, son of a Welsh immigrant and prominent — and rumbustious — coalminers' leader of the 1920's and 1930's.

KANSAS has the following, among several other counties: Edwards, Montgomery, Morris, Phillips and Thomas. It has small towns and villages of Lewis, Reece, Morganville, Phillipsburg, Milford, Conway, Conway Springs, and New Cambria.

KENTUCKY has counties of Lewis, Montgomery, Morgan, Owen, and Powell, and towns and villages of Fort Thomas, Jenkins, Newport, Lewisport, Lloyd, Hopkinsville, Morgantown, Newport, Owensboro, David, Emlyn and Morganfield and Morris Fork. There is too a Bonnyman — was that ever possibly Bonymaen? In Kentucky there is also a village called Emlyn, and an Oneida, named after the Welsh Settlement in New York State.

LOUISIANA has one county which may possibly be of Welsh origin, Winn (sic), Wyn or Wynn originally? There is a town called 'Welsh' in the county of Jefferson Davis named after the great Southern statesman, of Welsh stock. Louisiana has towns and villages called Evans, Jones, Jonesboro, Jonesville (the Joneses certainly liked Louisiana — or vice versa), Floyd, Glynn (sic), Morgan City, Montgomery.

MAINE. No counties with Welsh names, but towns and villages include Saint David, Bangor, Monmouth, Jonesport, Jonesboro, Lewiston (72,474 population), Pembroke and Winn.

MARYLAND has a county of Montgomery. A big suburb of Washington D.C. is called Bethesda, a name beloved in the Welsh valleys, and in fact named after a Presbyterian chapel in the area. Elsewhere in Maryland are Cardiff (510), Bowens, Berwyn Heights, Lewistown, Newport and Nanticoke (sic), Hughesville, Powellville, Price, Thomas, and Wynne.

MASSACHUSETTS. No Welsh-named counties, but Wales itself (852), Swansea (12,640), Swansea Center (950), Milford (13,740), North Pembroke (2881), Pembroke (11,193), and Phillipston. Among the many English and Indian names is Southwick, a village near to Brighton, Sussex, which has a big Welsh colony.

MICHIGAN has no Welsh-named counties, but has the big city of Flint, well known to Welsh-Americans from North Wales, with a population now of over half a million. Towns and villages in Michigan include Bangor, Edwardsburg, Hopkins, Jones, Lewiston, Beulah, Montgomery, Mount Morris, Jonesville and Williamston. There is a Flint River as well as the big city of Flint.

MINNESOTA has a county named Stevens, and towns and

16

villages called respectively Glyndon, Evansville, Morgan, Lewiston, Lewisville, Montgomery, Morristown, Newport, Hopkins, Williams, Morris, and Rogers. Despite these Welsh names, it will be shown later that one of the favourite places for settlement with the Welsh was Le Sueur County.

MISSISSIPPI has counties of Humphreys, Jones and Montgomery. Towns and villages with 'Welsh' names include Jonestown, Beulah, Morgantown, Morgan City, Thomastown, Thomasville, Pricedale, Johns and Edwards.

MISSOURI has counties named Barry, Davies, Howell, Montgomery, Morgan and Lewis. Towns and villages include New Cambria, Jonesburg, Lewistown, Beulah, Matthews, Montgomery City, Hopkins, Morrisville, Owensville, Gower, Phillipsburg, Rogersville and Williamsville.

NEVADA shows little sign of Welsh presence, having no Welsh names for counties, and only a little place called Montgomery Mount (inhabitants 10), and that would probably turn out to have been named after the Irish-American General of that name. And yet, when we get to the industrial section of this book, particularly on gold and silver mining, it will be seen that hundreds of Welsh miners worked in the Nevada mines — leaving no trace of their passage, or whether they were winners or losers. This State also has Reese River.

NEW HAMPSHIRE has no Welsh county names but a fair number, for a small State, of Welsh-named towns and villages. There is a Swanzey, spelled as pronounced, with a population of 4254. There is also an East Swanzey with another 500. New Hampshire has two Newports, but one or both of them may refer to Newport, Isle of Wight in England, which looks across the water at Hampshire. There is a large Morgantown with 13,625, and a smaller one with 3547, a Williamston, a Pembroke, and a village called Morrisville.

NEW JERSEY, not far from New York, has counties of Monmouth and Morris. It has towns named Morristown and Howell, and smaller towns of Monmouth Beach and Monmouth Junction. An intriguing name is Bellmawr. The 'mawr' is Welsh enough, as in Pennsylvania's Bryn Mawr. Mawr means 'big', so is Bellmawr a hybrid word meaning 'big bell'? But suppose 'bell' was a shortening of 'belle'? There is another Newport in New Jersey.

NEW MEXICO has no Welsh county names, and only two Welsh-sounding place-names, both small — Vaughan and Williamsburg. It is not likely that this particular Williamsburg has anything to do with King William. By the time that New Mexico left its Spanish heritage behind, and became one of the United States, it more likely came to refer to someone of the Williams ilk, possibly Old Bill Williams himself (see later).

17

NEW YORK STATE, beautiful New York State (more interesting to many British visitors than the Big Apple itself), has the counties of Lewis and Montgomery. Towns named here with Welsh names are all over one thousand population. More will be said about New York City in the body of this book, but New York State has Williamson, Williamsville, Mount Morris, Lloyd Harbour, Thomaston, Morrisville, Watkins Glen, and Montgomery.

To many Welsh, paying a first visit to New York, the first thing they would notice if they looked at the map, would be Jones Beach; others would be surprised, if they read the history books, at the very non-Welsh names of some of the places in New York State favoured by the Welsh immigrants, e.g. Utica and Oneida County.

NEBRASKA has a Thomas County, a Saunders County, a David City and villages of Newport, Lewellen (sic), Berwyn, Lewiston, Phillips, Powell, Prosser and Rogers. It is likely that not many Welsh came to Nebraska, but some of these villages may have been started by Welsh farmers and agricultural labourers, probably from North Wales. The same thing happened in other American States, and the villages grew to sizeable towns, or even cities. Not so in Nebraska.

NORTH CAROLINA has counties of Jones and Montgomery, and the town of Thomasville (15,230); smaller places are Bethel, Pembroke, Jonesville, Newport, Phillipsville, Matthews, Powell's Point, Powellsville, Lewiston and Johns.

NORTH DAKOTA, whose history was written by Elwyn B. Robinson, has a Williams County and place-names of Beulah, Conway, Denbigh, Gwinner, Reynolds and — Wales. It is interesting in this State that one of the non-Welsh names is Mandan, the name of the American Indian tribe long supposed to be descended from the 'Welsh discoverers of America' eight hundred years ago (see later). Mandan now has a population, mainly white, of 11,093.

OHIO has counties of Montgomery, Morgan and Williams. Its small towns include Lewisburg (1553), Newport (975), Owensville (707), Phillipsburg (831), Radnor (950) and Williamsport.

OKLAHOMA has counties of Hughes and Stephens, and a county called Ellis, which is common, both as a Christian name and as a surname in Wales. Towns and villages with Welsh names are not plentiful in this State, but there are a Jones (1666), Thomas (1336), and two small villages of Phillips and Humphreys. Bethel and Bethel Acres, with a 297 and 1083 population respectively, probably had Welsh connections.

OREGON seems to have been too far West for many Welsh to have reached there in settlement days. There are no Welsh county names, but towns called Monmouth with 5237 population, West Linn with 7091, Powell Butte (550) and Williams (750).

PENNSYLVANIA will take up quite a bit of space later as a very popular place of settlement with the Welsh, both in earlier agricultural settlement, and later industrial immigration. Thousands of Welsh came to live there, from the time of the Quaker Welsh of the late 17th century to 19th century emigration to Pennsylvania by coal-miners and iron and steel workers. County names in this State include Cambria and Montgomery. Quite a number of the Welsh place-names are in the Philadelphia area. You could not get much more Welsh than Bala-Cynwyd (6483) and Brynmawr (5737). Then there are Bangor (5425), Berwyn with a respectable 14,000 population, Colwyn with 3169, Crum Lynn (sic) (3700), Edwardsville (5633), Evans City (2144), the city of Haverford with a substantial 55,132, Hughesville (2249) and Hughestown (1407), Nanty Glo (sic) (4298), Montgomery (1902), Lewistown (11,098), Lewisburg (6376) and Newport (7747); there is little doubt that this Newport was named after the South Wales Newport.

Also in Pennsylvania, there are two Morrisvilles, one with 11,309 population and a smaller version with 1232. There is a Pencoyd (sic) (6650), a North Wales (3911), and a Phillipsburg (3700). There is a big Williamsport (37,918) and a Williamstown and a Williamsburg, each near the two thousand mark in population; it is quite likely however that one, two or all of these may be named after William III of England. Also in this state are Penn Wynne (6308) and Wynnewood (9200).

RHODE ISLAND founded as a State by Roger Williams, possibly Welsh, is yet a State with few Welsh place-names, especially after Pennsylvania. There is a Newport County and a Newport City, the latter having a population of 34,562; there is also a Newport East with 10,285, and a Phillipsdale with 2523. There is, predictably, in view of Roger Williams' religion and philosophy, a couple of appropriate English names Hope and Harmony, each having the same numerical chances with a population of 975. Also in Rhode Island are Saunderstown and Bowen Hill.

SOUTH CAROLINA. As will be shown later, prominent in the history of this State was the area known as Welsh Neck. There is no Welsh-named county, but there is a city of Williamsburg, which may however have been, again, named after William III. There are however a Swansea (691), Hopkins (300), Jonesville (1447) and villages of Pritchard, Prichardville, Lewis, Winnsboro and Winnsboro Mill, Floydala, a Jenkinsville, and islands of Johns, Pritchards and Morris.

SOUTH DAKOTA has counties of Hughes, Jones and Roberts, but apparently only Morristown (1444) as additional Welsh reference.

TENNESSEE has counties of Lewis, Montgomery, and Morgan. It has towns and villages of Morristown (20,318) the county seat, Jonesboro, Lewisburg and Morris Chapel.

TEXAS was presumably too far off and too far south during the main periods of Welsh emigration. Anyway, it was in Spanish hands during most of the relevant period, before Texas allied itself to the U.S.A. — or vice versa, as I gather the Texans prefer to put it. There is, of course Edwards Plateau, which takes up a lot of space, even for vast Texas. Yet surprisingly there are in Texas counties called Jones, Edwards, Lynn, Hopkins, Morris, Montgomery, Roberts, Stephens, Floyd and Ellis. There are few towns with Welsh names, even if Floydada is counted, so it seems that such Welsh as there were were scattered throughout the State. There are also on the map the towns of Lewisville and Phillips.

UTAH is best known to most British, and, I suppose, to most Americans, as the State of the Mormons. N. Anderson, in his book on them, calls them 'the desert saints'. As will be shown in later chapters, there were many Welsh among them. One of the Utah counties is called Morgan, and there is the large town of Price (6218) a county seat; small towns with Welsh names include Lewiston, Milford and Morgan. In Utah there is also a Lake Powell, a Price River and a Thomas range of mountains.

VERMONT has no Welsh county names but has Newport (4664), Morristown (4052), a smaller Newport and a much smaller Morristown, just a village. Morrisville however has a population of 2116. There are villages of Jonesville, Montgomery, Montgomery Center and Morgan.

VIRGINIA has counties of Floyd, Mathews, and Montgomery. It has towns and villages of Dillwyn, Hopkins, Jonesville, Floyd, Ivor, Gwynn, Lloyd Place, Newport, Matthews and Stephens City.

WEST VIRGINIA has a Lewis County and a Morgan County, a Hughes River and a Williams River. It has the City of Morgantown (29,431) which is listed as a county seat. Other towns and villages with Welsh names are Evans, Griffithsville, Lewisburg, Montgomery, Morgansville, Morrisvale, Selwyn and Vaughan. Also in this State, a favourite of mine, is Jenkinjones (all one word). Then there are Powellton, Price Hill, Prichard, Radnor, Thomas and Uneeda, the latter a corruption of the Welsh Uneida, New York.

WISCONSIN has a county called Price. It has the towns of Bangor, Bethel, Phillips, Evansville, Wales, Cambria, Roberts, Reesville, Milford, and Lewis. Many Welsh went to Wisconsin, and Welsh-Americans from this State still feature, as will be shown later, in lists of prominent people today.

WASHINGTON STATE, right up in the North-West corner of the United States, with Seattle not far from Vancouver, in British Columbia. Washington State has counties of Lewis and Stevens. Here we are by the Pacific, and yet, as with California and Oregon, there are some Welsh place-names. As argued earlier in this chapter, the presence of Welsh place-names must mean that some Welsh passed that way, and had enough influence or importance to leave Welsh place-names behind them. This was certainly true in Philadelphia, so if true in Pennsylvania, why not in Washington? There we find Bryn Mawr again, Evans, Usk and Prosser.

WYOMING. Total population 332,416. Liveable in, and beautiful. From Denver it is easy to get to this lovely State. It has no Welsh-named counties, but it has towns of Powell, Evanston and Evansville.

It would be interesting to trace all the place-names included in this chapter to their actual origins; this is not always possible, as these origins, occurring in troublesome times, were often lost in the mists of the past. For many States no attempt seems to have been made to trace all the State place-names back to their source. Happily, however, this has been done in some States, so this chapter ends with such attempts made for Pennsylvania, Minnesota and California.

A. H. Espenshade wrote his *Pennsylvania Place-names* in the early twenties of this century (1925). Early in his book appears the information that there had been a Saint Jones County in Pennsylvania up to 1683, at which date it became Kent County — a pity. The city of Lewistown, states Espenshade, was laid out by Samuel Edmiston on his own land in 1791, and named after his friend, William Lewis, a Welsh iron-master. Milford was laid out in 1796 by John Biddis, a Philadelphian of Welsh descent. Bangor was named after the Bangor in North Wales, from which so many of the Welsh slate-working immigrants came. Edwardsville was named after Daniel Edwards, the Welsh superintendent of the Kingston Coal Company. Hopefully, it will be clear that no attempt is being made here, even in dealing with Pennsylvania, to suggest that all towns and villages in this State had Welsh names; other researchers on different ethnic sources will find Espenshade a good starting-point.

One striking proof that a big State, even an industrialised one, still has its countryside and villages is shown by the author's statement that in Pennsylvania (1925) there were over 3000 post-offices; they could not all have been in cities and towns. Espenshade, certainly not Welsh-American, was struck by what seemed to him the typically Welsh names that he found in the State — Bryn Mawr, Cynwyd, Duffryn Mawr, Gwynedd, Haverford,

Lampeter, Merion, Nantmel, Pen Argyl, Radnor, Tredyffrin and Uwchland. He notes that Merion, as a place-name, had existed from before 1714, Haverford from 1722, Jenkintown in Montgomery County from the time of the Welsh pioneer, William Jenkins, who had settled there in 1697.

Nantmel was called after the village of Nantmel in Radnorshire, mid-Wales. Tredyffrin (town in the valley) described the location of the township. Uwchland was originally Uwchlan, meaning 'upland'. Cambria County had been called after the little settlement of Cambria, which quickly grew in size. Ebensburg was named after Eben, the eldest son of the Reverend Rees Lloyd, one of the pioneers. It became a borough in 1825.

Many Welsh from Pennsylvania moved on in later years to Minnesota. Warren Upham includes their new home-towns and villages in his 'Minnesota Place-names' (1920). For the Welsh communities in the State, he relied a lot on earlier histories of those communities by Thomas Hughes and Judge Evan Hughes. Cambria Township was given its name by another Hughes, Robert H. Hughes, reputed to be the first settler there before 1850. Jo Daviess Township was named after the courageous soldier, Joseph Hamilton Daviess from Kentucky, who was killed in the Battle of Tippecanoe (1811).

Many Welsh, as will be shown later, went to live in Blue Earth County, Minnesota; one of its counties was named after the legendary Isaac Shelby, whose family came from Wales. One town in the Blue Earth region was given the name South Bend by David Evans, while Matthew Evans gave its name to Effington in Otter Tail County. Evansville in Duglas County was named after its first mail-carrier, who was killed by Sioux Indians in 1862. May Township in Cass County was named for May Griffiths, the daughter of the county auditor. Jenkins Township in Crow Wing County was named after George W. Jenkins, a Welsh lumberman. In St Louis County, John T. Jones had a unique distinction — the local railway station was named after him, in recognition of his discovery of iron ore locally, which provided work for many in the mines. James Williams also provided a service for the community by operating a portable saw-mill; in Koochiching County, Williams Township was named after him.

California attracted wandering Welshmen in its early days; they were literally restless nomads in fact, because they were 'loners', to use current slang, wandering all over Colorado, Nevada and California as rumours spread of gold strikes, or even silver or other metals. Most of them of course had been miners back in Wales, or in the early coal-mines of Pennsylvania — trying to move from coal-dust to gold-dust. So most of them had come over the mountains to California, but some by sea, the so-called 'Argonauts' round the Cape. E. Gudde, in his *California Place-names,* looks at the townships where they could be found, generally in their later years.

Cambria in California is best known to American visitors from its proximity to the amazing San Simeon estate in San Luis Obispo County. According to Gudde, Cambria was originally called Slabtown, having been settled in the 1860's; even its rough-and-ready early settlers thought there was something missing in that name, and were going to change it back to Santa Rosa, the name of the estate on which the township had been built. A Welshman named Llewellyn got in first. He hung up the sign 'Cambria Carpenter Shop' over the doors of his business. People became accustomed to the Welsh name, or rather the Roman name for Wales, and 'Santa Rosa' was dropped. Another Welsh name on the map of California is Cardiff-by-the-Sea in San Diego County. No story there; Frank Cullen laid it out, and named it after the South Wales seaport, Cardiff.

Prosser Creek in California was called after William Jones Prosser, who kept an hotel there in the mid-nineteenth-century, according to the *Pacific Tourist* (1876). Mount Wynne was called after Sedman Wynne, former Supervisor of the Sequoia National Forest, who lost his life on duty. Another creek, Davis Creek, was named after David Davis, who settled there in 1860.

Prominent on the map in California is Owens River, which runs into Owens Lake. Both of these, and other Owens natural features in the area, were named after Richard Owens of Ohio, who was J. C. Fremont's second-in-command on the third of Fremont's historic expeditions. Owens Mountain on the other hand, was named after George W. Owens, also from Ohio, who came to California in 1862. Williams was the name of a small township called after a celebrated character, Billy Williams, who settled near Red Lake in the early days of last century.

Chapter 3

Prince Madoc and John Dee

MADOC and John Dee are grouped together in this chapter because they illustrate, in the field of Welsh Americana, the mixture of reason and unreason which characterises most of human history. Jointly they illustrate the mysterious and legendary in the composition of 'knowledge' at any period. What is believed to be true is seen as being as compelling upon events as what, at the time, could be proved to be true. Truth, at any period of history, is relative to available knowledge at the time — and, what is considered to be 'proof'.

In the Madoc story, 'proof' of the existence of Welsh-speaking Indians would scarcely meet modern scientific criteria. Nor today do stories of the Abominable Snowman, the Loch Ness Monster, or Unidentified Flying Objects — but belief in them is still widespread, despite our much greater accumulation of scientific knowledge. So, are we to smile at Queen Elizabeth I 'taking counsel' of John Dee because of his supposed astrological 'knowledge', or at highly-educated men two centuries later believing the 'Madoc legend' for emotional, not to say chauvinistic, reasons, rather than by logical standards? In both cases, additionally, charisma, the negation of pure reason, affected judgements — the charisma of forceful personalities.

MADOC AND THE DISCOVERY OF AMERICA (1170 A.D.)

There has recently (1983) been an international conference on the question — Who discovered America? The Vikings, of course, hundreds of years before Columbus? But could it have been Prince Madoc of Wales in the twelfth century? The first published work, in Tudor times, to affirm the discovery by Madoc (sometimes spelt Madog) was a pamphlet entitled *A True Reporte,* by Sir George

24

Peckham in 1583. It was elegantly written to support Elizabeth's claim to the New World. It was repeated in Humphrey Llwyd's *Historie of Cambria* the next year. Dr. David Powell of Ruabon in Wales gave much publicity to this account by Llwyd.

Several books have since been written looking at the legend and its variations. Fairly recent books have been by Richard Deacon *(Madoc and the Discovery of America,* 1967) and by Professor Gwyn Williams of the University of Wales *(Madoc: The Making of a Myth,* 1980). Deacon declares that by far the most support for the Madoc story comes from Hakluyt. The opinion of Richard Hakluyt was that Madoc landed in the West Indies. Other writers at the time thought the landing was much more likely to have taken place in Virginia. Another claim was for Mobile Bay in Alabama, where a memorial tablet to Madoc was set up by the local chapter of the Daughters of the American Revolution in 1953.

Deacon seems to agree with this latter suggestion. He quotes a letter by John Sevier, one of the founders of Tennessee. The letter, written in 1810, refers to a belief among the Cherokee Indians that there had been a Welsh-speaking Indian tribe. Their chieftain was supposed to have told Sevier that he had heard his father and grandfather speak of a people called the Welsh, and that they had crossed the seas and landed at Mobile. This quotation gives the flavour of much of the discussion of Madoc that, literally, went on for centuries. One initial difficulty in trying to test the credibility of the story is that Madoc was, as Deacon admits, a very common name in twelfth century Wales. Owain Gwynedd, the most powerful Prince of North Wales, had several sons, some legitimate, some illegitimate. At least one of each category was called Madoc (or Madog), as were other young men in Owain's Court. Deacon goes thoroughly into the question of which was the real Madoc of the ancient story. According to the *Encyclopaedia Britannica,* Owain Gwynedd died in 1170; a quarrel over the distribution of his father's estate so disgusted Madoc that he sailed to Ireland, and from there 'Westwards'. A year later, it was said, he returned to Wales, and assembled a group to colonise land he had discovered in the 'Western Seas'.

George Catlin, in his book on the *North American Indians* (1841) maintained that Madoc had reached the Upper Missouri River valley, and that his group were the ancestors of the Mandan Indians. At Louisville, Kentucky, there is still said today to be a tradition of Welsh-speaking Indians. There are about 350 Mandan Indians left today, living at Fort Berthold Reservation, North Dakota; nobody claims that they speak anything resembling Welsh. It could have been different in the old days, it is asserted. L. B. Wright in his *Elizabethans' America* (1965) said that Captain

25

Wynne, who met such Indians in 1608, wrote to his patron, Sir John Egerton, saying, "I travelled to a country called Monacan . . . the people of Monacan speak a far different language from the subjects of Powhatan, the renowned Indian chieftain. Their pronunciation is very much like Welsh, so that the gentleman in our company desired me to be their interpreter" (Wright, p.186). Deacon complains that the story of Madoc is one that has been sadly neglected by his own countrymen. He asserts that Welsh scholars have been much more sceptical than historians and geographers of other countries. On the other hand he admits that there were good reasons for the scepticism. Welsh experts had been fooled for many years by Iolo Morganwg's forgery of ancient odes. Edward Williams (the real name of the bard), with his friend, Dr Owen Pughe, wrote a series of articles in defence of the Madoc story. Through Owen Pughe, who was an honest researcher, Robert Southey the poet, heard the story, and published his ode *Madoc* in 1805. Deacon comments, "Poor Southey, he would have fallen for any story, whether in a tap-room or in non-conformist Wales."

Southey, speaking for Madoc, wrote, "We left the ship, And cleft with rapid oars the shallow wave, and stood triumphant on another world". Even Dr. Samuel Johnson appeared to believe the Madoc story and wrote a poem in Latin about him. Iolo Morganwg, carried away by his own enthusiasm, included his own version of the legend in what he claimed were genuine medieval texts, named by him the 'Triads'. It was eventually proved that the Triads were a fraud, which, according to Deacon, discredited the Madoc story for many years. What then are we to believe?

That was the question George Borrow asked himself when he went from East Anglia to North Wales in 1854. Borrow met a North Walian who had no doubts about the matter (George Borrow, *Wild Wales,* 1862). They were talking by Madoc's Bridge, supposed to have been built by Madoc in the twelfth century. Borrow spoke Welsh fluently, being a brilliant linguist. The old Welsh countryman told Borrow, "Madoc was a great sailor, Sir, and the first to discover Tir y Gorllewin (Land in the West)". Geoffry Ashe, in his *Quest for America* (1971) thinks that Madoc did exist, and was a renowned sailor — but would not go further than that. In 1858 the Welsh National Eisteddfod Committee offered a prize for the best essay on 'The Welsh Discovery of America' (later to be considered a rash and unpopular act). The prize was won by Thomas Steven, who, however, threw cold water on the story.

Whatever the truth of the legend, it served as a very useful support for Welsh pride and self-identity when morale needed boosting in a strange land and difficult times. This was very much the view of Professor Gwyn Williams. In his books on Madoc, as in his *Search for Beulah Land,* he examines the variations on the legend, the parts played by John Evans and Morgan John Rhys, and above all the function of the myth, in exciting and activating an important group of radical Welsh intellectuals during and after the French Revolution. Taking the two books together, Professor Gwyn Williams shows how very dynamic a belief can be, whether it is true or not. Its consequence moulded a large part of the history of middle-America, as did the North West Passage theory before it. "It was precisely here," said Professor Williams, "in the realms of the imagination and the spirit that the myth of the Welsh Indians worked its magic . . . Madoc had been the catalyst for the whole process."

Hartmann stated, "On January 13th 1804, an American President of Welsh ancestry, Thomas Jefferson, despatched a letter to another Welsh-American, Meriwether Lewis, containing a map of the Upper Missouri valley. The map had been prepared by a third Welsh-American, John Evans." Including Morgan John Rhys, that makes four 'of Welsh blood' involved in that portion of American history. It is an irony of history that John Evans, a Welshman who had left Wales, purely for personal reasons, to investigate the Madoc story, did much of his exploration for the Spaniards. To add to the irony, the head of the Spanish company that employed him was Jacques Clamorgan, described as 'a West Indian of Welsh descent'. The Spanish in the 1790's still occupied much of the central territory of America; they had suddenly realised that the British were pushing South from Canada, and had already reached the lands of the Mandans, whom Evans was seeking for his own Madoc-intoxicated purposes.

JOHN DEE THE MAGICIAN

Many accounts have been written of the Elizabethan Age, the age, not only of Shakespeare, Sidney and Marlowe, but of Drake, Frobisher and Raleigh. All were vigorously inspired by their Tudor Queen. She had a keen eye to the expansion of her dominions overseas. In this constant aim, she depended greatly on John Dee. Dr. John Dee, according to the British *Dictionary of National Biography,* was born in London in 1527, but belonged to the ancient family of the Dees of Nant-y-Groes, Radnorshire. He himself had drawn up a genealogical table, tracing his family back to Roderick the Great, Prince of Wales in the Early Middle Ages. He went to St John's College, Cambridge, and graduated there in 1544. When Trinity College, Cambridge (where our present Prince of Wales was educated) was founded in 1546, he was one of the Founding Fellows, as Reader in Greek. So much for his orthodox background. The rest of his background was anything but formal or orthodox.

Robert Lacey describes him as "the mysterious Welsh wizard whose astrological magic had been consulted, in 1558, to set Elizabeth's Coronation date". The *Dictionary of National Biography* describes him as "mathematician and astrologer". He left Cambridge to visit scholars and scientists all over Europe. He had met astronomers and geographers like the great Mercator. In Europe he had studied charts showing European ideas of where the North-West Passage was situated. From Europe he had brought the cross-staff, or balestila, an instrument for measuring the height of the heavenly bodies. "He was," said Lacey, "the guru of Elizabethan exploration, and all the world came to his house at Mortlake, London, to examine his wonderful instruments." (R. Lacey, *Sir Walter Raleigh,* 1973.)

He was visited by Drake, Frobisher, John Davis, the Gilberts and Raleigh, merchants of the Muscovy Company . . . and even by Elizabeth herself. He had been taken into her service at an earlier date. He was said to have consulted with her Court physicians about her health. He was a strange mixture of magician and scientist, perhaps illustrating the difficulty of separating magic and science at that period. "Her Majesty was in fact more interested in the doctor's reputed dabbling in the black arts than in his solid scientific achievements." (Lacey, p.59.) Lacey continues, "With his long white beard and black skull-cap, he looked the very image of a black magician." The mystery that surrounded him was augmented by the rumour that, on his European trips, he was acting as a secret agent for England. Most people feared him, many disliked him, but the Queen thought highly of him, and all the great sailors of Elizabethan England respected and consulted him.

Admiral Morison says of Dee, in connection with Frobisher's voyages, "He spent many days in the Spring of 1576 on board *Gabriel* and *Michael,* instructing the pilots in navigation, and in the use of the new navigational instruments. Some of the latter had certainly helped Frobisher to obtain his remarkably accurate latitudes." (S. Morison, *Great Explorers,* 1965, p.282.)

Captain John Davis, persuaded by the Gilberts to make another search for the North-West Passage, called on John Dee. "Talke was begone," said Dee, "of the North West Straights Discovery," writing of this first visit by Davis. The latter made three voyages to the North-West Atlantic, and added considerably to British knowledge of the Arctic.

Queen Elizabeth visited John Dee in 1580, and asked for a geographical description of the new countries in the West, which she claimed. He presented her with two large rolls of charts, accompanied by descriptions. "It was the huge chart of the North American coastline, which Dr John Dee had prepared in 1580 that provided the basis for Walter Raleigh's North American strategy. You can still see the chart in the British Museum today." (R. Lacey, *Life of Sir Walter Raleigh,* p.59.) There were many Welsh at Queen Elizabeth's Court. The Tudor Queen was keenly aware of her Welsh heritage (having, for instance, established Jesus College at Oxford for the Welsh). John Dee must have been one of the strangest, but also one of the most influential, of her Welsh subjects.

Chapter 4

The Welsh In Early America

EVERYBODY knows about the *Mayflower* landing, in what is now Massachusetts, in mid-November 1620. William Bradford was one of their members. He tells of their first moments on American soil. "They fell upon their knees, and blessed the God of heaven, who had brought them over the fast and furious ocean, and delivered them from all the perils and miseries thereof, againe to set their feete on the firme and stable earth, their proper element . . . They now had no friends to welcome them nor inns to entertain or refresh their weather-beaten bodys . . . They marched through Boughes and Bushes, and under hils and vallies which tore their verie Armour in peeces; we found at last Springs, and drunke our first New England Water with as much Delighte ever we drunke drinke in our lives." Of his companions, he said, "What could they see but a hideous and desolate wilderness full of wilde beestes and wild men?"

George Wilison gives a vivid account of the *Mayflower* voyage and the founding of the Plymouth Colony (G. Wilison, *Saints and Strangers,* 1966). He maintains that a clear distinction must be made between the Pilgrims who began building the town of Plymouth in 1620, and the Puritans who came ten years later to settle fifty miles north of Plymouth, with Boston as their centre.

What part did the seventeenth century Welsh play in these developments, that is, in Massachusetts? The answer, is simply, very little compared, for instance, with the part they played later in Pennsylvania. A minority of the Pilgrims came from the English Midlands, via Holland, where they had spent some time in exile. The majority of the passengers came from London and south-east England. The Captain of the *Mayflower,* Captain Christopher Jones came from Norwich. It is tempting to claim Captain Jones

30

for Wales, but this has to be resisted, as he was East Anglian through and through.

In the earliest days of the Pilgrims at Plymouth, some settlers moved out of Plymouth itself and founded Rehoboth and Swanzey, soon changed to Swansea. So, who then named these townships with such Welsh names? Certainly not the original settlers, Mrs Elizabeth Tilley, John Howland, Thomas Willett, Mary Browne, Samuel Eddy and others, none, so far as is known, with 'Welsh' names. It was several years before Welsh Baptists came to join them, and found these Welsh place-names there already. So here we have a real puzzle — who named Swanzey and Rehoboth? The latter name is said to be Hebrew for 'enlargement'. This may seem appropriate for a growing settlement; it really however referred to 'spiritual enlargement'.

We will be dealing with John Miles and his Baptists when we come to the chapter on 'Religion and the Welsh Emigration to the United States'. It would, however, be convenient to say something about Swansea (Mass.) at this point, for two reasons: firstly because Swansea-Rohoboth was the only Welsh settlement that developed in Massachusetts, and secondly because Swansea developed in a fashion that was unique in the United States. Coming from a caste-ridden Britain, most migrants looked for freedom and some degree of equality, or at least equal opportunity, in the New World. Not so at Swansea (Mass.). (There were to be other American Swanseas.) Citizens were to be divided into three classes. Fixed classes decided several aspects of the life of the township. Top class members received three acres of land, second class two acres, and third class one acre, and so on in these proportions, as land became cleared. If anybody got into trouble, offenders of the top class paid a fine of £3,,12 shillings each; second class paid £2,,8 shillings and third class paid £1,,4 shillings each per offence. Committees of the town kept the system going, for the period that it lasted, by degrading and promoting at discretion — there was a little social mobility (Otis O. Wright, *The History of Swansea (Mass.), 1917*).

In the last quarter of the sixteenth century and the first quarter of the seventeenth century, a search for new territory went on over vast areas, from Labrador to the West Indies. "Yet, even in the time of Columbus," states Professor David Williams, "we read of one, Lloyd, described by contemporaries as 'the most skilful mariner in all England' " (D. Williams, *Short History of Wales, 1977*). Admiral Samuel Morison complained that "Canada and the United States seem to be full of racial groups who wish to capture the 'real' discovery of America for their medieval compatriots." (S. Morison, op. cit. p.341.) Wesley F. Craven

31

states, "An enormous bibliography has been built up of works devoted to the place in American history of the Jew, the German, the Welshman, the Scot, the Irish and others." (W. F. Craven, *The Legend of the Founding Fathers,* 1956, p.172.) Craven asks, "What bothered them?" He answers the question himself. "The Anglo-Saxons seemed to be on the point of taking over the legend of the 'founding fathers'. Other groups demanded a place in this vast history."

The Welsh were not slow in demanding such a place, notably in the Madoc story. Cautious historians, Welsh included, generally agree with Alan Conway, "Doubtless there were Welsh among the early colonists, but the first sizable immigration by the Welsh was not until the late seventeenth century." (A. Conway, *The Welsh in America,* 1961, p.2.) This may be so, but one still wonders at the scores of Welsh names that occur in accounts of early explorations. Thus D. B. Quinn refers to the third voyage by Frobisher, a narrative of which was written by Thomas Ellis, a crew-member, in 1576 (D. B. Quinn, *England and the Discovery of America,* 1974, p.217). Was Ellis Welsh or London Welsh, of whom there were many in the time of the Tudor Queen? Shipping magnates in Bristol at that time were Rice Jones, Thomas Jones, John Thomas and Hugh Elliot. Veteran seaman, Phillip Jones gives an account of the voyages of Cabot, who sailed round parts of Hudson Bay, in a manuscript now in the British Museum (Quinn, p.142).

There is no doubt at all, of course, that in Elizabethan England the main impetus for Atlantic exploration came from the rich London merchants, and from the Queen herself, supported by the arguments of Hakluyt, John Dee, and many others who believed in England's destiny in the New World. Richard Hakluyt had been encouraging the English to look 'Westwards' for several years. In a dedication to Sir Philip Sidney of his book *Divers Voyages touching the Discovery of America,* he wrote of "those temperate and fertile parts of America which, being within six weeks' sailing of England, are as yet unpossesed by any Christians, and seem to offer themselves unto us. Lasting riches do wait upon them that are zealous for the advancement of the Kingdom of Christ". The enemy Spaniards had the same idea.

Acting on this precept, Captain John Davis made two voyages to North America at the end of the sixteenth century. His little fleet called in at Iceland, then pressed on Westwards to Gilbert Sound. One of the ships was called *Sunneshine;* the purser of the *Sunneshine* was a Welshman called Henry Morgan (long before the dreaded Henry Morgan the pirate). Morgan traded for sealskins

32

with the Esquimaux, then said Morgan, "Divers times they did weave us on shore to play with them at the foot-ball, and some of our men did caste them downe as soon as they did come to strike the ball" (August 1586). "This is the first recorded international football match," said Admiral Morison. He also noticed this first recorded instance of rough play (S. Morison, op. cit. p.341).

Very much further South, in the Magellan Straits, Francis Drake, sailing round the world, went with his men onto an island — just about six years before the above-mentioned football match. There they killed and ate three thousand penguins, which, said Drake, "the Welchmen called Pengwin, meaning 'white head' " (modern Welsh Pen Gwyn); the trouble is, it has been shown, that penguins have black heads, not white heads. Nor is it clear that Drake had Welshmen in his crew — he could have been recalling something that he had heard earlier. There had, however, been a Captain John Thomas in Drake's fleet. He was captain of the *Marygold* (30 tons 16 guns). On October 7th, 1577, stated Morison, running off the Chile coast, the *Marygold* disappeared with all its crew. "Those on the *Golden Hind,*" said Morison, quoting Drake himself, "did heare their feareful cryes." (Ibid. p.686.)

Such a tragic end may have overtaken some of the very early settlers in Virginia, in one of Sir Walter Raleigh's attempts to colonise there, at Roanoke (D. N. Durrant, *Raleigh's Lost Colonies,* 1981). The names of some of those who went out with Raleigh, and were never heard of again after 1587, include Edward Powell, Thomas Stevens, Thomas Ellis, John Jones, Griffin Jones, Winifred Powell, and Jane Jones.

The Elizabethan obsession with exploration in the Atlantic, and colonies in America, lasted on into the seventeenth century. "Interest in North America continued to increase during the early years of the seventeenth century, until almost any account, true or exaggerated, found eager readers." (L. B. Wright, *Elizabethans' America,* 1965, p.15.) The doctrine that God had destined the English to be a power in the New World increased in popularity. Lewis Hughes, a Welsh minister, writing home from the West Indies in 1615, said "The King of Kings hath kept these islands from the King of Spain, and all the other kings in the world, till now that it hath pleased His Holy Majesty to bestow them upon the King of England." (Ibid. p.202.)

The King of Spain had long been tormented by Drake and other English mariners and privateers. The latter term in effect meant royally licensed pirates. A couple of totally unlicensed pirates were Simon Fernandez and John Callice, not Welsh, but who used Welsh ports, Cardiff and Penarth in particular, to sell captured ships, some of which were Spanish, taken as prizes in the Atlantic.

At these ports they also sold whole cargoes, and bought new ships and provisions (Quinn, op. cit. p.248). Probably they took on board Welsh crew members as well, some of whom no doubt jumped ship, an old naval custom, at the West Indies and headed for the United States.

Some official early voyages were certainly manned by Welsh sailors, and occasionally captained by experienced Welsh mariners. Thus in 1617 the Earl of Warwick sent out two ships to explore the Caribbean. One of these, the *Lion,* was captured by Thomas Jones, whose voyage culminated in 'sheer banditry', as Professor Andrews put it (C. M. Andrews, *The Colonial Period of American History,* 1934, p.47).

A more famous, and more respectable Welshman was Sir William Vaughan, whom Andrews described as "a fantastic Welshman, one of the most picturesque colonial characters". Vaughan lived at Torcoedn in Carmarthenshire, South-West Wales. He had become obsessed with the idea of a Welsh settlement in Newfoundland, as he saw the Bristol and Devonshire fishing-fleets departing across the Atlantic. Being wealthy, he was able to send out two colonies to Newfoundland. One he called Cambria Colches and the other Golden Grove. "Vaughan was of a strongly literary turn of mind, colourful and imaginative," remarks Professor Andrews. Sir William went out himself in 1622. While there he wrote, as mentioned in the introduction, *Cambrensium Cariola,* and also *The Golden Fleece.* The first of these was said by Andrews to be the earliest work written in America.

The head of one of the two colonies was a Southampton mariner, Captain Richard Whitbourne, explorer, adventurer and whaler, a remarkable man in his own right; in his younger days he had fought against the Spanish Armada. He wrote works which were as comprehensive and vividly written as those of Vaughan. Whitbourne was very much under the influence of Sir William. Remarkable men both but not able to meet all the difficulties of settlement in bleak Newfoundland, especially the weather. A pity Vaughan had not fixed his enthusiastic gaze a thousand miles further South. As it was, Vaughan returned home, and the whole scheme failed within a few years; not that this was the only one to fail, even where climatic conditions were better, as in Virginia.

One of the lesser known of explorers of North America in the early seventeenth century was Captain Thomas James. Like many others, he was obsessed with the idea of the North West Passage to the Orient and its reputed riches. Helped by the merchants of Bristol, he continued his exploration of the Arctic area. Oddly enough, the name of his ship is not known, but its Master was Arthur Price, who sailed with a crew of twenty-two. At one point along the icy coast, as Captain James said in his account of the voyage, "We got to this little cove which I called by the Master's name of my ship — Price's Cove." (Captain Thomas James, *Strange and Dangerous Voyages,* 1633, edited by Commander R. B. Boddiley, R.N., 1928.) Although Captain James did not give the names of all his crew, there must have been several Welsh there for, "*1st March. 1632.* The first of this month, being St. David's Day, we kept Holiday, and solemnised it in the Manner of the Ancient Britons, praying for the Happiness of His Royal Highness, Charles, Prince of Wales." (Ibid. p.123.)

Several of these early expeditions to the North-East of the American continent had this aim of finding the North-West Passage. At the time when Captain James was looking for it, financed by Bristol merchants, Captain Luke Fox led a rival expedition, financed by London merchants. Both expeditions started in 1631. The North-West Passage was as much of a motivating myth to the English as the myth of Madoc and the Welsh Indians was to the Welsh. Sir Thomas Button of Duffryn, South Wales, had been affected by the English myth, for he commanded an expedition sent out even earlier (1612) with the dual purpose of looking for the lost Henry Hudson, and taking part in the North-West Passage quest. A neighbour of Sir Thomas was Sir Robert Mansel of Margam, Vice-Admiral of England (D. Williams, *A Short History of Wales,* p.45).

The *Mayflower,* and ships immediately following, *Fortune, Anne,* and *Little James,* had passengers named Rodgers, Williams, Adams and Morgan. Unfortunately for our purpose, C. E. Banks of the Massachusetts Historical Society shows that Thomas Rodgers came from Saint Bartholomew, John Adams from Aldgate, Benedict Morgan from Clerkenwell, all three in London (C. E. Banks, *The English Ancestry of the Pilgrim Fathers,* 1962). But there are plenty of London Welsh now, and there were plenty in the smaller London of early Stuart times. Could one of the above-named, or other Welsh back in London, have had influence enough to name Swansea and Rehoboth (Mass.)? There is no proof of this in a specialised article by George Stewart of California (G. S. Stewart, *Men's Names in Seventeenth Century Massachusetts,* 1948), but the possibility remains. When the first political document was drawn up at Cape Cod (Mass.), there were at least five Welsh names on it (A. Morton, *New England Memorial,* 1826).

Other Welshmen were already in the New World when the *Mayflower* landed. In 1606 the Plymouth Company had sent 143 emigrants to Virginia under Captain John Smith. More came the next year in three ships under Captain Newport. Of those who landed at, or near, Jamestown, twenty or more were said to have

36

had Welsh names. As Professor Hartmann says, "That there were many Welsh scattered among the early English settlers one can safely assume from the presence of many Welsh surnames among the settlers of these colonies." (E. G. Hartmann, *Americans from Wales*, 1967.) S. E. Morison stated, "America was discovered by accident, not wanted when found, and early explorations were directed to finding a way through it or around it" (S. Morison, op. cit. p.76). Some Welsh undoubtedly had a part in this strange beginning of a great nation.

Brief mention has already been made of early settlement in Virginia at Roanoke, written up under the appropriate title *Raleigh's Lost Colonies*. To American historians this became as much a mystery of settlement on land as the *Marie Celeste* was at sea. It is safe to say that nobody to this day knows what happened to them, some of them with real Welsh names, though various theories have been put forward. More certain information is available about later attempts to settle Virginia, also involving some Welsh.

The settlement at Jamestown, Virginia, already mentioned, prospered though not without grave initial difficulties. Every American child knows the story of Captain John Smith, and how his life was saved by Pocohantas, daughter of the American Indian 'King' Powhatan. The story is not so well known this side of the Atlantic. Captain John Smith was chosen as 'President' of the infant colony at Jamestown as early as 1608. "There was added to his Council Captain Waldo and Captain Peter Wynne, two ancient soldiers and valiant men, but ignorant of the business, being newly arrived." (E. Arber, *The Travels of Captain John Smith*, 1910.) Wynne was the name of a very well-known and aristocratic Welsh family; he was in fact sent over to be on the Council. There was added to the Council slightly later Captain Nathaniel Powell who had earlier made a visit to Roanoke. He had come to Virginia, described as 'a worthy gentleman', with Captain John Smith. The veteran Captain Nathaniel Powell was among those slain by Indians in 1622, along with five other members of the Council, and scores of others. Already in earlier years the colonists had had experience of the Indians.

The Indian King Powhatan had divided his territory into shires or provinces, each under a chieftain or 'werowance'. One of these chieftains, a werowance rejoicing in the name of Wowinchopunck, was seen 'skulking' with a company of braves around the small blockhouse at Jamestown. A letter from Captain Wynne to his friend and patron Sir John Egerton, described what happened next. "Captain George Percy, Governor of the town, sent forth Ensign Powell and Ensign Walker to make surprise of him, if they could possibly, and bring him alive into the town, but they, not finding him at any such advantage, yet loath to lose him or let him escape altogether, set upon him (he being one of the mightiest and strongest savages that Powhatan had under him, and one who had killed treacherously many of our men). Powell, running upon him, thrust him twice through the body with a sword" (L. B. Wright, op. cit. p.213). So it seems that, in this very early period of Virginia's history, a Wynne and two Powells played their part.

A. H. Dodd makes some important points in his study of early Welsh migrants to America (A. H. Dodd, *The Character of Early Welsh Emigration to the United States,* 1953). Some of them, like Captain Wynne, came from rich families, but most of them, states Dodd, were servants, going to America with English families, that is, in the days before the mass migrations in the late seventeenth century. Once there, of course, they did not necessarily stay with these families, but made their own way in life, often heading Westwards. Dodd here crosses swords with J. A. Doyle; the latter, in his book on the Middle Colonies, said that not many Welsh stayed long in America beause of the language barrier. Dodd challenges this view. He points out that the language factor did not stop the Welsh going to Elizabeth's Court, or to the Irish settlements. The Welsh, he states, were highly prized as servants in London and America, often holding some of the higher positions in rich homes.

We have just been looking at early Virginian history. Dodd gives an example of his main points from this infant State of Virginia. In 1642 Howell Powell went out as 'headright' to Hugh Gwyn. Powell and his family prospered, and moved from Virginia to Maryland. There he left his name on the map in Howell's Point and Howell's Neck. "He was the first identifiable Welsh settler known to have made a permanent home in the future republic." (Dodd p.7.) Both Howell Powell and Hugh Gwyn, who financed him, came from Brecon, mid-Wales. Owen Williams of Caernarvonshire went out in 1664 as a 'planter' to Virginia. Dodd suggests that he may have been an ancestor of the Thomas Williams, described as a Virginian planter, who fought under George Washington.

Politics back in Britain sometimes affected emigration. Thus a Welsh Catholic, Francis Trafford of Denbighshire, went out to Maryland in 1640, but soon returned home to support Charles I when the Civil War broke out in England; other Welsh in America, Catholic or Protestant, may have returned home to fight on one side or the other.

One remarkable thing was how often the Atlantic was crossed, so soon after the *Mayflower* crossing. The ships remained small, the Atlantic vast and dangerous, yet in the records one reads of intrepid characters, often Welsh nonconformist ministers, crossing and recrossing the ocean. In those days, ties with the old country must have been strong indeed.

We have looked early at Virginia, as some of the first attempts at settlement in the United States proper, as distinct from Canada or the West Indies, occurred there. Virginia in its early days was not a paradise for settlers. In 1615 James I had appointed a commission to send out English criminals to the colony (R. B. Morris, *Government and Labor in Early America,* 1946). There is little evidence that this actually occurred, but it showed the opinion held of the territory. Slaughter by Indians led to 350 deaths in 1622, including John Rolfe, the husband of Pocohantas. By mid-century, however, a high degree of law and order had been established. Permanent institutions of law and government had been set up, and individual Welshmen, among others, were in posts of considerable responsibility at an early period. Virginia became a self-governing colony in 1652. Samuel Mathews was prominent on the Governor's Council very soon; Francis Morgan was a York County Court Justice from 1645 onwards (W. F. Craven, *The Southern Colonies in the Seventeenth Century,* 1949, p.267). These men must have been known, and appreciated, at an earlier date to have earned their eminence in the State. The same applies to Richard Wynne, who was a Justice of the Peace in Virginia (1660) and Hugh Gwin, who sat in the Virginia Assembly as a representative for the new Gloucester County.

This was not surprising, as individual Welshmen, like individual Scots and Irish, not to mention the English, of course, were finding their way in the New World from 1635 onwards. Professor Hartmann has done research on some of these early Welsh-Americans who came alone, and not with the Pilgrims or the Saints, or with later group-migrations. He shows that several parts of the Eastern Seaboard had Welsh visitors, some who went back home, but some who stayed and were the ancestors of later Welsh-Americans. Some of the latter, in the nineteenth century or this, traced their family-tree back to those early Welsh immigrants, either by using family records (which will be illustrated later) or by using the services of professional genealogists. Some fascinating facts have been revealed by both these methods.

In the Southern colonies, Hartmann shows that Robert Lewis went to Gloucester County Virginia (1635), John Price to Henrici County, Virginia, even earlier (1620) and Phillip Thomas to Virginia in 1651 (op. cit. p.57). John Jones and Robert Jones came to Virginia some time after the mid-century. Rhys ap Thomas went to Maryland at the same period. In the Northern States, the same thing applied. "To New England in the seventeenth century came

Griffith Bowen and his son Henry, the first settlers of Woodstock, Connecticut. Alexander Evans settled in Springfield (Mass.) in 1640. Thomas ap Jones went to Weymouth (Mass.) in 1651, James and Miles Morgan to Boston in 1636, the Reverend John Jones to Concord (Mass.) in the 1630's, Evan Thomas to Boston in 1640, David Yule, father of Elihu Yale (Founder of Yale University) to Boston with his mother in 1637, Thomas Flint to Salem (Mass.) in 1642, Richard Rees Morgan to Boston in 1660." (Ibid.)

Speaking of these and other 'individual' immigrants, to, for example, the Middle Colonies, including New York and Long Island, Hartmann says, "Probably all of these people merged quickly into the great body of their English-speaking neighbours, so that only the existence of Welsh surnames gives a clue to their proper identity." (Ibid. p.40.) Hence the value of family records, sometimes revealing an astonishing continuity, as with the long chain of judges in the Jones family of Long Island (see later). Later in the seventeenth century, we hear of grants being made in North Carolina, as the State was being opened up for settlement. As in Virginia, several of the Welsh had come as servants to rich English families. Some nevertheless soon established themselves as reliable and hard-working people, who could safely be trusted with grants of land. Thus Henry Jones, who had come to America as a servant, was granted a hundred acres of land in 1672. Robert and Mary Thomas shared a grant of land (670 acres) with Thomas Clutterbuck, who was probably their master (1671). Evan Jones (servant) was awarded seventy acres of land in 1672 (W. F. Craven, op. cit. p.350).

More evidence that Welsh were involved in mid-seventeenth century life in responsible, if not always high, positions comes from Maryland. In this State, for example, there was a dispute in 1640. Involving a Margaret Brent, it concerned arrears of pay due to soldiers. Evidence was given in Court by Lieutenant William Evans and Captain John Price. They must have been in the State at an earlier date, to have been commissioned so early in the history of the State (M. P. Andrews, *The Founding of Maryland,* 1933, p.125). Similarly, in the same State, in 1662 there was a strange case of an important letter that had clearly been tampered with, and its seals broken, in its passage through several pairs of hands. One pair of hands belonged to Thomas Evans, who apparently was able to show that the letter had left *his* hands intact. It was a letter from Governor Calvert to Mr Edward Lloyd. It was about a Commission to negotiate with the local Indian tribe; Lloyd was a member of that Commission (ibid. pages 213 and 233). Also involved in Indian affairs at that time was Thomas Mathews, who must have been in the territory for some time to have acted as interpreter for 'Emperor Pascatoway'.

Later in the century, Kent County, Maryland, sent a protest to King William III of England shortly after his accession (1689), about actions taken by Coode, the official Proprietor. The letter was signed by leading families of Maryland, including the Evans family. How long had they been there to be recognised as a leading family? It should also be noticed that the Clerk of the Assembly at that time was John Llewellyn.

Likewise noteworthy was an incident at the end of the century, when friction had developed between Protestants and Catholics (there were many of the latter faith in Maryland). A Protestant Declaration was issued; among the signatures to this were the names of John Llewellyn himself and Phillip Lloyd (ibid. p.309). L. H. Gipson (*The British Empire before the American Revolution,* 1936) described the Lloyds as "one of the great land-owning families of Maryland".

Wertenbaker pointed out that "the rulers of Virginia after 1630 were the hardiest of surviving planters" (T. J. Wertenbaker, *Planters of Colonial Virginia,* 1922). This was probably true of the more prosperous in each of the original States. Samuel Mathews, mentioned earlier, was certainly one of Nature's survivors. In 1637 Mathews, and the clique to which he belonged, fell foul of Governor Harvey. He sent them to England, to be tried by the Court of Star Chamber on several charges. But Harvey soon found himself deprived of office; the accused returned to Virginia. Twenty years later Mathews' son became Governor of Virginia.

The family histories of several Welsh-American families in New York, Virginia, Pennsylvania, and elsewhere show that the Welsh were no novices at survival. Proof of this can be found in the chapter devoted to brief biographies.

Chapter 5

William Penn and the Growth of Pennsylvania

WILLIAM PENN was born in London on October 14th 1644. "His father", says Paul Wallace "was a young naval officer, Captain William Penn . . . said to have had Welsh as well as English blood in his veins." (Paul Wallace, *History of Pennsylvania,* p.34.) Professor Hartmann is more precise on the matter. "Penn's grandfather was a Welshman, John Tudor, who was called Pen-Mynedd (of the hill-top) in Wales; when he left Wales, he took the name Penn." (E. G. Hartmann, op. cit. p.43.) Captain William Penn became an Admiral under Oliver Cromwell. Young Penn went to Oxford University and became a Quaker. The famous diarist, Pepys, knew Admiral Penn, and took young Penn and his sister to the theatre. "Returning from the theatre, the Father of American Quakerism left his sword behind in the coach." (A. Bryant, *Samuel Pepys,* p.171.)

In Cromwell's time, George Fox, the Quaker, had made many converts in Wales, particularly in the counties of Radnorshire, Monmouthshire, and Montgomeryshire (as they were called up to 1974). Persecution in Wales, after the return of Charles II, fell mainly on the Quakers, who, at the Court of Great Sessions, Bala, North Wales, were threatened with burning (David Williams, *History of Modern Wales,* 1977, p.12). Their leader in Wales was Richard Davies; one of his converts was Charles Lloyd, the rich squire of Dolobran. The Quakers decided to emigrate to America, where the English Quakers were going under William Penn's leadership. No sooner had Penn obtained the grant of Pennsylvania from the King than the Welsh Quakers bought from him 40,000 acres of land; they left for America in 1682.

42

When they reached Pennsylvania, Charles Lloyd's brother, Thomas, joined them. The brothers were to play a big part in the early history of the State. Thomas Lloyd acted as Deputy-Governor for William Penn when the latter was absent from the colony. We will return soon to Penn and the Quakers, but note that at the time the Welsh Quakers left for America, the Baptists of mid-Wales also left Wales, and settled on the outskirts of Philadelphia (1683); they were joined later by other Baptists from West Wales. The latter soon left, however, and moved further down the Delaware River, buying 30,000 acres of land. So, at the same period, Welsh Quakers and Welsh Baptists were settling near each other in Pennsylvania. Professor Williams comments, "So numerous were the Welsh in Pennsylvania in the early 18th century that it was sufficiently profitable to publish books in America for them" (ibid. p.124). It is estimated that, between 1682-1722, over 2,000 Welsh had settled in Pennsylvania alone.

Pennsylvania, incidentally, was given its name by royal fiat, quite contrary to the wishes of William Penn. He personally objected, as a Quaker, to the use of the family name, which to him seemed un-Quaker-like vanity. He proposed to call his province 'New Wales'. Penn was over-ruled by the King, who had a great respect for his father, the Admiral. The Welsh Quakers had been much influenced by a pamphlet by Penn, printed in 1681, advertising his new domain. They had been thinking of emigrating to America since 1675; Penn's pamphlet was probably the deciding factor. One of their leaders, John ap John, had approached William Penn personally on the matter.

The area first purchased from Penn was later increased by another 50,000 acres. "The Welsh Quakers were unlike those from England, who as a rule were plain people, small farmers, tradesmen, artificers . . . The Welsh Quakers were from the best social classes," said C. M. Andrews (op. cit. p.301). The land the Quakers purchased was known variously as 'the Welsh Tract', 'Cambria', or 'New Wales' by the Quakers themselves. William Penn had his own way about at least part of his province. "The Welsh Quakers left a deep impression upon the region of their occupancy, as the place-names of Merion, Radnor and Haverford show." (Ibid.) Yet another term for the Welsh Tract was the 'Welsh Barony'; it was located to the North-West of Philadelphia, in what was then a very fertile valley, lying in the present-day counties of Montgomery, Chester and Delaware.

The famous Gwynedd settlement came with a second wave of Welsh Quakers. It was in Montgomery County, about eighteen miles West of Philadelphia. It developed mainly as the result of a visit back to Wales by Hugh Roberts. At his instigation William

John and Thomas ap Evans bought 7820 acres and sold it in small batches to the North Welsh Quakers who arrived in 1698. Others joined them later from Wales, and the Gwynedd area was settled between 1698-1720. William Penn visited the area himself in 1701 to see how things were going. Some temporary meeting-houses were built, soon to be replaced by new ones as numbers increased.

One of their number, Edward Foulkes, wrote the only description of the Quaker emigration, and this was translated from the Welsh by his grandson, Howard M. Jenkins, many years later; it included the genealogy of the Foulkes family, and also the Evans and Roberts families, in his account of the Settlement (H. M. Jenkins, *The Gwynedd Settlement*, 1884). All the Welsh present in the area at 1711 appended their names in a petition in that year for a road to be built from Gwynedd to Philadelphia. H. M. Jenkins stated that the first settlers in Gwynedd were Edward Morgan, a tailor, and John Jones, a carpenter, both before 1710.

From 1734 onwards the character of the settlement changed, with an influx of German immigrants. There was eventually intermarriage — and occasional friction — between the immigrant groups. "Gwynedd," said Professor Hartmann. "became one of the most prosperous areas of Pennsylvania." That was later; at first there was a great deal of hardship and hard work. "Na ty, nac ymoger" (neither house nor shelter) said, for example, John Jones' father when he first saw the settlement (Paul Wallace, op. cit. p.59). Along with the Germans came other ethnic groups from Europe, all seeking to name their little settlements after places back home. "Dutch, Swedes, English, Welsh, Germans, Scots and Irish, all embroidering their homesickness into the tapestry of new towns." (Ibid.)

"The first great wave of immigration (following Penn's pamphlet) came from Wales," states Paul Wallace. "Hundreds of ruddy-faced thick-set and bright-eyed Welshmen came in hopes of planting a new Wales under the aegis of William Penn, who was said to have been of Welsh descent." (Paul Wallace, op. cit. p.59.) These early Welsh immigrants were mostly farmers, but there were men of wealth and education among them, like the several branches of the Morris family. Wallace points out that second and third generation Welsh in America tended to move to the cities, entering commerce and the professions. "Before 1730 most of the physicians in Pennsylvania were Welshmen. William Penn's own physician was Dr. Wynne; later on George Washington's doctor was Dr. John Jones." (Ibid.) The first medical book written in the United States was by Dr. Thomas Cadwalader. Professor Wallace points out that the Welsh could not keep entirely to themselves, as they had first intended. He himself considered that the English and Welsh in Pennsylvania were both strengthened by the mingling of the two races. He adds however, "The Welsh, as a distinct people, are still remembered there by the surnames they have scattered over the State, such as Jones, Cadwalader, Morris, Davies, Richards, Griffiths, Evans, Hughes, Rees or Rhys, and Llewellyn . . . and place-names such as Gwynedd, Meirion, Radnor, Haverford, Brynmawr . . . Best of all is the strain they contributed — intense, artistic, intellectual and physically vigorous." (Ibid. p.59.)

Most of the Quaker Welsh in the Welsh Barony area near Philadelphia were gentry or yeomen farmers. Some were wealthy enough to have brought their own servants from Wales. In 1685, however, came an unwelcome event to them, in the form of interference from the provincial authorities who drew a line between counties, dividing the Welsh Barony into two parts; in 1690 the colonial government abolished the civil authority of the Welsh Barony, setting up regular township government. This was contrary to the original agreement between John ap John and Penn. The Welsh had to give in. "Thereafter," says Hartmann, "Penn was scarcely a popular person within the confines of the Barony." (See Hartmann, *The Welsh Society of Philadelphia.)*

In the very early days, the Quakers worshipped under the trees, or within their homes if the weather was wet; their first proper meeting-houses, log at first, then stone, were at Meirion, Haverford and Radnor. An interesting account of the Quakers in early Pennsylvania, including the Welsh, comes from Charles S. Browning (*The Welsh Settlement of Pennsylvania,* 1912). He mentions the Meirion Meeting-house, which he said was completed in 1695, and still there in 1912. It was, he said, symbolic of the number of Welsh Friends from Merionethshire, North Wales. Browning, himself a Quaker, gave details, from Quaker records, of the Welsh delegates who met Penn. They included three doctors of medicine: Dr. Griffith Owen of Merionethshire, Dr. Edward Jones of Bala, Dr. Thomas Wynne of Flintshire. These three doctors and delegates Bevan, Roberts, Ellis, and Owen went from Wales to Pennsylvania, and helped the Settlement to become established. They had all originally been inspired by John ap John, but he himself, owing to ill-health, did not go to Pennsylvania.

The Merion township started with a purchase of 5000 acres of land by the Thomas and Jones Company at a cost of £100, subscribed by seventeen Friends from Merionethshire. They sailed together in the *Lyon* from Liverpool. Dr. Jones was chosen as their representative in the Pennsylvania Assembly. In Browning's book are listed twenty-six American descendants of Dr. Edward Jones. Similarly there are listed forty descendants of John Cadwalader, a young Welsh Quaker schoolmaster in the party. These included Dr. Thomas Cadwalader, Colonel Lambert Cadwalader, General John Cadwalader, General Thomas Cadwalader, Judge John Cadwalader, Dr. Charles Cadwalader, and Admiral Cadwalader Ringgold, at the time that Browning wrote. So the earliest settlers by no means faded from history, as some writers have asserted, and their descendants had distinguished careers. Some of the earliest and most prominent families were soon united in marriage, such as that of Dr. Edward Jones' son Jonathan, to Gainor Owen in 1688. The young teacher, John Cadwalader, was on the City Council, and a member of the Pennsylvania Assembly until his death in 1734.

The original land bought from William Penn was all sold out to Welsh Quaker immigrants by successive Land Companies, seven altogether. The second of these Land Companies (Lloyd and Davies Company) had sold land to the famous Quaker brothers, Charles, Thomas and David Lloyd; the first two were graduates of Jesus College, Oxford. Charles Lloyd and his wife had been in prison for years because of their faith. So had others in subsequent parties, such as Dr. Thomas Wynne, a celebrated physician in London, before being jailed for six years for being a Quaker. He was one of the many London Welsh who came to America; the story of the Welsh-Americans would indeed be incomplete if it were limited to only those Welsh who emigrated direct from Wales. Shortly after this Welsh Quaker emigration, much of Welsh emigration to the United States, particularly among the more educated, was directly inspired by the London Honourable Society of Cymmrodorion, founded, it must be remembered, as early as 1751. Dr. Thomas Wynne came over, appropriately, in the *Welcome;* he became a justice of the peace in Pennsylvania, and a Representative at the State Assembly. He died at Lewes, Sussex (Pennsylvania) in 1692. Most of the Quaker settlers came from North Wales, but the third Land Company sold also to settlers from Llantrisant and Carmarthen.

While discussing 'the Welsh in the United States', one has to preserve a sense of moderation and proportion. Professor Paul Wallace helps towards this by reminding us of the heterogeneity of the Pennsylvanian population, even three hundred years ago and onwards. "The people who now inhabit Pennsylvania are, as they have always been, a heterogeneous lot, the Indians who were here first, Europeans of all kinds — Dutch, Swedish, Finnish, English, Welsh, German, Swiss, Scottish, Scotch-Irish, straight Irish (sic), French, Italian, Jewish, Greek, Austrian, Hungarian, Polish, Czechoslovakian, Armenian, with an infusion of African and Oriental." (Paul Wallace, op. cit. (Foreword).) No wonder that Penn had in mind the idea of the 'melting-pot', with his belief that freedom flourishes best in a diversified society. Reading the list above, one cannot become too narrowly ethnocentric about any one group, Welsh or otherwise.

There were times, no doubt, when Penn could have done without some of his Welsh colleagues, useful as they were in general. The Lloyd brothers, Thomas and David, were both in high office, and both forceful characters. Thomas Lloyd, for example, refused to pass letters-patent at the order of the Council to commission five provincial judges, as he considered the commissions, to use his own words (and spelling) "more moulded by ffancy than fformed by law" (C. M. Andrews, op. cit. Vol. III, p.309).

Controversy with David arose from his refusing, in very scornful language, to deliver certain records of the provincial court for the inspection of the Council. There were very heated debates about this in Council, which deeply distressed William Penn (L. Sharpless, *Political Leaders of Pennsylvania,* p.55). Penn was particularly worried by the fierce and continued quarrels between followers of James Logan and David Lloyd, "the fiery Welsh leader of the popular party in the Pennsylvanian Assembly". Lloyd in fact tried, without success, to get Logan impeached for treason. Thomas Lloyd meanwhile was President of the Council 1684-1688, and Governor-General in 1691. (Note that John Evans and George Thomas had been Deputy-Governors.)

To Thomas Lloyd, Penn wrote, "For the love of God, me and the poor country, do not be so litigious and brutish." (S. Morison, *Oxford History of the American People,* p.128.) William Penn had written to his Council, "I am a man of sorrows, and you augment my griefs, not because you do not love me, but because you do not love one another." Part of the trouble was with what Joseph Kelley called Penn's "incredible propensity for picking the wrong people" (J. Kelley, *Pennsylvania,* 1980, p.59). Kelley continues, "He chose a wholly incompatible group to run the colony, the cantankerous Nicholas More, the highly unpopular James Claypole, the anti-proprietory David Lloyd . . . and John Eckley, whose prime interest was in pressing the contentions of the Welsh, on the West Bank of the Schuylkill, that their land was a 'barony' independent of local courts and taxes." David Lloyd was also the champion of these highly independent Welsh "those ancient Britons as they sometimes called themselves, who boasted no Anglo-Saxon blood and claimed genealogies traceable to Adam." (Kelley.)

Since a substantial number of non-Quakers in the lower counties, and some other groups, also disputed his authority, "Penn's 'holy experiment' turned from a dream of harmony to a nightmare of conflict" (R. C. Simmons, *The American Colonies,* 1976, p.143). But Penn was tough, experienced and patient — he knew that the

47

price of freedom was much argument. On the whole, states Admiral Morison, people got on reasonably well with each other in the 'city of brotherly love'.

Pennsylvania continued expanding and increasing in population during the eighteenth century. "Pennsylvania grew at an astounding rate, surpassing that of any other colony, and telescoping into a few years, developments that took place over much longer periods in slower-moving societies." By the end of the century a drive to settle the west of the State was in full flood. On that flood came a new wave of Welsh settlers. The lead was given by that Baptist minister from Glamorgan already mentioned, namely Morgan John Rees or Rhys (later to call himself Rhees). He had emigrated to Pennsylvania in 1792; he was responsible for the formation in 1796 of the Cambrian Company. This company acquired land in West Pennsylvania for a new Welsh settlement, of which Beulah was to be the centre; later Ebensburg became the main centre. Mention has already been made of Llanbrynmair, Montgomeryshire, from which so many came to the United States. A large group from this village made their homes in Cambria. Later still some Welsh from Llanbrynmair, under Ezekial Hughes, moved West to Paddy's Run, Ohio, of which more later.

George Roberts remained in Ebensburg and, many years later, wrote a vivid account of the early settlements in *Y Cronicl*. A pamphlet extolling the virtues of the Cambrian settlements was issued in 1800. It was worded as a "letter from Welsh immigrants in Cambria to their brethren in Wales". The pamphlet praised the soil in the area "rich enough to bear all kinds of grain, and very good for hay and pasture, well adapted for the making of cheese and butter" (E. Abbott, *Historical Aspects of the Immigration Problem,* 1926). "We have a market for everything we have to dispose of at Beulah . . . Our end in establishing this settlement was for the general good of the Welsh, particularly that they may have the privilege of hearing the gospel in their own language; there are in Cambria, preachers of different denominations living together in peace and amity . . . within the last four years upwards of one hundred families have come to our neighbourhood." Back in England, William Cobbett did not think so much of the project. He attacked the pamphlet (in his *Porcupine Gazette*) as "a base and infamous trick to decoy the poor Welsh from their homes to go and augment the population and the value of land at Cambria, where Theophilus Rees and his relation Morgan Rees have purchased great quantities of land, and where they have already ruined hundreds of poor creatures." (Quoted in Abbot p.28.)

Professor Gwyn Williams has shown how the push towards Cambria in Western Pennsylvania, and to Beulah in particular, was the result of the merging of the Madoc legend with the fiery radicalism of the 1790's. The success of Ebensburg, and the sad failure of Beulah, have to be seen in this wide ideological context. The full story is vividly unfolded in Gwyn Williams' *The Search for Beulah Land.* Ezekial Hughes and Rees Lloyd were the leaders of a first party to make its way there, after appalling difficulties, reaching Beulah in 1796. A second party, under Morgan John Rhys himself arrived there in 1797.

Ezekial Hughes, then 26 years old, had organised the first party at Llanbrynmair, North Wales. It took two years for his party to reach America, after many perils, including a violent storm which dismasted their ship. "As the *Maria* at last sighted the Delaware, the Captain turned to Rees Lloyd and said 'Well, Mr Lloyd, there's no need to preach and pray any more. We come from the sea to the river.' " Whereupon, as Rees Lloyd pointed out with wry satisfaction, the *Maria* ran aground (Gwyn Williams. p.126).

It was in the autumn of 1796 that the first party of settlers crossed the Allegheny Mountains to reach the wilderness of western Pennsylvania. They had come up from Philadelphia by boat, and then on foot. They found their way by compass through the vast forests until they reached their goal. Many years later Rees Lloyd, the Pontypool minister, wrote that his first home in Cambria was a little cabin covered with spruce, and snow two feet deep, where the town of Ebensburg came to be built. The total significance of the expeditions to Cambria was well put by Gwyn Williams. "Madoc then, playing on the minds of the Dissenter leaders, could turn emigrants into Children of a Cymric Israel . . . with Morgan John Rhys as their Moses." In the Welsh periodical that he had produced, Rhys encouraged the Welsh in their adventure, as if he spoke for Madoc himself "Dyma ni yn awr ar daith ein gobaith" (here we are now on the journey of our hope).

This whole period, say 1790 to 1820, is particularly interesting, not only in the context of the Madoc legend, or even its great effect upon the renaissance of Welsh identity, but also its influence upon Welsh-Americans in the nineteenth century. This necessarily brief reference to it here cannot do justice to the role of the Madoc myth in Welsh emigration to the United States at that time. Relevant here is the part played by the London Welsh of the period, as told in the *History of the Honourable Society of Cymmrodorion* by R. T. Jenkins and H. T. Ramage (published by the London Cymmrodorion, 1951).

Although many of the Welsh who came to Philadelphia were well off, there were many initial difficulties about the land claimed from the wild. Edward Jones, who had arrived on the *Lion* wrote to his friend John ap Thomas back in Wales, "we are short of our expectations by reason that ye town is not to be builded at Upland . . . we are enforced to take ye Country lots . . . the people generally are Swedish . . . we are among the English, which sent us both venison and new milk." *(Memorial History of Philadelphia,* 1895, p.35.) "The Welsh had been among the first to respond to Penn's call, recognising him as one of their own kin . . . that the Penns of England came from Wales is plain. Penn is as Welsh as Wynn."(Ibid. p.63.)

The arrival of John Evans, aged about 26, as appointed Deputy Governor of the State, was a disaster. Evans was definitely not the man for what was to some extent a Quaker community. "Penn's reliance on the clannishness of the Welsh was not prudently attended with the remembrance that the Celtic temper is liable also to domestic quarrel." (Ibid. p.67.) Deputy Governor Evans and William Penn Junior were drinking at a tavern when a row started. Griffiths Jones and Anthony Morris, the Mayor, came in to try and make peace, but the crowd sided with Evans and Penn. An unpleasant scene developed. Not the best publicity for the Welsh Deputy Governor in a city where the leading families were the Lloyds, the Morrises and the Cadwaladers. John Evans was soon sent back to Wales.

In a later section more will be said about the remarkable Cadwalader family, which had so much to do with the growth and development of Philadelphia. Very well known in eighteenth century Philadelphia was Dr. Thomas Cadwalader, two of whose sons fought as officers in the American War of Independence. The Morrises, as we have seen, came from the same Welsh Quaker stock (at one time London Welsh). Their descendants in the United States are said to number over 30,000. The settlements in Pennsylvania kept adding to their population, and developing off-shoots in new settlements, with Welsh folk among the various ethnic groups swarming in all areas after the American War of Independence. In eastern and central Pennsylvania the pioneering days were over; most of the new immigrants bought established farms abandoned by earlier settlers who were pushing West, either in search of adventure or joining new settlements, such as those in Ohio, in the mid-west. Lastly in Pennsylvania came new settlements in the Portage area, namely Palmyra, a small additional settlement at Green Township, Indiana County, twelve miles from Ebensburg, the township of Neath in Bradford County, and small settlements at Spring Brook in Lackawanna County and at Clifford in Susquehanna County, most of them having some Welsh.

The Welsh, being a numerically smaller group to start with, were increasingly out-numbered, not only by the English but by other ethnic groups. Thus the Bucks quote the 1790 Census to show "the bewildering complex of national origins" apparent in, for example, Western Pennsylvania by that date (S. J. and E. H. Buck, *The Planting of Civilisation in Western Pennsylvania,* 1939). Taking figures for 'heads of family', of the 12,955 white families in the five western counties of the State, about 37% were still of English origin, 7% Welsh, 17% Scottish, 19% Irish, 12% German, while 8% were of other origin. In the five counties, Welsh proportions were stronger in Washington County with 9%, Allegheny County with 8% of the population 'heads of family', Bedford and Fayette counties each with 7% Welsh 'heads of family' and Westmoreland with only 3% on that index.

As mentioned earlier, Pennsylvania may not have become the spiritual paradise that Penn would have wished to see, but signs of a civilised community were increasing. At times Penn had despaired and complained of "the scurvy quarrels that break out . . . to the Disgrace of the Province, there is nothing but Good said of the Place, and little that's Good said of the People." Penn adhered however to the family motto that his Admiral father had adopted — 'he kept his tiller true'. The political foundations of the new State, for all the quarrels, were sound. As well as agricultural developments in the counties, commerce and industry were both expanding in Philadelphia. The capital city was becoming the financial centre of the British colonies in America, and was gaining recognition in Britain and Europe as an important city with an expanding foreign trade.

Prominent in the early industrial developments in, or near to, Philadelphia was the Morris family. Anthony Morris and Company established the Durham Iron Works up the Delaware River as early as 1727. The Cornwall iron-ore mine became the greatest source of iron ore in America at the time. Miners were brought over from Wales, even at that comparatively early date, to work in the mines and furnaces, as Paul Wallace pointed out *(Pennsylvania,* p.202). This was to anticipate the next flush of Welsh, as Pittsburg developed in the next century.

The cultural life of Philadelphia grew as its commerce and industry grew. Amongst those who contributed to Philadelphia's early cultural advance was Lewis Evans, who produced the first good map of the State. Beautiful buildings were being erected in what is now Old Philadelphia; these included James Logan's country home, Stenton, and Hope Lodge, completed at mid-century by Samuel Morris. Of the Morris family it is probably Robert Morris who is best known in Pennsylvanian history. When America won the War of Independence, the meetings to draw up the federal Constitution were held in Philadelphia. Benjamin Franklin, then 81 years old, headed the Pennsylvanian delegation.

Alongside him in the delegation, which had a total of eight members, were two Morrises. One of them was the aristocratic Gouvernor Morris; the other was Robert Morris, who in 1781 had set up the Bank of North America. For three years he had been Superintendent of Finances for the State, Gouvernor Morris being his assistant. Later Robert Morris came to be known as 'the Financier of the American Revolution'.

In early Philadelphia a large proportion of the City Fathers were Welsh, including Mayors Edward Roberts and Robert Wharton. The oldest Welsh Society, to honour Saint David, started in Philadelphia. It was there that Ellis Pugh, a stonemason and a Quaker, wrote *Annerch i'r Cymru* (Salute to Wales) in 1721. It was in Philadelphia that Abel Morgan produced the first Welsh concordance to the Bible (1730). "The English and the Welsh together were responsible for the pattern of civilised establishment in Eastern Pennsylvania." (L. B. Wright, *The Atlantic Frontier, 1607-1763,* 1947, p.223.) "Several thousand Welshmen — many of them substantial citizens, lawyers, farmers and artizans, founded homes in the Welsh Tract, and made useful contributions to the progress of the colony . . . fiercely independent, hating tyranny from church or state, the Welsh contingent provided some of the colony's most zealous protagonists of liberty." (Ibid.) Even today one of the sights of Philadelphia is the Powel House, purchased in 1768 by Samuel Powell, first mayor of the city after the coming of the new Republic. The St. David's Hotel in the St David's district still welcomes guests.

It has been shown that several developments in the expanding State of Pennsylvania involved Welsh immigrants. Their influence in the State continued through their descendants. Examples of this will be given later in discussing religious factors in Welsh immigration. To anticipate somewhat, in matters outside the field of religion, the Pennsylvanian Railway Company, mid-way through the nineteenth century, laid its railroad through Welsh Quaker territory. One of its directors gave Welsh names to stations on the line from the great Broad Street Station; trains went through Merion, Narberth, Wynnewood, Ardmore, Haverford, Brynmawr, Radnor, St. Davids and Berwyn.

At Brynmawr College, student hostels were named Merion, Radnor, Denbigh and Pembroke. Welsh links with the Old Country, 'yr hen wlad', were maintained, not only by post, but by the little ship *Union* that plied regularly between Philadelphia, Cork and Swansea for many years. While keeping up links with Wales, the Welsh of Pennsylvania at that early period were still keeping up Welsh customs and, of course, the Welsh language itself; as we have seen, the first book in Welsh in America was by

52

the Welsh Quaker, Ellis Pugh. He had come from Dolgelley, sailing from Milford Haven in 1686.

While most Welsh in the State were leading normal, respectable hard-working lives, there were some, perhaps more colourful, but less respectable exceptions. Professor Wallace of Pennsylvania tells of one of the State's earliest and best known rogues. "Best known of all Pennsylvania's outlaws was David Lewis, quixotic and very much in the Robin Hood tradition . . . " (even to the story of the poor widow and the wicked sheriff). "Lewis was tall, handsome, well-mannered, strong but gentle — crimes of violence he abhorred." Nevertheless he was known as Robber Lewis (the Welsh seem to have transferred to America their gift for picturesque nicknames). The worthy religious Welsh of both city and countryside were no doubt glad to see the end of the Welsh highwayman when he died in 1820 (Wallace, op. cit. p.175). Yet Twm Shon Catti might have got on well with Robber Lewis if many years, and many miles of ocean, had not separated them. Even his critics would not have liked the manner of Robber Lewis's death. Shot in the arm, he would not have the arm amputated; gangrene set in, and he died a painful death.

Pennsylvania was thus filling up with population, and expanding into its western areas; other parts of the Eastern United States were developing their own settlements, townships and civic institutions. Space does not allow a detailed look at all these developments. Something has been said in earlier pages about the beginnings of Massachusetts. Pennsylvania has been given considerable space, rightly so, especially as Welsh Pennsylvanians often influenced cultural developments in other States. Maine, Connecticut, New Hampshire, New Jersey, Rhode Island, New York State, Virginia, North and South Carolina, all of these places have been the subject of separate histories.

We can only consider a few of the Welsh influences and interests in these States as they developed in this early period. In fact, in some of them the Welsh were there only in small numbers, but they were often in influential families, best dealt with in the biographical section of this book. On the other hand, New York State, like Ohio, was one of those States where the Welsh came in appreciable numbers. Whether many or few came to any State, it must be remembered that, as shown in an earlier chapter, all States had some Welsh settlers who left a heritage of Welsh names.

Already mentioned have been educational innovations with some Welsh connections, such as Brynmawr College at Philadelphia. Yale University likewise had such Welsh connections. Thomas Yale and his wife lived at Plas Grono, near Wrexham, North Wales. At his death, his widow, Anne, emigrated to Boston (Mass.) She married again and with her new husband Thomas Eaton, moved to New Haven, Connecticut. Her son by her first marriage, David, returned to Boston. There he in turn married, and had a son, Elihu Yale (1648). This son went to London, and started an extremely profitable career with the East India Company. Enormously wealthy, he returned to Britain from India, and settled at his grandfather's home in Plas Grono, Wrexham. He managed to combine being High Sheriff of Denbigh with running a diamond business in London. A college had been started at New Haven, Connecticut in 1700. The rich Elihu Yale used some of his wealth to build up the infant college into a great University; he sent, for example, numerous books and pictures to help the new college. The church at Yale is said to be modelled upon the parish church at Wrexham.

The foundation of Brown College, Rhode Island, which beame Brown University, owed a lot to Morgan Edwards of Pontypool, a Baptist minister who became pastor of the church at Pennepek, Philadelphia. He founded the college at Rhode Island, and persuaded his friend, Dr. William Richards, to present it with a library. Edwards, who wrote several books about the early settlers, useful as sources, was buried in Pencader Cemetery, Delaware.

Another College with Welsh connections was William and Mary College, Virginia, as old as Yale, if not Harvard. The great Welsh poet whom George Borrow admired so much, namely Goronwy Owen, born in Anglesey, was ordained as a priest but took up a teaching post at William and Mary in 1758. Admittedly he did not stay long there, for reasons which will be given later in this book. He, however, fulfilled his original ambition of becoming a priest by becoming Rector of St. Andrews Church, Virginia. He lived a very lonely and unhappy life there, for his wife and child had died on the voyage out to America. Incidentally, according to Professor David Williams, his salary as Rector was paid in tobacco, 18,000 pounds of it per annum (D. Williams, op. cit. p.37).

The Welsh, in the melting-pot that Penn had foreseen, usually tried at first to preserve their language. They had also, however, to become fluent at English, if they were not so beforehand (this is where the many London Welsh who went out had an advantage). In this respect they became subject, like all Americans, to a standardisation in the use of the English language. Boorstin maintains that, transported to America, English speech tended to become more uniform. John Pickering, as early as 1816, noted "greater uniformity of dialect throughout the United States than is to be found throughout England". In Virginia in 1724 the Reverend Hugh Jones observed that "the Planters, and even the Native Negroes, generally talk good English without Idiom or Tone, and can discourse handsomely upon most common subjects''. William and Mary College, where Hugh Jones was Professor of Mathematics, was particularly concerned that students spoke with a standard and correct accent. Hugh Jones desired that ''a Publick Standard were fix'd to direct Posterity, and prevent irregularity and confused Abuses and Corruptions in our Writings and Expressions''. Benjamin Franklin amongst his many and varied interests, also wanted a standard American language — but with a constant respect for the traditional English language. It is interesting to note that this Welshman, Hugh Jones, had considerable influence on the development of the American language, as did another clergyman, a Scotsman this time, the Reverend John Witherspoon, President of Princeton University, in the journal *The Druid* (1781). Incidentally, Hugh Jones, as a Reverend and a Welshman, felt himself impelled to give his opinions on a wide range of subjects, as we see in the Boorstin index (D. J. Boorstin, *The American Colonial Experience*, p.301).**''Jones. Reverend Hugh:** On the Church of Maryland, on commerce, on hiring ministers, on knowledge, on language, on smallpox, on tobacco and religion, on Virginia clergy, on Virginians.'' In America, as in Britain, the Welsh were seldom tongue-tied or inarticulate, whether in English or in Welsh — as George Borrow, English of the English, noted in his mid-nineteenth century *Wild Wales*.

Awareness of language was linked to awareness of American identity. This was much affected by the dynamic spread westward of American civilisation. Boorstin (op. cit.) said that never before in a civilised country had physical and intellectual expansion been so clearly synonymous. ''The crowning symbol of this American identity was the Lewis and Clarke Expedition, conceived and fitted out by Jefferson.'' Conceived, it may be noted, by one of Welsh stock and carried out largely under the leadership of another of Welsh stock. The sense of American identity was reinforced by early geographical and historical accounts of the various States as they emerged e.g. Belknap's *History of New Hampshire* (1791). Here also was a Welsh contribution in Samuel Williams' *History of Vermont* (1809). As we have seen, several of the Welsh ministers who led their flocks to the New World had to carve their way through impenetrable and hostile lands; often they wrote up their experiences as a contribution to knowledge, and a warning to successors of the dangers to be expected. These accounts, taken as a whole, were a valuable addition to knowledge of the United States, and to the sense of American identity.

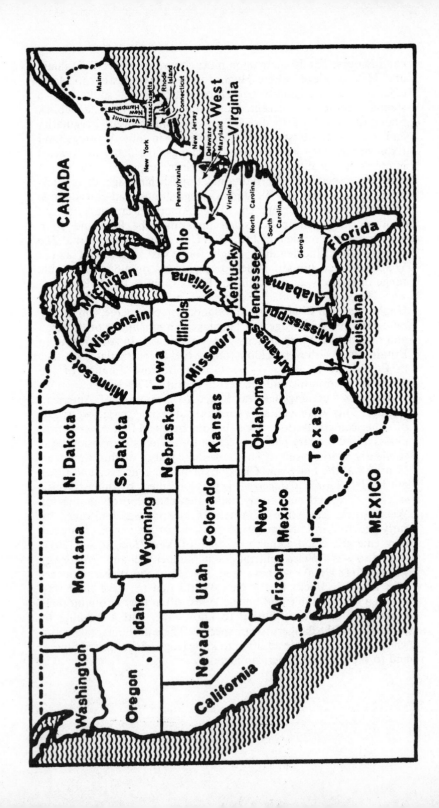

Chapter 6

Religion and Welsh Emigration to the United States

OFTEN during the seventeenth and eighteenth century, and into the nineteenth century, church and chapel members followed their pastors into the New World. As well as the drive of a shared religion, the pastor was often the only educated man in the local community. These pastors were usually men of outstanding gifts of leadership, vision and determination. They featured in the opening up of the United States as prominently as any explorers, soldiers or backwoodsmen. The tale of American expansion is littered with the names of these reverend and inspired men. This was particularly so at periods when intense religious feelings, often curbed and frustrated in the home country by the State, led to new waves of immigration into America.

Generally in the seventeenth century the driving faith was that of the Quakers or the Baptists, but often Presbyterians and other denominations, including Anglicans, were involved. Thus several Welsh 'gentlemen of good note' went out with Robert Blinman of Gloucester at an early date (1639), when he became a pastor at Pilgrim Church, Marshfield, New England (A. H. Dodd, op. cit. passim). Marmaduke Matthews was upset by an adverse report from the Bishop of Saint Davids, so left Wales to become a pastor at Yarmouth, Massachusetts. One member of Blinman's party was William Thomas who later became pastor of a chapel near Plymouth (Mass.) (T. Hutchinson, *History of Massachusetts Bay,* 1936 edition).

Several of these pastors in the early days took some members of congregations with them, or the latter joined them at a later date, heeding the advice of their pastors on travel, money etc. Religious motives were often the most important in British emigration to the

United States. The settlers in Boston and Plymouth (Mass.) were almost entirely motivated by their religion, and the persecution that had followed from it. The Quakers, as an example of this, have already been discussed in the chapter on Pennsylvania. There were, however, big differences between individual States in the matter of religious belief and religious tolerance. It might be interesting therefore to start this chapter by comparing Virginia and Rhode Island with Massachusetts, to illustrate the latter point.

"Compared with the Puritans of New England," comments Boorstin, "the Virginians were not passionate about religious dogma, for the simple reason that they knew nothing about it. George Washington, though an active vestryman, probably could not have told the difference between the Church of Virginia and any other, except that the Established Church stood for moderation in all things, and was the bulwark of decency in his community." (D. J. Boorstin, op. cit. p.157.) Boorstin gives a typical Virginian example of such moderation. William Fitzhugh, a prominent member of Virginian society, himself an Anglican, lived happily beside George Brent, a Catholic; Fitzhugh even considered a scheme for importing Catholics to a settlement of their own. Boorstin explains that the Virginians did not like 'revivalist fireworks'. When the militant Presbyterians invaded Virginia in the 1740's, the Reverend Patrick Henry described their ways — "They thunder out in awful words and new-coined phrases — cursing and scolding, calling the old people 'Grey-headed devils' . . . and 'lumps of hell-fire' etc." Prominent among these "Enthusiastic Preachers" was Samuel Davies, who was doing the rounds of meeting-houses, filling them with Welsh eloquence. The Church authorities made an example of him and curtailed his activities. They did not want a "network of religious agitators presided over by some super-pastor" (Boorstin). To show their impartiality, the Church of Virginia later sent fifty Baptist revivalists to jail, not for their beliefs, but for "disturbing the peace".

Incidentally, while not admiring his style of preaching, the worthies of Virginia owed a good deal to the Reverend Samuel Davies, at a time when its very existence was threatened. In 1755, the threat from Indian tribes, always menacing, became much more dangerous. "All the frontiers of Virginia," according to Lewis Evans, a contemporary observer, "had been reduced to one universal waste by the burning, murdering and scalping committed by the Indians." Virginian counties started raising troops to meet the horrific situation, in Hanover County particularly. Prominent in the defence measures was the Reverend Samuel Davies; most of the troops raised were recruited by him, and he was described at the time as "the best recruiting officer in the district". It was in a sermon to the company he raised that he made the famous prophetic statement, often quoted, "I may point out to the public that heroic youth, Colonel George Washington, whom I cannot but hope Providence has hitherto preserved, in so signal a manner, for some important service".

In helping to secure the safety of his State, Davies was also helping to preserve the identity and continuance of his Presbyterian Church within that State. "Samuel Davies, with his benevolence, good sense, moderation, eloquence and winning personality, was a steadying force for the Presbyterian Church in those critical years." (R. L. Morton, *Colonial Virginia,* 1960, p.677.)

Rhode Island and Roger Williams. The story of Rhode Island and Roger Williams really started in Massachusetts. This was the most staid and strict of all the New England States. In 1631 there came to the infant Colony someone whom the *Cambridge Modern History* describes as "a brilliant, energetic, attractive young Welshman". Professor David Williams is not convinced of Roger Williams' Welsh background, but some American authors agree with the *Cambridge Modern History;* it is possible that he came of London Welsh stock, or from one of the numerous families with a Welsh background living in other parts of the United Kingdom. C. M. Andrews describes him as "temperamentally excitable . . . divinely mad", as one of the divines of the time called him, "often hasty in speech and indiscreet." (C. M. Andrews, op. cit. Vol II, p.59.) He was only twenty-eight when he came to Massachusetts, contrasting strongly with the elderly sobersides of that colony. There was not only a temperamental gap, but a generation gap.

Perhaps a more serious matter in those days, he repudiated leading doctrines of the Puritan body, as C. M. Andrews clearly demonstrates. As the *Cambridge Modern History* puts it, "He differed as much, in Christian belief, from the divines of Massachusetts as they did from the Church of England." He held in an extreme form the doctrine, utterly repudiated by Puritan teachers as a whole, that the secular power must not control nor in any way meddle with religion. In October 1635 he was brought before the General Council of the colony. He refused to alter his views, and was banished from Massachusetts.

Massachusetts' loss was Rhode Island's gain. He purchased from the Indians a tract of land and formed a settlement which became Providence. Later he went back to England to obtain a grant from the Commission of the Long Parliament. This incorporated Providence, Portsmouth and Newport under the title of Providence Plantation; later this became more commonly known as Rhode Island. Of his leadership at Rhode Island, C. M. Andrews says, "Roger Williams welcomed the coming of the humble and unwanted folk who had been unable to find peace at either Plymouth or Massachusetts Bay, and who were, like himself, at war with the orthodox and conventional in life." (Ibid. Vol II, p.6.)

All authorities seem to agree with Admiral Morison that Roger Williams was the most beloved of colonial founders prior to William Penn. "The Indians," says Morison, "whose language he studied, lodging with them in their filthy, smoky homes, adored Williams. He respected their individuality, protected them against land-hungry members of his race, and never tried to convert them unless they asked for it." (S. Morison, *Oxford History of the American People,* op. cit. p.68.)

The Baptists, whom he joined eventually, followed his lead in standing for religious liberty. To understand how the Baptists came to Massachusetts, and eventually much of the States, particularly the South, it is necessary to go back to events in Wales at the time of Cromwell, in the mid-seventeenth century. After the Civil War and the execution of Charles I the Puritan Committee of Plundered Ministers sent Morgan Llwyd and Vavasour Powell on a mission of investigation to North Wales (1648). Meanwhile John Miles, a Baptist Minister, went from his London church to Ilston in Gower, near Swansea. Other Baptist chapels were set up at Llanharan, Hay, Carmarthen and Abergavenny. At the Restoration (of Charles II) John Miles and the South Wales Baptists fled to America.

One reason for making a preliminary mention of the Baptists at this point is the above-mentioned link with Roger Williams. Another reason for doing so is that John Miles (sometimes spelt Myles) was typical of a regular occurrence in Welsh-American history, the naming of new homes after the 'old country' homes; this was referred to in the opening chapters. There is a special interest in John Miles and his party, in that much of the earlier Welsh immigration into the United States, long before the immigration of industrial workers, was from North Wales.

When Miles, an Oxford graduate, and his Baptists came to Massachusetts, they settled first (1663) at Rehoboth in the Plymouth Colony. They soon moved because of quarrels with the Plymouth authorities. The latter however gave them a grant of land, and they eventually settled at Swanzey, later to be changed to Swansea. This was about ten miles from Providence, Rhode Island. Miles remained pastor of the Swansea church until his death in 1683. By the end of the century, four other Baptist churches had been built in the area. "Their descendants," states Hartmann "are still numerous in the vicinity, and the church (in 1967) is still active." (Op. cit. p.42.) Perhaps the best known descendant of John Miles was the late General Appleton Myles (1839-1925), Chief of Staff of the United States Army during World War I. Rehoboth had been incorporated in 1645 and Swansea in 1667, with John Miles junior as its first Clerk. "The motive to Swansea settlement," states the Reverend Otis Wright, "was religious freedom." (Otis O. Wright, *The History of Swansea (Mass.), 1917.*) Swansea (Mass.) is best known in America as a major casualty in 1675 when the Indian chieftain, King Philip, killed many Welsh.

On the Atlantic seaboard, in Delaware and South Carolina particularly, the expansion by the Baptists and the Presbyterians was especially interesting. The Delaware Welsh Tract dated from a boundary dispute between William Penn and Lord Baltimore. Penn granted 30,000 acres to Welsh settlers in 1701. The land was soon taken up by Baptists and Presbyterians. Iron Hill Baptist Church and Pencader Presbyterian Church soon became nuclei of Welsh settlement (Richard Cook, *The Delaware Baptists,* 1880, W. T. Skinner, *History of Pencader Presbyterian Church,* 1899).

Iron Hill Baptist Church was called after a discovery of iron-ore in the district. Immigrants came there from Wales itself, particularly from Pembroke and Carmarthen. The church became the centre for Baptist expansion, North and South. For over seventy years the pastors of Iron Hill were native Welshmen, preaching in Welsh. Oliver Evans, the inventor, came from this church. Another of its sons, Able Morgan, founded the first Baptist College in America.

Pencader Presbyterian Church became for many years the centre for American Presbyterian expansion; its founders were West Walians from Carmarthen. The church produced outstanding Presbyterian leaders in David Evans and his cousin, Thomas Evans. Another such outstanding leader was Samuel Davies, already mentioned in connection with Virginia.

In North Carolina there was a small Welsh settlement in Hanover County, but there was a much bigger Welsh concentration in South Carolina at Pee Dee River. Delaware Welsh Tract sent settlers south, and the South Carolina Assembly granted them 173,000 acres of land (1735) on both sides of the Pee Dee River. A company to share out the land was started by Jenkin and Owen David (to become one of the leading families in South Carolina). This so-called Welsh Neck colony, mainly of Baptists, occupied very rich agricultural land. Prominent in the colony was the rich settler James James. The Welsh Neck Baptist Church was founded in 1738, its first pastor being Phillip James, son of James James. Welsh Neck Baptist Church became the mother church to thirty-eight Baptist churches in South Carolina. In most areas of the United States, the Welsh were in the forefront in the struggle against slavery — South Carolina was the exception.

The really big migrations of Welsh under the leadership of their pastors came in the last quarter of the seventeenth century. There was widespread Welsh Quaker migration, as already mentioned in the earlier chapter on Pennsylvania, under the leadership of John ap John and others, followed by Baptists from Radnor and West Wales, leaving, as Dodd put it, another trail of Welsh names. As settlers died, left for the West or returned home to Wales, the settlements renewed themselves by new immigrants from Wales. An Association of Baptist churches had been established by 1706, with headquarters in Philadelphia (A. H. Dodd, op. cit. p.15). In 1756 this association set up the Baptist Hopewell Academy in New Jersey. By 1765 the Baptists had founded a college at Providence, Rhode Island, which later became Brown University. Baptist minister, Morgan Edwards, went back to Wales to get subscriptions for the college. "A Welsh foundation for Brown can be claimed on better grounds than for Yale." (A. H. Dodd, op. cit. p.15.)

By the 1760's there were a dozen or so Regular Baptist churches in the colonies south of Virginia, all having loose ties with the Philadelphia Association. Henceforth the older Baptist communities in the South were to be joined, and sometimes 'plagued' as they put it, by the Separate Baptists. This was the result of the 'Great Awakening' of the later eighteenth century. In 1754 a number of new-type 'Separate Baptists', led by Shubal Stearns, left New England 'to put new life' into the Baptist cause further South. They moved into Sandy Creek, North Carolina, and into Virginia south of the James River.

By the end of the century the Separate Baptists had expanded vigorously throughout Virginia and both the Carolinas. The reactions of the older 'Regular' Baptists, mainly of Welsh stock, to this new influx were somewhat mixed. But it was a Welshman, David Thomas, who set out on an evangelist mission that consolidated the Baptist Church in the South. They became the strongest denomination in an area which had been mainly Anglican (D. Benedict, *History of the Baptist Denomination,* 1850). Another Welshman, Lewis Richards, was typical of the new religious enthusiasm that came with the Great Awakening. He had originally gone to Georgia as a Baptist minister, but became well-known as an 'enthusiastic' preacher throughout the Carolinas, Virginia and Maryland, also keeping constantly in touch with his religious friends and mentors in Wales.

In the old pattern, several congregations from Wales followed their pastors out to the New World after the American Revolution. Some of these came from Bala, which A. H. Dodd described as "the very Mecca of North Wales Methodism". We have seen earlier how Morgan John Rhys in 1794 had led his South Wales Baptists to Western Pennsylvania. Morgan John Rhys had been known in Wales as a distinguished intellectual, a rebel in both religious and political matters (J. T. Griffith, *Morgan John Rhys,* 1910). Like many of the Welsh pastors he had a dream of settlements where his Welsh followers might enjoy religious and political freedom in the new American environment. Another Welsh minister, Rees Lloyd, a Congregationalist, had been one of the advance party for Morgan John Rhys. He did much to ensure the success of Ebensburg, whereas Morgan John Rhys died in 1804, and thus did not see the sad end of Beulah.

The leadership, and encouragement to find a new home in the States, so common amongst Welsh pastors in the 'agricultural' migrations, continued on into the nineteenth century, when group migrations were mostly 'industrial' in nature. Ministers were moved by the poverty and unemployment in Wales, but also welcomed the chance to spread the different versions of the Christian faith in pastures new. Accordingly, as more and more Welsh communities looked towards the West of America, pastors in the home country and in America sought to help their compatriots in the movement toward the West. Welsh religious leaders, with help from knowledgeable Welsh-Americans, visited the Middle and Far West to find out for themselves what conditions and opportunities were like for those Welsh wanting to emigrate to the States. What had applied to the older-style farming-immigrants came to apply as much to the new industrial workers of the nineteenth century.

The Reverend Samuel Roberts was well-known in Wales for his efforts to encourage emigration to the United States. Another Congregational minister, Michael Jones of Bala, had considered going, with his congregation, to Wisconsin; instead they made history by starting the famous Welsh colony in Patagonia. This important event, is of course, outside the scope of this book.

Morgan John Rhys had put his religious principles into practice, by cooperating, as a Baptist, with ministers and their followers of other denominations. These other denominations were mainly the Congregationalists and the Calvinistic-Methodists (more often known in the United States as Welsh Presbyterians). These denominations were the most numerous in membership; Quakers and Mormons were decidedly minority groups. All the big denominations were represented in the new-founded settlements of Oneida, New York State, where there were many Welsh. In Oneida, as elsewhere, these Welsh nonconformists agreed to worship together in so-called 'union-churches' until their respective numbers increased sufficiently to justify separate churches. In some cases numbers did not increase, so they continued, united by Welsh ties and language, in the union churches, mainly on the Congregational pattern.

Harmony did not however always prevail amongst the non-conformist denominations, Welsh or otherwise. Furious quarrels sometimes broke out on doctrinal matters. "Yet," says Hartmann "there were many characteristics of the religious life of the Welsh settlers that were decidedly similar, so similar in fact that all three denominations conformed to a general pattern of religious expression . . . that can best be described as 'the Welsh way of life'. It had dominated the behaviour pattern of the Welsh in Wales; it became transplanted to America, and governed the lives of the Welsh settlers over here as well." (Op. cit. p.104.)

Sunday was the big day of the week for the Welsh communities. The church was the acknowledged nucleus of the settlement. "Its affairs and its activities were the dominating interest of the Welsh immigrants, beyond the normal problems of earning a living." (Ibid.) A very puritan regime was maintained in most Welsh settlements.

It has been said that the 'hiraeth' (home-sickness) was more for the preachers and the chapels of the old country than the scenery (Berthoff, p.159). The preaching sessions were the high-points on Sundays, and great preachers were powerful figures. Former Governor Arthur H. James of Pennsylvania told Professor Hartmann that, on many occasions in his youth, he remembered his father and his Welsh cronies debating the merits of the Sunday sermon. "Heaven help the preacher who turned up with too many Biblical inconsistencies in his sermon, for Welsh congregations, brought up in Sunday Schools as children, then years of chapel, knew their Bible." (Hartmann.) Much use was made of the hwyl; of this W. Jones said, in an article, "Their preaching is usually marked by a great variety of intonations . . . the judicious use of it is confined to the more passionate or pathetic parts of a sermon" ('The Welsh in America', Atlantic Monthly, 1876). But it was pointed out that "the hwyl was not the only thing that counted: the sermons had to be well thought out, with plenty of Biblical references".

Second only to the service, with its sermon, was the Sunday School. "It was the Sunday Schools that had made the Welsh a literate nation, for they were established at a time when there were no opportunities for elementary education of the masses in the homeland." (Hartmann, p.106.) Professor Hartmann gives one of the best general descriptions of this 'Welsh way of life' in his chapter 'The Welsh-American Cultural Community — its Religious Aspect'. There is only room here to refer to his section on

A contemporary newspaper notice

'congregational singing'. "Abundant singing there was at every religious service, or any other social activity of the Welsh in America. A unique feature was the use of four-part harmony, the ability for which seemed inherent in the Welsh nature."

Closely connected with this was of course the Gymanfa, still today a favourite occasion in the life of Welsh-Americans. Dr. Daniel J. Williams stated, "The Gymanfa when convened in regular session was a great gathering in the historic days of the Welsh settlements — local choirs and congregations rehearsed special hymns — generally there was an invited delegate or preacher from Wales." (D. J. Williams, *One Hundred Years of Welsh Calvinistic Methodism,* 1937.) Estimates of the crowds present ranged from three to six thousands. "The Welsh hwyl pervaded the multitude, as the preachers swayed the crowds with Welsh eloquence." (Ibid.)

The Welsh preachers, who really came into their own on these dramatic occasions, were generally men of great stamina and determination. Thus the Reverend Lewis Williams travelled on foot over the mountains of Pennsylvania in the 1850's from Carbondale settlement to the settlements of Wilkes-Barre, Hazleton and Pottsville. He walked fifteen to twenty miles on Sundays to preach to three, four or five congregations. The Reverend E. B. Evans, Congregational minister at Scranton, travelled on foot on one occasion all the way from Pittsburgh to Pottsville, a distance of three hundred and fifty miles. He left Pittsburgh on a Monday evening, and arrived at his destination on the Friday evening (D. Jones, *Memorial Volume of the Welsh Congregationalists,* 1934). The Reverend Edward Jones, Calvinistic Methodist, travelled thousands of miles on foot in Ohio, to organise new churches and to strengthen weak ones. In 1835 he walked from Cincinnati to Palmyra. On this trip he was overtaken by a severe storm — roads were mere tracks through the woods. During the storm he removed his shoes for fear of losing them in the sticky clay.

By the 1830's the Welsh churches of the three main denominations were numerous enough to justify national organisation. The Calvinistic-Methodists had district presbyteries and state synods, with a national convention. Baptists and Congregationalists organised only regional associations.

We have already looked at the early days of the Welsh Baptists in the United States. Starting from the earliest church at Swansea (Mass.), they spread widely, and by 1840 there were 117 Baptist churches in the U.S.A. with marked Welsh memberships or associations. Some were still going strong in the early part of this century, especially in the coal areas of Pennsylvania. After the mid-nineteenth century, there were five regular Baptist conferences in America: in New York, Eastern Pennsylvania, Ohio and Western Pennsylvania, Wisconsin, and 'Trans-Mississippi West'. The Welsh Baptist journal, *Wawr Americanaidd,* shows how important these conferences were to the Baptists at the end of the last century.

The Congregationalists were more numerous than the Baptists, with over 228 churches at the end of the century, including churches in New York, and at Utica and Steuben in New York State, the famous church at Paddy's Run in Ohio, as well as Radnor Church, also in Ohio. In the State of Pennsylvania there was the historic church at Ebensburg, earliest of all the Congregational churches, a church at Carbondale, and another at Neath, with a fourth at Minersville.

The Calvinistic-Methodists (Welsh Presbyterians) were even a little more numerous than the Congregationalists, with 236 churches. Their earliest church had been Pencaerau at Remsen, New York (1824) with another in New York City itself shortly after (1826); Remsen soon had another Welsh church, Penygraig (1827), and a third, Capel Ceryg, in 1831. Other early churches of this denomination were in Pennsylvania (four before 1834), Utica, New York, and Cincinnati, Ohio.

Naturally a good deal of attention has been paid to the Welsh nonconformist churches in the United States. Yet in any consideration of the religious aspect of Welsh immigration into the United States, the Anglicans must not be forgotten. So far they have only been mentioned in connection with Virginia. But, as Nelson Burr has shown (N. Burr, *Historical Magazine of the Episcopalian Church,* June, 1939), Welsh Anglicans (or Episcopalians, to use the American term) played a large part in American religious life. Burr, for example, considered that, by 1700, Welsh Episcopalians were as numerous as Baptists in Pennsylvania. Burr goes as far as to say, "An inclination to consider the Episcopal Church in colonial Pennsylvania and Delaware as 'English' is soon corrected by the documents, which reveal the startling fact that to a large extent it was 'Welsh'. In 1695 an important event in Episcopalian history was the foundaton of Christ Church in Philadelphia. "The coming of the Reverend Evan Evans in 1700 to serve as pastor of Christ Church was of great significance to the future of Welsh Anglicans." (Ibid.) As a result many Welsh immigrants were retained for the Anglican or Episcopalian persuasion who might otherwise have left it. "Within two years Evans' congregation numbered over five hundred, of which a substantial number were Welsh."

Many of the Welsh of the Gwynedd settlement in Pennsylvania were Anglicans. They built their own Trinity Church at Oxford in that State. In Radnor, enough Welsh Episcopalians had settled to encourage Evan Evans to inaugurate St. David's Church. Another Christ Church had been founded in Swansea (Mass.), the old Welsh settlement near Plymouth, as early as 1846, as Otis Wright stated in his *History of Swansea (Mass.).*

The Welsh in the Mormon Church came to be located mainly at New Zion on the banks of the Great Salt Lake, Utah, though later many found their way into Salt Lake City itself, and had their own special areas there. This was, however, after a long and truly epic journey from Wales. Dan Jones from Flintshire played the leading role, as far as the Welsh Mormons were concerned. He had emigrated to America in 1840, going West to Illinois in the first place. Very soon he was piloting a vessel, the *Maid of Iowa,* transporting settlers to the West. If he had never become a Mormon, he would still have had a historical role in the vital early history of American river-transport. His knowledge of the Ohio and Mississippi Rivers later became invaluable. In 1843 an event happened that changed the whole course of his life. In that year he took a party of English Mormons from St. Louis to Nauvoo, Illinois. He met Joseph Smith, one of the leaders of the Mormon sect, and became converted to the faith; he so impressed the elders, the Saints, that he was invited to join their council, the Quorum of Twelve (Kate Carter, *The Welsh in Utah,* 1949).

In 1845 he went on a mission to his homeland, but saw more of South Wales than his native North Wales. With Jones went his wife and other missionaries. From Merthyr Tydfil he organised a Welsh District of the Mormon Church. His mission included the tasks of writing pamphlets on Mormonism, and undertaking preaching tours throughout Wales. By 1848 he had made over four thousand converts. In 1849 he returned to America with some of these. They proceeded to Iowa, and then across the Great Plains and the Rockies to Utah. Immediately they were allocated a site in Salt Lake City itself; it was referred to at the time as the Welsh settlement. Some of the party went on to a site in San Pete County.

He made a second missionary tour of Wales in 1852. Having brought another party of converts to Utah, he remained at Provo, in that State, until his death in 1861. "He was an eloquent and magnetic speaker in both Welsh and English. Jones was the instrument which converted thousands of his countrymen. He was known among his fellow Mormons as 'the Father of the Welsh Mormons'." (Hartmann, p.74.)

More Welsh Mormons came to Utah from 1849 onwards, their settlements being in the 15th and 16th wards of Salt Lake City, at Wales, at Spanish Fork, and at Williard. Naturally, some of them being miners back in Wales, headed for mining-areas of Utah such as Carbon County, Ophir and Winter Quarters. "So great was the Welsh influx that the official historian of the Mormon Church estimated their numbers as 25,000." Professor Taylor mentions the large numbers of Welsh Mormons who came from Merthyr Tydfil, and also many from Swansea (P. A. M. Taylor, *Expectations Westward,* 1965). He considers that the Mormon leaders suspected that some had joined the Mormon faith as an aid to emigration. In a *Report from Swansea* (1896), quoted by Professor Taylor, it was said "Many enquire about emigration before they are baptised. We expect to baptise quite a few more by emigration-time, many of whom are in comfortable circumstances, intend to join the Church, sell off and emigrate." In 1854, the President of the British (Mormon) Mission, in charge of British emigration parties, was

Samuel W. Richards, who would know well the situation in South Wales. Once started however on the long trek, there is considerable evidence that a substantial number of the Welsh stayed the course, however mixed their original motives. Kate Carter asserts that the Welsh played a considerable part in Mormon affairs, especially on the musical side. Evan Stephens, for instance, composed much of their music. One Welsh immigrant, John Parry, formed the original group which became the world-famous Mormon Tabernacle Choir.

A dramatic incident in the history of the Welsh Mormons, one that constituted the major religious defection from the ranks, was the Morrisite affair. "Joseph Morris was an uneducated Welshman converted to Mormonism in 1849; he emigrated to Utah in 1853. He had been farming in isolated Weber County for six years when he began to have visions, and to hear revelations of himself as the seventh angel spoken of in the Revelation of St. John." (Irving Stone, *Men to match mountains,* 1963, p.266.)

Brigham Young did not take him seriously, and ignored him. But in his own little local community, about a hundred of his neighbours believed him, including the local bishop. In 1861, Bishop Cook publicly announced his allegiance to Prophet Morris. Young excommunicated them both, along with some lesser followers of Morris. Weber County flared up. Soon there were six hundred who claimed to be Morrisites. According to the Rocky Mountain News of the period (still a leading Denver newspaper) affidavits were presented to the Salt Lake Chief Justice, claiming that Prophet Morris was holding four dissident members as prisoners. The Salt Lake City Marshall went to investigate, and reported that Morris was guarded by at least a hundred armed men. Robert T. Burton, a prominent Mormon leader in Salt Lake City, went to Weber County with 250 Mormon militia. Thus came to an end the most dangerous schism within the ranks of the Mormons. It will be shown later that the Mormon community flourished, and within that community many of the descendants of the original Welsh pioneers. At the present time, Professor Dennis of the Brigham University, Utah, is carrying out a special study of the Welsh contribution to the movement.

Chapter 7

Welsh Agricultural Emigration to the United States

IN THE seventeenth and eighteenth centuries the flocks led by the adventurous Welsh ministers of various denominations were largely farmers and agricultural labourers, along with the wealthier emigrants who could afford to buy large tracts of land. These early Welsh emigrants were often referred to as 'Welsh agriculturalists', a sufficiently comprehensive term (W. S. Shepperson, *The British Emigration to North America,* 1957). The movement of these Welsh agriculturalists over the years to different parts of the States did not constitute a steady flow, but a series of waves, the first of which was that of the Welsh Quakers and Baptists, mainly to Pennsylvania in the 1680's. Then came a long gap, over a century, before the next wave; some 'individual' emigration, of course, continued from the more adventurous, and sometimes more prosperous, Welsh.

It may help to clarify what follows if we briefly list these 'waves' at this point:

(i)   the 1680 emigration mainly to Pennsylvania, referred to above;

(ii)   the 1795 emigration from Llanbrynmair, Montgomeryshire, to Beulah and Ebensburg in Cambria County, Pennsylvania;

(iii) further 'agricultural' migration in the 1830s, first to Pennsylvania, and then on to Ohio;

(iv) direct migration to Ohio in the 1840s, and the movement on to Illinois, Iowa, Wisconsin and Minnesota;

(v)   the first migration led in the 1850s by Samuel Roberts from Llanbrynmair to Brynffynon in Eastern Tennessee, to be followed within a few years by several other parties — all to be sadly disillusioned.

70

While these waves, or group-emigrations, can be seen as separate events, there are, to change the metaphor, threads which connect them. Thus, they all had common economic causation, based on distress in the homeland; they all had cultural factors based on intense 'Welshness' and yearning for independence. Several of them came from that one special spot, Llanbrynmair in Montgomeryshire. Professor Shepperson points to the uniqueness of this little place in North Wales in the story of Welsh emigration to the United States, indeed one might say, considering its size, in the story of all 'ethnic emigration' to America. "The Parish of Llanbrynmair in North Wales is today, as it has been for hundreds of years, a romantically fascinating but materially unrewarding farming community in the rain-swept hills of Montgomeryshire . . . during the nineteenth century few European communities can be more closely associated with the United States . . . its inhabitants migrated to the United States in staggering numbers." (W. S. Shepperson, *The Life of Samuel Roberts,* 1961.) During the period 1794-1801 alone, more than a thousand Welshmen sailed for America, many of them from Llanbrynmair (see Richard Williams, *A History of Llanbrynmair,* 1889). It would be very interesting to know how many citizens of the United States of America today could trace their ancestry back to that one little village in North Wales.

Another common thread in the story of Welsh farmers and agricultural labourers, on their way to becoming Americans, would be the factor of leadership. The story could not be told without looking at the personalities of men like Edward and William Bebb, John Morgan Rhys and Samuel Roberts. Without in the least diminishing the importance and the undoubted charisma of the latter two, or of the Reverend B. Chidlaw, a special case might be made for the central role of the Bebbs, father and son. Later in this chapter attention will be paid to the pioneer, Edward Bebb. For the moment, because of his important role in the history of Ohio, something will be said about William Bebb. "Bebb's active mind and serious nature led him to become schoolmaster, lawyer, and finally politician and statesman." (Shepperson, p.32.) It might be considered that he was more practical, and less of a dreamer than some of the other leaders; on the other hand it could be asserted that he was every bit as much a dreamer, but had the politician's necessary ability to recognise the limitations of the practical. He became Governor of Ohio in 1846. The abilities he showed in being elected to that position, and the power that position gave him made it easier for him than for others, to make some dreams, at least, come true. "He nurtured much of his Welsh culture, and formulated plans which he hoped would allow for large-scale

71

Welsh migration to America." (Ibid. See also Herbert Bebb, *The Bebb Genealogy*, 1944.) In addition to his own efforts, he had family connections useful to the Welsh cause. For instance his cousin, another William Bebb from Llanbrynmair, helped him in 1847 to cater for another batch of sixty from the home village. They had come out under the leadership of this second William Bebb. The two William Bebbs together visited Illinois and Wisconsin to see if other sites were possible.

Another cousin of Governor William Bebb was Samuel Roberts, the celebrated S. R., as he was always called. When planning the East Tennessee settlement of Brynffynon, S. R. did not hesitate to use this useful contact with Governor Bebb. The latter in fact visited Sam Roberts in Wales in 1855 to talk the whole matter over, along with yet another cousin, Richard Roberts.

Increasingly after 1820, the agricultural settlement movement in the States by North Walians began to overlap with industrial migrations by South Walians, but that will be discussed later. Throughout the nineteenth century, there were two parallel developments relating to Welsh immigrants. Firstly, as the century rolled on and communications improved, many Welsh immigrants went directly to the mid-West or even further West. Secondly, others came to the old rallying-point, Pennsylvania. Some stayed there; others moved on. The greater numbers of Welsh in Pennsylvania had led to the founding of the Welsh Society at Philadelphia. This was in 1798; there had been a previous society, the Saint David Society, but that had faded out. The Welsh Society, throughout the period, helped Welsh immigrants, whether they stayed in Pennsylvania or moved on. Some who stayed in the East helped in efforts to improve communications to the expanding mid-West. Thus, at the beginning of the nineteenth century some Welsh immigrants settled in Mohawk Valley, New York State, turned away from farming, and helped to build the new Erie canal. A flood-tide of new immigrants from Wales came in 1817, when Britain was hit by much unemployment, with the end of the Napoleonic War. Demographic and economic forces in Wales in any case, as Conway shows, were forcing Welsh farmers to look towards America. "With the opening of the Nineteenth Century there had begun a new era in Welsh emigration . . . an increase in population in every shire in Wales at every census until 1841 intensified the seriousness of the situation in the rural areas." (Alan Conway, *The Welsh in America: letters from immigrants*, 1961.) Conway tells of the fewer farms in Wales available for sale; this resulted from the consolidation policies pursued by the richer farmers. Some, landless and hopeless, migrated to the Welsh industrial areas. Others turned to the U.S.A., news of which

72

featured largely in the denominational journals, and in the newspapers.

It was not only economic and demographic factors that impelled farmers and agricultural workers towards America at this period. They coincided with cultural factors, psychological factors some might say, where a nation found its soul and craved for independence of thought and action. Professor Gwyn Williams, as already shown, has explained much of this cultural impetus in his books on Madoc and Beulah. Others have added to this explanation the force of religion, claiming that the radicalism of Welsh nonconformity itself did not need the support of myth to provide a driving force. In a section of one of his books, headed *'The Welsh Agriculturalists'*, Shepperson states "During the hundred years prior to Victoria, Wales had witnessed a complete social transformation, generally attributed to the Methodist Revival, which had stimulated the Welsh people to maintain their language; this in turn resulted in a new output of literature and a school of mighty pulpit orators." (W. S. Shepperson, op. cit. p.32.) This again had intensified the demand, argues Shepperson, for better educational and social conditions. "The realisation that there was a land beyond the sea where the hated Anglican clergy influenced neither Church nor State stimulated the self-assertiveness of the Welsh, intensified the dissatisfaction with home, and made the glories of America apparent." (Ibid.)

The agricultural settlements that were still springing up in Pennsylvania in the early nineteenth century were matched by similar developments in New York State, centred around Utica. As with Cobbett in England, there were those in America who warned of the difficulties for immigrants, like Hugh Jones of Utica. "Be happy in your own country," he told his parents (Alan Conway, op. cit.). But William Davies (letter dated 24th September 1821) liked Utica, "a smart and thriving village with several chapels and churches". By 1832, John Lewis was informing his nephew that Utica was a large and fine town, "It has 8000 inhabitants, including many Welshmen, and more than forty Welsh preachers. Many Welsh are coming over continually." (Conway, p.64.)

New York State went on attracting Welsh 'farming immigrants'. For the Welsh, like the Irish, the 1840's were 'the hungry forties'. In Wales there were high rentals for farms, and crippling charges at new toll-gates on roads. Many in agricultural districts were living on the verge of starvation. There was a burning desire in North and West Wales to own one's own land — and land was being sold cheap in the U.S.A. Welsh farmers and agricultural labourers flooded into Utica and Steuben up to the outbreak of the American Civil War. Oneida County rapidly filled up, so then Lewis County welcomed Welsh farmers at Turin, Leyden, Greig and Collinsville. At places in other New York counties such as Cattarangus, Herkimer and Madison, farms had been vacated by American farmers 'heading West'; many of these were taken over by the immigrant Welsh, as by other immigrants. David Maldwyn Ellis gives a detailed account (D. M. Ellis, *Landlords and Farmers,* 1946), especially of Oneida County from 1795. Their progress from that date was earlier reviewed by Paul Evans — (*The Welsh of Oneida County,* 1914). Karl Wittke, in his multi-ethnic study, confirms that nearly all who came to Oneida County were Welsh (*We who built America,* 1944, p.31).

Welsh people, entering America through New York at the end of the eighteenth century and the beginning of the nineteenth century, generally went by sloop to Albany, up the Hudson River in New York State. From Albany they usually proceeded to Utica by flat-boat and then overland to Steuben. This was part of the Oneida settlement, along with Remsen township. This area was not much good for crops, so it specialised in dairy-farming. Some Welsh farmers farmed north of Steuben in Lewis County. A survey made in 1812 showed that, in an area fifteen miles long and ten miles wide, with Steuben as its centre, there were approximately seven hundred Welsh settlers and their families.

Over the years, New York State became as heterogeneous as New York City itself. Referring to the continuity of occupations today in New York State, Professor David Maldwyn Ellis writes, "One can find German Mennonites on the farms of the Black River Valley, Italian truck-drivers round Rome and Canastota, French Canadians in the North Country, and Welsh farmers in Central New York State." This brief excerpt, from an authority on New York, illustrates how ethnic roots and memories can persist, even in the most ethnically mixed areas.

A later and most interesting chapter in D. M. Ellis's work shows how Welsh folk in New York fitted into the early nineteenth century political scene.

"Between 1825-1855, Catholic Irish, French Canadians, German and French immigrants voted overwhelmingly for Democratic candidates who had traditionally befriended immigrants. On the other hand, English, Scottish, Welsh and Ulster Irish rallied round the Whig (now Republican) candidates." (D. M. Ellis, *New York, State and City,* 1979, p.205.) These Welsh were clearly not as radical as those who had headed for Beulah under Morgan John Rhys.

Alan Conway gives a vivid account of how these Welsh emigrants travelled from Wales to the United States (op. cit. p.150). By the mid-nineteenth century, Liverpool handled most of the emigration trade. The best-known emigration agent in Liverpool was N. M. Jones, known by Welsh emigrants as 'y Cymro gwyllt' (the wild Welshman). "As fellow-emigrants," says Conway, "the Welsh would seem to have been clannish, condescending, and stiffnecked, but generous to those in need, genuinely sorry when deaths occurred aboard ship, and occasionally revealing an ability to laugh at themselves" — which was refreshing, adds Conway.

The majority of Welsh farmers and small-holders preferred to remain near the older settlements of New York State (where they acquired a reputation for making excellent butter) and Pennsylvania. Some left the countryside, as in Pennsylvania and Ohio, for the towns and trades, commerce and the professions. Other farmers stayed on the land, but sometimes moved out into mid-western and northern States, often taking the place-names Utica and Oneida with them.

Meanwhile new settlers from Wales kept coming throughout these important years of the mid-nineteenth century. As early as 1803, settlers from Radnorshire moved into Delaware; others reached rural areas near Pittsburgh at Centreville, which kept receiving immigrants from Cardiganshire and Aberystwyth. Immigrants from Montgomeryshire kept arriving at Van Wert County, Ohio. The Reverend B. Chidlaw regularly visited Wales to recruit settlers for the latter State.

The Welsh in Ohio. The first Welshman in Ohio, according to the Reverend D. J. Williams, was a Welsh missionary to Shawnee and Delaware Indians in 1772-73 (*The Welsh of Columbus, Ohio,* 1913). The first permanent Welsh settlers came under the leadership of Ezekial Hughes and Edward Bebb, a remarkable couple of Welshmen. They had started from Llanbrynmair in 1795 with a party of fifty people, and had walked from North Wales to Bristol, where they boarded the *Maria*. After considerable initial difficulties and hardships, they arrived at Delaware Bay and Philadelphia. "These settlers," said D. J. Williams, "became the pioneers of Ebensburg and Cambria County, Pennsylvania, and of Paddy's Run, Ohio."

Hughes and Bebb had, as agreed, brought them to Philadelphia, where some of them settled in Dyffryn Mawr (the Great Valley) west of Philadelphia, while others continued with the two leaders to Ohio. Paddy's Run became the mother-settlement for Ohio. Paddy's Run may seem an incongruous title for a place to become so important for Welshmen. It really was named after an Irishman called Paddy, who died by drowning. The Welsh took a fancy to the name, and would not have it changed (later however it was called Shandon).

A strange story concerns Bebb, one of the two pioneering leaders. Having, with Hughes, brought the party to Paddy's Run,

Bebb started back to Ebensburg in Pennsylvania as a start of the long journey back to Wales, to claim his boyhood sweetheart, Margaret Owen. Instead, he found her at Ebensburg, a widow. She had married another man, had come with him from North Wales to Pennsylvania, where this first husband had died. Bebb married her. In 1802 their son William was born, the first white child born in Butler County, Ohio, and destined later to become, as we have seen, the Governor of the State of Ohio.

Out of Paddy's Run, itself a rich, fertile settlement, growing food for Cincinnati, grew other settlements. Two of the settlers from the failed settlement of Beulah, West Pennsylvania, namely Theophilus Rees and Thomas Phillips, led a party from Beulah to Paddy's Run. From there they went on to Licking County and Granville Township, Ohio. The whole of this area became known as 'the Welsh Hills'. "From 1803 to 1820 there was a constant stream of Welsh people coming into the community, and a Welsh colony was the result." (D. J. Williams, p.23.)

By 1823 there had been added to Licking County the settlements of Gallia and Jackson in Jackson County. Gomer settlement in Allen County (1833), and Venedocia settlement in Van Wert county (1848) were to follow. There was also the Radnor settlement in Delaware County, Ohio. This had been founded by David Pugh from Radnorshire in Wales. He had come to Baltimore in 1801. He bought 4000 acres of land in Delaware County, Ohio, from Dr. Samuel Jones of the Pennepek Church in Philadelphia. He sold the land in 100-acre lots to Welsh immigrants.

Several of the settlements in Ohio had interesting histories, as D. J. Williams showed. The Gallia settlement in Jackson County, for instance, had been a French settlement, hence the name. The Welsh settlers, who had struggled hard to get that far, had had a totally disastrous journey, mainly by boat. The French persuaded the Welsh to go no further, but to join with them. Meanwhile the boat the Welsh had come in was mysteriously destroyed. Some of the Welsh thought it was the act of the French, as a means of keeping them in the settlement, which needed men for the hard work, and defence against the Indians. Whatever their suspicions, the Welsh stayed. Moreover the Franco-Welsh settlement flourished. The Reverend Edward Jones went home to Cardigan in Wales to enlist more settlers for the infant settlement — after he had inspected both the settlements in Jackson County, Gallia and Jackson Town. He praised them highly, and many from Cardiganshire went to Jackson County, Ohio. The Reverend D. J. Williams said that it was frequently referred to as "the Cardiganshire of America".

The Welsh preferred, if possible, to settle with Welsh from their own areas back home, or neighbours they had known in previous

Welsh-American settlements in the Eastern States. Hence Gomer settlement, Ohio, was manned mainly by people from Montgomeryshire. The Welsh folks in Venedocia, Van Wert County, Ohio, were mainly friends and relatives of Edward Bebb; his son William encouraged this trend when he became Governor of Ohio in the 1840's. It helped that they were nearly all of the same religious denomination, Calvinistic-Methodists. Some areas of the Welsh Hills were conclaves of South Wales Baptists.

Most of these Welsh of Ohio had come to Paddy's Run first, and spread out from there. Thus the Montgomery people in the Allen County settlement of Gomer had bought land at Paddy's Run (for $1.25 per acre). "They named it Gomer after the Biblical figure generally accepted by the Welsh as their common ancestor — and often referred to themselves as 'Gomermen'." (E. G. Hartmann, *Americans from Wales,* 1967, p.69.)

In the chapter on Religion and Welsh Emigration to the United States, much was said about the role of Welsh preachers in encouraging emigration to America. A striking example was the Reverend B. B. Chidlaw. He had been brought to Radnor, Ohio, from Wales at the age of ten. As a youth, he went to Miami University at Oxford, Ohio, walking 125 miles to get there. He went home to Wales to do a refresher course in Welsh, before becoming minister of a Congregational church at Paddy's Run. "He was a great agitator," said D. J. Williams, "of 'America for the Welsh'." (Op. cit. p.47.)

Chidlaw was missionary for the American Sunday School Union for many years. He visited Wales in 1836, publishing a pamphlet to encourage emigration to Ohio. He knew all the Welsh settlements in the United States through his Sunday School work. He gave in this pamphlet *(Yr American),* written in Welsh, full details of the journey from Wales to Ohio. D. J. Williams stated, "the Reverend Chidlaw brought hundreds to America, and enjoyed the role of a beloved elder patriarch of the Welsh people in America for the rest of his life." (Op. cit. p.69.) We have already seen that the Reverend Edward Jones had similarly publicised Gallia-Jackson, north of present-day Gallipolis, which had over 6000 Welsh by 1860.

As we have noted above, there were always some Welsh with a farming background who would leave the land for the big cities. Columbus, Ohio, was no exception. It attracted the younger men and women from the Welsh farming areas. The population of Columbus grew from 700 in 1815 to 18,554 by 1860. Radnor and Welsh Hills settlements were within thirty miles from the capital. A Welsh chapel catered by 1823 for the many younger Welsh in Columbus who had moved in from the farming districts. From

77

1840 more came from Wales itself, once more mainly from Llanbrynmair; they were some of the many Welsh who came from Wales to the United States under the influence of the famous Samuel Roberts.

Finally on Ohio, 'the religious way of life' of the Welsh, described elsewhere in this book, was still prevalent to a high degree when D. J. Williams wrote *The Welsh of Columbus, Ohio,* in 1913. He made special mention of Yr Ysgol Sul (Sunday School) and the Cyfarfod Ysgolion (Sunday School Meetings) so important for the Welsh in Columbus and its surrounding areas at that period.

A difficulty in any field of research concerning eighteenth and nineteenth century United States, is this: as the States multiplied, developed and filled with people, they split up, with potential new States first becoming 'Territories'. This is a difficulty that one finds in looking at the Carolinas in historical times, likewise Virginia, Kentucky, Tennessee and other Southern States. It was the same with Connecticut, Long Island, New York and the 'Middle States' generally, with different States competing for territory. So it was in the developing Northern mid-West States somewhat later.

Michigan was the subject for several years of agitation for sub-division. Prominent in this agitation were Morgan Martin and G. W. Jones (F. L. Paxson, *History of the American Frontier,* 1924). In 1836 their campaign bore fruit with the recognition of **Wisconsin** as a separate Territory, later to become a separate State. G. W. Jones, in Congress as a Wisconsin delegate, was still not satisfied. He went on to sponsor a further division, and the result was Iowa, added to recognised States as a Territory, for recognition as a State in due course (ibid. p.292).

It was at this period that Indiana experienced the New Harmony experiment of Robert Owen, the famous Welsh industrialist and would-be social reformer (see biographical section later). Robert Dale Owen had been at New Harmony with his father. When the social experiment failed, Robert Dale Owen stayed on in the United States, eventually becoming a Congressman. He kept his ideals, but tried to adapt them to the American way of life. In his autobiography *Threading my way* he tells of his part in the creation of the famous Smithsonian Institute. As Congressman for Indiana, he helped to liberalise women's status there.

Wisconsin was described by Alan Conway as particularly attractive to Welsh immigrants, many settling in or near Racine. The first settler to reach Waukesha County, Wisconsin, was John Hughes; he was joined by relatives and friends from Cardigan and Montgomery counties in Wales. Another settlement for the Welsh in Wisconsin was that of Welsh Prairie. Most Welsh settlers came to the State in the 1840's and 1850's, and were truly pioneers, cutting down forests and clearing the land for cultivation. They were often joined by second-generation Welsh-Americans from the older settlements. Thus Samuel Lewis came to Wisconsin from Massachusetts, to become superintendent of Schools (1837).

When John Hughes and his group arrived in Waukesha County, they settled in the township of Genesee, where, within two years, there were nearly a hundred Welsh settlers. The general area came to be known as 'Wales', with a village of that name as its centre. There were another hundred Welsh at mid-century at Racine, including the villages of Mount Pleasant and Pike Grove. Welsh Prairie, mentioned above, was in Columbia County, centred on the village of Cambria.

Another Welsh community in Wisconsin was in Winnebago County, near the large town of Oshkosh. More Welsh arrived from Wales and the older Welsh settlements to extend this centre further into the backwoods. Oshkosh issued a Centennial Report in 1947. It stated, "Wisconsin is recognised as one of the most Dutch and German States in the Union, but to supplement them, God led a strong delegation of genuinely religious Welsh to the State". Nothing is known about German and Dutch reactions to this statement. The Centennial Report is interesting in tracing the original nine Welsh settlers of 1847 through their lifetimes, and the lives of their descendants, right to the end of the century. The Report was particularly proud of the record of Oshkosh Welsh in what it calls 'the War against slavery'. By 1860, Oshkosh had a Welsh population of 800, of whom 52 went to fight for the North, nineteen of them losing their lives in battle.

Smaller Welsh settlements started in other Wisconsin counties in the 1840's, notably in Sauk, Jefferson, La Crosse, Rock and Iowa Counties. It is interesting that La Crosse County with its old French name, had two settlements with very Welsh names — Bangor and Blaendyffryn. Sauk County had a settlement called Spring Green, which became the home town of the famous Welsh-American architect Frank Lloyd Wright. He was known not only all over the United States but all over the world, especially perhaps in Japan. He had a long life (1869-1959) so was famous through many generations. His mother, Anna, was the daughter of Richard Lloyd Jones "one of a clan of Welsh preachers, teachers and farmers living in South Wisconsin" *(Dictionary of American Biography)*. "Frank Lloyd Wright inherited, from his mother and Welsh ancestry, the love of learning, passion for teaching, the fervour of temperament and the imaginative power that were to form the substance of his personality and genius." (Ibid.) His imaginative ideas on structure and appearance of buildings influenced architecture all over the world. Perhaps his most famous two creations were the Imperial Hotel, Tokyo, which survived the great earthquake of 1923, and the famed Guggenheim Museum in New York.

Another Welsh-American citizen of Wisconsin, famous all over the United States in his day, was Jenkin Lloyd Jones (1843-1918). He was actually born in Wales, at Llandyssil, Cardigan. As an infant, he came to America with his parents, who went to live in Wisconsin. As a young man, he served in a Wisconsin regiment in the Civil War — and lived to see the end of World War I, a long life, like Frank Lloyd Wright. After the American Civil War, he went to a theological college in Pennsylvania, graduating in 1870. He was pastor of the All Souls Unitarian Church, Janesville, Wisconsin, from 1874-1883. He organised an All-American Congress of Religion, which was very successful. He was noted for his administrative ability, and was awarded several honorary doctorates from universities. He wrote several books, and lectured throughout the United States, particularly on the peace movement.

Beyond Wisconsin lay **Minnesota** with its famous twin capitals Minneapolis-St. Paul. Minnesota, like Wisconsin, attracted many Welsh; some in fact just moved across the State line from Wisconsin. More came from greater distances. "Here," states Professor David Williams, "came Welsh from Utica, New York State, from the Ohio settlements, as well as from Wales, especially Cardigan and Merion, Caernarvon and Anglesey." (Op. cit. p.61.) A group of Welsh ministers, the Reverends Thomas Hughes, David Edwards and Hugh Roberts, gave a vivid picture of the Welsh in Minnesota at the mid-nineteenth century (*The Welsh in Minnesota,* 1895). Maps in their volume show clearly the main Welsh settlements in Blue Earth and Le Sueur Counties; settlements had names Otawa, Sharon, Cleveland, Kasota, Eagle Lake and others somewhat exotic to our eyes; only one Welsh place-name, Cambria, but many Welsh people, spread through the dozen original settlements.

In May, 1849, Major John Owens, came to St. Paul from Cincinnati, and started Minnesota's first newspaper. In the same year Thomas Thomas from Pontypool, South Wales, came to the capital cities as a building contractor (which he had previously been in New Orleans) and helped to build some of the early buildings of the two cities.

Welsh immigration into Minnesota owed a lot to the propaganda efforts of David Evans and Richard Davies. Through them John Jones, Griffith Jones, John Roberts and Enoch Mason came to St. Paul in 1850, and four more Welshmen joined them in 1851; all these were farmers, so they soon moved to the Blue Earth settlements up the Minnesota River. They went by ox-wagon to Le Sueur and the bigger Blue Earth settlements.

In 1862, Abraham Lincoln's government, in order to speed up settlement in 'new territories', passed an Act granting 160 acres of land each to genuine settlers. But that same year, undoubtedly inflamed by the Act, the terrible Sioux tribe made war on the settlers of Minnesota. Hundreds of men, women and children, many of them Welsh, were slaughtered. Welsh immigrants joined up with the military to defend Fort Ridgeley, and the mainly German settlement of New Ulm, against the Sioux attacks. The Sioux uprising was eventually suppressed in 1864.

Illinois This is a State that Buley says did not increase its population much before what he called the 'Great Migration', starting from about 1815, after the American War with Britain had finished (R. C. Buley, *The Old North-West,* 1951). Ninian Edwards had come from Kentucky where there were many Welsh scattered through the State, several of them Edwards family-members originally from North Wales. Buley described him as "kindly, charitable, but at the same time pompous and overbearing". In the period 1815-1825, an important time for Illinois, he clashed frequently with his chief opponent, Jesse Thomas. The latter had been elected as territorial delegate to Congress in 1809 (i.e. before recognition as a full State). So, in early Illinois we have, mainly at loggerheads, an Edwards and a Thomas; a new and important member of the local Council was a Jones, namely John Rice Jones, Rice being a frequent variation on Rees or Rhys, indicating Welsh stock, especially when linked with a 'Welsh' surname. The young son of John Rice Jones had been assassinated in the street; one political group tried to put the blame for this on the local land commissioner, another Jones, Michael Jones. The latter was later acquitted of the crime. A third Jones among the top men in the early organisation of Illinois was Obadiah Jones.

T. C. Pease describes the early days of Illinois as "a system of aristocratic political factions", so some of the men mentioned above were far from being poor men (T. C. Pease, *The Story of Illinois,* 1925). Pease described Ninian Edwards as Governor "adroitly refusing to take sides with any faction, basing appointments to office, as far as he could, upon popular referendum" (Pease, p.105). The whole area was known at the time as 'the old North-West', between the Ohio and Mississippi Rivers, and south of the Great Lakes. The area in the first years of the nineteenth century was in a state of flux. In the first decade of the century Illinois was still part of Indiana Territory, from which it emerged as a separate political unit in the midst of the most bitter political quarrels. One such intense controversy concerned Davis Floyd (a typical Welsh-American combination of names) who was convicted of a misdemeanour. A licensed pilot on the Great Lakes, of whom several were Welsh, he had many friends who were convinced of his innocence (B. W. Bond, *The Civilisation of the Old North-West,* 1934). Heated argument occurred in the Council, and in the streets, about his case.

John Rice Jones, already mentioned, was a striking figure in local politics in Illinois. Bond describes him as "the brilliant Welsh lawyer and orator who held a number of important posts in government" (ibid. p.186). Jones was an excellent French scholar, and was sympathetic to the original French settlers in Illinois, helping them adjust to the changing conditions of the State.

It was obvious that someone like Ninian Edwards, even though rather 'pompous and overbearing' was needed to heal the vicious divisions in the new State. Bond said of him, "Governor Edwards was balanced in his views, with a knowledge of men and of frontier needs that was drawn from practical experience". He also had an ample fortune, and could afford to stand aloof from greedy quarrels (Bond, p.193). What is clear from a study of this period in one State is that those who appeal for a recognition of the non-English elements in the growth of America have a fair case. Louis B. Wright admits, "The portion of North America which later became the United States was so dominantly English in its background that other elements in its composition are frequently overlooked" (op. cit.). In other words, just looking at Illinois, the Joneses, Edwards, Thomases, Floyds and other Welsh names may rightly be noted; naturally the Scots and Irish would pick out their own participants in the complicated processes of American history. That brings us to Ezra Owen and son (J.R. Haydon, *Thomas Owen: Chicago's True Founder,* 1934).

Ezra Owen was born in Virginia in 1770, the son of a Welsh immigrant to that State, one of the Virginian Owen family. Like so many Virginians, Ezra Owen migrated to Kentucky, fighting in the Indian Wars there alongside Daniel Boone, and becoming a major. With this rank and nearly forty years of age, he migrated to Illinois. His military skill, learned from Daniel Boone, made him a very useful and welcome person in that State. He was particularly good at training raw recruits. Ninian Edwards as Territorial Governor had the power to give accelerated promotion; he had the reputation of never giving a job or promotion unless it was deserved. In this case, he made Ezra Owen Quartermaster Major of the State army.

Owen soon settled down to these new army duties, plus other official duties for the Legislative Council. He still found time to build a local jail at Kaskaskia, an important need in early Illinois. In 1819 he was appointed Justice of the Peace (perhaps as a reward for building the jail). Ezra had brothers who, in the course of several years, dispersed to California and other States.

Ezra's son, Thomas, was born in Kentucky in 1801, before Ezra came to Illinois. At twenty-one years of age, Thomas Owen was elected Sheriff of Randolph County, Illinois. He had a farm of 160 acres a few miles from Evansville. He married into a prominent local family, the Hotchkiss family, and had close ties also with the Kanes, the Menards and the Mathers, "wealthy, prominent and politically powerful as a group", as Haydon described them. Thomas had also two cousins, Lemuel and Levi Owen, well-known local farmers and prominent citizens.

In 1825 Thomas Owen made the first census of the county and, at the age of 29, was elected as Congressman for Illinois. Thomas, a Catholic himself, had a large part in founding Notre Dame University. At about the same time (1830) he was made Indian Agent, a very important post at that place and time. Many things were happening at that time in the Chicago general area, of importance for the history of the city. Cook County was just being set up, and Thomas Owen (full name Thomas Jefferson Vance Owen) was made its first School Commissioner. Chapter 2 of *Chicago's True Founder* is headed *'Owen saves Chicago'* — as dramatic as any newspaper headline. The meaning of the chapter-heading is that Thomas Owen used his post as Indian Agent to prevent the war that the Indians were threatening in 1832.

Haydon explains the true gravity and seriousness of the Indian threat, which could indeed have been calamitous for Chicago. "Thomas Owen," said Haydon "held a commanding influence over the United Tribes of Potawatami, Chippewa and Ottawa Indians. His administration reflected an invincible firmness towards the red men, on matters of principle and orderly government, combined with a disposition to take infinite pains to satisfy their legitimate desires. He stood prepared to fight any white man who prevented justice to them." (Haydon, p.119.)

For several reasons the infant Chicago was in a state of chaos in 1833. Thomas Owen was elected President of the Board of Trustees, i.e. Chief Executive, to bring about orderly government, in which he succeeded, as he had done in preventing another Indian War.

Professor Hartmann, using the 1900 Census figures, places Illinois fourth in the list of numbers of Welsh-Americans at that date, after Pennsylvania, Ohio and New York. (The Census gave figures for Welsh immigrants and their American-born children.) For Illinois in 1900 these were respectively 4366 and 7514, making a total of 11,878. We shall see later, that Hartmann disagrees with these figures, as not counting grandchildren and preceding generations of Welsh stock.

83

It is impossible in the space available to give much detail for every State in Central and North-West U.S.A. Place-names on the list in Chapter 2 would indicate some Welsh presence in them, and only a few supporting facts are given here. In any case the greater concentrations, in Minnesota, Ohio and other States have already been described. What we are dealing with now is the recurring incidence of smaller groups, and indeed often lone individuals, the latter particularly common in the Rocky Mountains.

Right from the earliest days, some Welsh from the Eastern Seaboard moved West, depending on where the 'frontier' or 'wilderness' had reached at any time. In the early nineteenth century pioneers of all nationalities were still extending the frontiers. Some Welsh had reached Iowa between 1838-1840. The first of these, according to the records, had come from Ebensburg colony, west Pennsylvania. They settled in the area later to become Iowa City. Later groups from the East, and some from Wales itself, settled in Louisa County and Iowa County in the early 1840's. Fourteen years later a bigger Welsh settlement developed at Howard County, bordering on Minnesota. Cyrenus Cole stated that, when Iowa was set up in 1834, the Chief Justice appointed was William Morgan, who must have already gained high repute in the area (Cyrenus Cole, *History of the People of Iowa,* 1923). At the first elections, George W. Jones was elected. In his autobiography he admitted that he had tried to get one county named after himself, and another after a Welsh doctor friend, Dr. Linn. In both cases he succeeded. Jones became a United States Senator, but was defeated in elections in later years.

In the years before the American Civil War, a score of Welsh families had settled in the Emporia district of Kansas. Some had come in 1856; others joined them later. Towards the end of the century, more Welsh came to Kansas, chiefly to Osage and Lyon Counties, to the townships of Osage City, Burlington, Reading and Arvonia. Those Welsh who chose to settle in Missouri had been attracted by work for the new railroads that were being built at mid-nineteenth century. In Missouri these included the Hannibal and Saint Joseph line. Small Welsh settlements developed, in connection with railway work, at Bevier and New Cambria in Macon County and at Dawn (Welsh for 'gift') in Livingstone County.

We have already come across some celebrated Welsh-Americans who became Governors of States, in Colorado and Ohio, for instance. The same thing occurred in the State of Missouri, when, at a critical time in the State's history, a Welshman, Sterling Price, became Governor. Sterling Price (1809-1867) was born in Virginia, son of Pugh Williamson Price, and descendant of John Price, who emigrated from Wales to Virginia in 1620. Sterling Price studied law, and became a member of the legislature for his State. He was elected for the United States Congress, but decided that he did not like the political scene; instead he opted for the military life. He became Colonel of Infantry in a Missouri regiment in the 1846 Mexican War. He was promoted to Brigadier-General and became Military Governor of Chihuahua in Mexican territory.

The experience of being a military governor must have convinced him that he had some talent for administration, if not for law itself. Anyway, he gave up army life and became Governor of Missouri in 1852. In that capacity he concerned himself with the reorganisation of the school system, made much more land open to settlement, and took a big part in the national drive to railroad construction at mid-century, vital in the opening-up of the Western United States. Then came the Civil War.

Sterling Price was heedful of his Southern origin, and in any case did not like the attitudes of some Northerners, despite his position as Governor. So he joined the Southern Army, and defeated Northern forces at the Battle of Wilson Creek (1861). There he showed high military ability, and again in the same year, when he marched North with his regiment, and captured 3000 of the enemy at Lexington. After a few later reverses, and a quarrel with Jefferson Davis, Head of the Southern States (and like Price, of Welsh stock) he withdrew to Mexico and private life.

Wyoming. From early to late nineteenth century, there was no lack of Welsh folk in Wyoming, although it was not one of the States with a history of large Welsh group immigrations. As early as 1807, there is frequent mention in the histories of Ezekiel Williams. In that year he was commissioned by the authorities to escort a Mandan chief back to his home. Expecting trouble from other Indian tribes, Williams had a party of 115 men in his company. Having delivered the Mandan chief, Williams rashly went to Blackfoot country to hunt and trap. There his party was attacked, and five were killed. Williams and the survivors then decided to make their way to California by South Pass. Again they were attacked by Indians, this time Crows; they lost five more men. Several more Indian attacks reduced the numbers of whites until only Ezekiel Williams and two other men were left.

Green River, Wyoming, became from mid-century the focus and central point of State development in Wyoming. "Green River was the home of a number of important men who played a big part in the territorial days and the early days of statehood." (I. S. Bartlett, *History of Wyoming,* 1918.) Green River was founded as a township in 1868, and for years after that, according to Bartlett, remained 'the frontier', still a very wild area. Amongst the 'important men' mentioned by Bartlett were Edward J. Morris, P. L. Williams and William Richards. The latter became Governor of Wyoming in 1895. The State was by that date very conscious of its identity, and in that year formed a Wyoming State Historical Society to preserve its history, its secretary being Robert C. Morris.

Another famous Morris in Wyoming history was Mrs Esther Morris, reputedly of Welsh stock. She was one of the earliest pioneer women in the area, and had originally come from Illinois. At her husband's death in Illinois, she joined her three sons in Wyoming in 1869. She came to live with them at South Pass, then a gold-mining town. She became the first woman Justice of the Peace in the area, a lively mining district, which kept her busy on the Bench, dealing mainly with bar-room brawls. This she did for many years, but also spent much time in the Anti-Slavery movement. She lived on to the age of ninety.

Wyoming experienced 'trouble', as it was usually put, from the Indians, particularly in 1867 when Red Cloud attacked Fort Kearny with 3000 warriors. It was defended by Captain James Powell, possibly one of the Powell stock well known among the Welsh as regular Army officers, several from Virginia or Kentucky. In 1869 another Powell, Major John Wesley Powell, left Green River on his famous expedition to the Grand Canyon by the Green River itself. No suggestion has been made, despite the surname, that this illustrious Powell was Welsh, but there was another Powell in his party, Walter Powell, who is said to have been of Welsh descent.

Wyoming, as it became a settled State, attracted more people, including Welsh, to less dangerous and adventurous tasks. Thus the State Auditor of Wyoming in 1894 was a William Owen. In 1907, Nathaniel Seymour Thomas, from the Welsh area of Philadelphia, became Bishop of Wyoming. John Williamson Price, of the well-known Tennessee Price family, his father a cotton planter, became the doctor for Laramie Town and the Colorado Railroad Company. William Rodgers, born in South Wales in 1862, was the son of a Welsh miner who came to the United States in 1869. At a Missouri coalmine, he cut coal until his death. His son William also worked as a miner for eleven years. He then gave up mining, found several other jobs, established himself in the community, and became a member of the School Board. He became the County Treasurer at Green River, and served for a time as Postmaster. He then became a Director of the Wyoming First National Bank, and also of a Green Bend general trading company. He married a Miss Isabella Pierce from North Wales.

South Dakota had a small influx of Welsh farmers in the 1880's — probably one of the last of the purely agricultural migrations by the Welsh, that had started two centuries ago. This late migration was mainly due to W. E. Powell, who was agent for the Chicago, Milwaukee, St. Paul and Pacific Railroad. Powell was a remarkable man. Not only did he have this top job with the railway company, but also he wrote Welsh poetry said to be of high quality, mixed freely in Welsh circles and societies and spent much time and energy in encouraging hundreds of Welsh to come to the State at the end of last century. One of the largest of the Welsh settlements was named after him (near present-day Ipswich). This South Dakota settlement of Powell was described in the *Cambria Journal* for April 1894. Other Welsh settlements in South Dakota, mostly based on the inspiration of W. E. Powell, were in Plana, Canova, Plankinton and Spain (S.D.).

Oregon was another State, far out to the North-West, that attracted a small party of Welsh to a settlement, Beaver Creek, not far from Portland. As Powell had played a big part in introducing Welsh to South Dakota, so did David Thomas for Oregon. His advertisements in the Welsh-American newspaper, *Y Drych* (the Mirror) produced Welsh customers for the timberland he had for sale. Some, in 1884, came direct from Wales when they heard about the advertisement. Most came from other Welsh settlements in the States. Apart from the timber trade the area of the settlement became quite famous for fruit-growing.

Nebraska received Welsh settlers in Richardson County at Prairie Union in 1867 and later in counties of Gage, Platte, Keyapaha and Wayne. By this date, so-called 'agricultural immigrants' were being supplemented by 'industrial immigrants', with workers, Welsh or otherwise, switching from one type of work to another, when unemployment threatened. This was exactly what had happened in New York State in earlier days. In the case of Nebraska, most of the 'industrial immigrants', who became farmers when convenient, had originally come to build the railroads.

Chapter 8

Welsh Nineteenth Century Emigration to Industrial America

THE movement Westwards in the United States coincided with the coming of the Industrial Revolution in England; it did not take long for it to jump the Atlantic, and enthuse the eager and inventive Americans. They had plenty of practice in tackling the many problems of the 'Wilderness' and the 'Frontier'; many of these had called for, not only ingenuity and endurance, but scientific knowledge. The latter was being provided by the expanding educational system in Boston, Philadelphia and other Eastern cities. Oliver Evans, although to a large extent self-trained, was one of America's first inventors; he has been described as an inventive genius almost a century before Edison. Oliver Evans was born in the Welsh Tract, Delaware. His grandfather, Evan Evans, had been sent to the United States by the Bishop of London to try and build up the Anglican faith there. Oliver Evans developed several inventions adapted for the needs of an expanding frontier. Before there were any proper roads on the frontier, expansion often depended on river transport, as Lewis and Clark had discovered in 1804. Evans invented a high-pressure steam-engine for river-boats as early as 1816. That was just the start of his contributions to the new industrial era.

By mid-nineteenth century, before the Civil War, industrial developments were rapid in the **Eastern United States.** The Welsh had a fair share in these developments. "The technical skills of the Welsh furnaceman and miner," said Alan Conway (*The Welsh in America,* 1961, p.8) "became highly valued in places like Scranton, Wilkes-Barre, Carbondale and Pittsburgh, which became the meccas of the industrial worker, as Ohio, Iowa, Illinois and Wisconsin had been for the farm labourer and tenant-farmer."

Official figures for immigration into the United States were available after 1820. In the decade 1820-1830, only 170 Welsh were recorded as entering the United States as immigrants. By 1850 that figure had gone up to 1261, and in the decade 1851-60 as many as 6319 Welsh had entered as immigrants, most of them 'industrial'. The figures for Welsh industrial immigration for each of the decades in the period 1881 to 1931 was in excess of 10,000, with a sharp drop down to only 731 for the 1930's, indicating the Depression.

Industrial immigrants in the first third of the nineteenth century were mainly miners. Many went over with very little idea of the conditions awaiting them. They were often, as Dodd shows, helped by the Welsh Society (as of course Germans and Irish and other ethnic groups were by their own societies). Many of the new Welsh arrivals at Philadelphia were at first settled seventy miles up-river at Pottsville (A. H. Dodd, *The Character of Early Welsh Immigration to U.S.A.*, 1953). "Here they were established," said the secretary of the Welsh Society, "under the guidance of our benevolent fellow-member, and true-hearted Welshman, Joseph Simmons" (a local big employer). Commenting on the miners amongst the first immigrants, M. L. Hansen stated, "The Welsh era in the history of American mining had begun." (M. L. Hansen, *The Atlantic Migration*, 1941, p.144.)

Skilled Welsh iron-workers came to work in new industrial towns like Scranton and Wilkes-Barre. The accent was on 'skilled'; the American employers (several of whom were themselves Welsh) wanted only the best, the pick of the industrial workers of South Wales. Before the end of the century, it is estimated that there were 5000 natives of Wales in Scranton alone (David Williams, *Wales and America*, p.81). But it was not only the ordinary skilled workers at the furnaces who were Welsh; some of the leaders in the iron and steel industries in Eastern United States were likewise Welsh. One was David Thomas; another was William Jones. David Thomas had been very experienced (and inventive) in the Welsh iron works. He left for America in 1839, invited by an American company to set up a new type of furnace, largely his own invention, in the great anthracite coal area of Pennsylvania. He became the Superintendent of a large iron works, many Welsh coming over to join him.

William Jones was the son of a nonconformist minister who had left Wales in 1832. William Jones became an army captain during the Civil War. After the War he became general superintendent of the Andrew Carnegie steelworks at Pittsburgh. He was both a highly efficient manager and a great inventor in his chosen field. "Much of the Carnegie fortune was due to him, and his own income was enormous, but," states Professor David Williams, "he was also a man of great humanity. When he was fatally injured in an accident in the steelworks, aged only fifty years, he was greatly mourned by his workmen, and by all the Welsh people of the United States." (*Wales and America,* p.83.)

Other Welsh immigrants of the period, with skilled industrial experience went to the copper works at Baltimore, which at one time was manned almost entirely by Welsh; many of these came from Swansea and Llanelli. The more adventurous of these left later to work in the copper and silver mines of Colorado and California. North Wales had mainly exported farmers and agricultural workers to the young American States. But North Wales had long had its slate-mines, really the only industry of North Wales at that time. Faced with industrial recession back home in Wales, many slateworkers departed at mid-century to work in the slate quarries of Pennsylvania at Bangor, which became the centre of the American slate industry.

One marked result of the increasing industrialisation of parts of the United States was the transformation that occurred at some of the old Welsh agricultural settlements. A big change came over the historic settlement of Ebensburg (Pennsylvania). It quickly became an iron and coal centre. Johnstown, also in Cambria County in Pennsylvania, became a focal point for Welsh industrial immigration. This process of transformation was even more dramatic in Indiana County in the same State. At Green Township, not far from Ebensburg, coal and iron deposits were found on the very farms of Welsh immigrants, according to Hartmann.

M. L. Hansen (op. cit.) mentions three additional factors that accelerated migration from Wales. One was that fares across the Atlantic came down in 1817, with the modification in that year of the British Passenger Act. Another factor was the extra pressure on Welsh farmers by the New Poor Law Act 1834, with its additional tax burden; thirdly there was the inflexible and hated tithe system that led to the Rebecca riots.

Industrial life started to change the immigrant scene in a quite literal sense. From the 1840's to the end of the century, the newer Welsh communities of Armstrong County in East Pennsylvania, followed by those of Clearfield, Westmoreland and other counties, became largely industrialised, with Welsh miners and iron workers from South Wales flooding in during mid-century. As in South Wales, coal mines existed in happy (using the word only in its economic sense) proximity to iron deposits. At first, in the United States, the coal deposits were bituminous; as in South Wales, there was a big technical distinction between bituminous and anthracite coal. The anthracite coal of Swansea Valley, South Wales, for instance, still had markets when the bituminous coal valleys of the Eastern areas of South Wales became depressed for lack of markets.

Anthracite coal, still confining ourselves to Pennsylvania for the moment, was discovered in East Pennsylvania. Rapid developments occurred in the area, with anthracite towns such as Carbondale, Pottsville, Minersville soon becoming well-known, not only in America but in South Wales. Referring to Carbondale, Berthoff, one of the leading authorities on industrial immigration to the United States, states "The weathered mountains and valleys, above the anthracite measures, suited Welsh miners," and adds, "Among the anthracite miners of Carbondale, the Welsh stood out for their neat and comfortable homes." (R. T. Berthoff, *British Immigrants in Industrial America,* 1953, p.125.)

These developments were paralleled in other counties in eastern Pennsylvania in the 1860's and 1870's. Thus Carbon County and Luzerne County became as well-known as Schuylkill County, where Pottsville and Minersville were situated. When anthracite coal was discovered in East Pennsylvania, two more counties that became well-known to South Wales miners were Wyoming and Lackawanna counties. The name of Scranton, as already shown, had from 1845 become familiar to many Welsh. "By the beginning of the post-Civil War period, Scranton had the largest Welsh immigrant population of any city in America." (Hartmann, op. cit. p.83). The peak year of Welsh immigration to this east Pennsylvania area was 1890. It is estimated that, in the Wyoming and Lackawanna Valleys, about twenty per cent of all the Welsh in the United States could have been found at that date. Wilkes-Barre alone had over 8000 Welsh immigrants and a total Welsh population of over 21,000.

In the later nineteenth century, as we have seen, Welsh emigration to the States came mainly from South Wales. Towns like Merthyr Tydfil, Dowlais, Aberdare, Tredegar and Mountain Ash had their own Emigration Societies by 1869 to help members emigrate to America. In the 1870's emigration to the U.S.A. was also being encouraged and helped by the North Wales Quarrymen's Union. On the other side of the Atlantic, the need for more skilled labour had led to the American Emigrant Company of New York, which advertised for skilled labour in English and Welsh newspapers.

The expansion of the American railroad system also led to a demand for skilled labour; it was not just a matter of sheer muscle-power, building the thousands of miles of railway tracks leading West, or from California and Oregon States Eastward to meet up. The American railroad companies gave much prominence to their need for skilled labour in the Welsh press — worded in both Welsh and English. As the railroads pushed on westwards, so did Welsh immigrants, like of course many other ethnic groups; the Chinese, who were numerous, generally came via California, the Irish from the East Coast cities or direct from Ireland. As far as the Welsh were concerned, the result of this westward expansion, with the railroads taking the place of the covered wagon, was the setting up of new Welsh settlements at places such as Arvonia, Emporia, Powys and Bala in Kansas. It can be seen that American-style names were springing up in Welsh settlements alongside the more traditional Welsh place-names. Similar developments for Welsh railway-workers took place in Platte County, Nebraska.

Meanwhile, in the last half of the nineteenth century, new immigrants, Welsh included, were still coming in to settle all along the Atlantic seaboard. There were, of course, no longer big groups of Welsh, like those who had come to South Carolina earlier. Yet Vermont, for instance, at the 1880 census had 514 Welsh immigrants (compared with 2253 from England, 1003 from Scotland and 396 from Germany), Maine had 283 from Wales at that date, 3716 from England, 1397 from Scotland and 688 from Germany. These figures were quoted from the Census by Brewer, to give some idea of the proportions of ethnic-group immigration at that period (D. C. Brewer, *The Conquest of New England by the Immigrant,* 1926).

New York State had in the early 1830's welcomed some Welsh to help build the first local railroads. In 1837 economic depression slowed up railway building for some time, so some of the Welsh joined fellow-countrymen in farming in the State. Some of these new farmers noted that in a few areas of New York State there were coalmines. "The Welshman had a traditional fear of being landless, so, instead of entirely forsaking his farm, he became part-farmer, part-miner." (Robert Ernst, *Immigrant Life in New York,* 1965, p.2.)

In New York City itself, some Welsh had established themselves, small in numbers compared with other immigrant groups. Ernst states that the Welsh and the Scots gravitated to the West Side of the city. In 1833 there were two Welsh churches in the fourteenth Ward and soon two more in the tenth Ward. The Welsh were served at mid-nineteenth century by two newspapers — *Y Drych (The Mirror)* and *Cambro-American.* About a sixth of the several hundred Welsh in New York City were in the building trade; another sixth were in domestic service, and rather fewer in the clothing trade. There were similar industrial developments in Ohio. Bituminous coal and iron ore dominated the scene in the new industrial Ohio. Welsh skilled workers came from the 1840's onwards to coal-mining areas in Meigs County, at Minersville,

Pomeroy and Syracuse. At a later stage others came to the Ohio counties of Lawrence, Summit, Perry, Hocking, Portage and Athens; by 1870 small Welsh communities grew up in several of these areas.

Just as at Green Township, Pennsylvania, so in Ohio, at the old Gallia-Jackson agricultural settlement, there was a conversion from an agricultural scene to an industrial one. At Gallia-Jackson it was iron ore that brought the transformation: this happened during the 1850's. Blast furnaces were soon in operation, two of them, Jefferson and Cambrian, owned by Welsh firms and manned by Welsh iron-workers. "Some of the original settlers (mainly farmers) who became associated with the iron industry became some of the wealthiest citizens of southern Ohio." (Hartmann, p.80.)

Two Ohio counties, Trumbull and Mahoning, met up with two West Pennsylvanian counties, Mercer and Lawrence, to form a vast new industrial area, with Youngston, Ohio, as its metropolis. At mid-century the area was developing coal-mines and steel works, all magnets to Welsh immigrants. Professor Hartmann, throughout his *Americans from Wales,* uses Welsh chapels as an index for Welsh settlements — a very useful device for a very religious age. By 1880 there were at least nineteen Welsh chapels in this great industrial area; this was also shown by the Reverend D. J. Williams, who likewise made use of the 'Welsh chapel index' in his Ohio survey. Not unrelated to this Welsh chapel index is the fact recorded by Berthoff that "Except for the Welsh, British Americans intermarried with native Americans to a greater degree than did other immigrants . . . Of the farmers only the Welsh chose to band together in their own communities . . . in the towns the Welsh similarly gravitated to a few wards of a city." (Berthoff, op. cit. p.134.) This latter remark could be well illustrated from New York City and Salt Lake City. D. J. Williams makes the same point about Columbus, Ohio.

This 'cliquishness' largely justifies Professor Hartmann's insistence that to get a full picture of Welsh-American life at that period you needed to take, not only, as some statistical tables do, Welsh immigrants and their children, but grandchildren, and possibly even following generations, as 'Welsh stock'.

One reason for the special 'togetherness' of the Welsh was, of course, the Welsh language, which to many first generation Welsh-Americans in the old days was largely their only language. According to my old grandmother, her brother, who emigrated to Pennsylvania during the Presidency of President Garfield, knew no more English than she did — which was no more than a few score words. Even when Welsh immigrants became Americanised enough to become bilingual, the Welsh language persisted for historical reasons. Even in later days, the Reverend D. J. Williams maintained that, at the time he wrote his study of Ohio (1913), it still took three generations for an immigrant Welsh family to lose its use of Welsh in the family circle. No doubt similar factors affected other immigrant groups such as Germans, Italians or Poles, including a shared history in each case, which the language at first seemed to symbolise. Thus many farmers in the last decades of the nineteenth century, who came direct from Wales, shared common memories of their long struggle for disestablishment of the Anglican Church in Wales. Shared also was the hold that the idea of America had long had upon the democratic and idealistic Welsh. "The type of democratic society in America which they had read about formed a marked contrast to caste-ridden Britain." (Hartmann, p.75.) In the last half of the last century, those Welsh who looked westwards over the Atlantic Ocean had been much impressed by the humanity of Abraham Lincoln and the Northerners, who had fought for the liberation of the Negro slaves in the Civil War. This idealistic aspect has been strongly emphasised by Gwyn Evans in his Madoc and Beulah books.

A more practical point was that information, in the last quarter of the century, on how to get to the United States had been much improved by the extremely convenient handbook, written in Welsh by the Reverend Robert D. Thomas (*History of the Welsh in America,* 1872). A Congregational minister, he knew America well, and his guide (1872), preceded by a short history of the Welsh in America to that date, was just what intending immigrants needed. *Hanes Cymry America* gave all the necessary information for the immigrant, plus much encouragement to make the first move.

The industralisation of Pennsylvania and Ohio was followed in many other parts of the United States, attracting from Wales miners and steel workers to territories different from the old traditional settlements, and often additional, and more far flung, than the industrial areas just discussed. Thus bituminous coal areas developed from 1850 onwards in West Virginia, Maryland, Iowa, Kansas, Missouri, Colorado. Usually coalminers moved on when coal seams became exhausted, or turned to more glamorous fields with the discovery of gold or silver. Sometimes former coal-towns remained on the map, with some Welsh still remaining in places such as Soddy, Bevier and Flint Creek.

Welsh coal-mine managers of considerable experience often led the way in opening up new coal areas, as did Daniel Davis at Knightsville, Indiana, Anthony Howells at Massillon, Ohio, and others in Alabama and other bituminous coal districts. Back in the East, there was, in anthracite coal and iron, the famous David

Thomas, known as 'the iron-master of America', with his blast furnaces at Allentown and Danville, Pennsylvania (see earlier). At the end of the nineteenth century, prominent in the Black Hills of Wyoming was the town of Cambria, owned by the Cambria Fuel Company. It was said at the time that the town lay on top of four million tons of bituminous coal. One prominent Welsh citizen of Wyoming at the time was David Willard Jones. He was born in Pennsylvania in 1882, son of David Jones, who had emigrated from South Wales. David Willard Jones went back to the Swansea Valley, South Wales, to learn colliery management. He then returned to America, was a rancher in Montana for a time, then qualified as an accountant, and became manager of the Sheridan Railroad Company.

Butte, Montana, with its huge copper-mining industry, attracted many Welsh miners, and in due course a Welsh chapel appeared to serve their traditional spiritual (and choral) needs. The Welsh Presbyterian Church there lasted until 1947. Its activities, and the Welsh population it served, were well described in an article in *Cambrian* (E. R. Williams, *Butte, its Welsh People and Welsh Church,* June 1909).

The Californian Gold Rush was an inevitable attraction for the more adventurous of Welsh miners. David Hughes described the small settlements in California in his *Welsh People of California* (1923). Sorting out where various Welsh were at any particular time would be a difficult task, as there was much frenzied mobility once the Rush started, and several Welsh were already mining in Colorado and Nevada. They seemed to have tried their luck, generally speaking, in one or more of the three States as rumours flew around about felicitous strikes, often reported, for instance, in the *Rocky Mountain News.*

There were undoubtedly Welsh in California even before the Gold Rush started, as David Hughes mentions, or as recorded in R. G. Cleland's *History of California* (1923). Thus the Chairman of the California River Authority in 1821 was named Floyd, a name common among Welsh immigrants; he must have been there some time to have attained that post. Isaac Williams, said in some books to be of Welsh extraction, had for years been a trader in Santa Fé, New Mexico; before that he had been a fur-hunter in the Rockies. In later life he settled down in California, twenty-five miles inland from Los Angeles. Further north, in San Francisco, Mary Floyd Williams had been active in the Vigilance movement that cleaned up the city in 1856; she had lived there several years, and in later life wrote a book about San Francisco and the crime-wave that had led to the Vigilance movement.

Prominent among the gold-mining centres where Welsh miners

are definitely known to have been was Placerville. Other such settlements, somewhat smaller, were Camptonville in Yuba County and North San Juan in Nevada County; in the latter county were the small Welsh settlements of Empire Flat and Burchville. Sierra County had large numbers of small gold centres, some with picturesque names — Port Wine, Whiskey Diggings, Brandy City indicate that this was not exactly a teetotal area. Still in Sierra County, there were Holldan Flat, Scala Diggings, La Porte, Monte Cristo, Forest City and Pike City. In Touleme County there was Yorktown. All of these are known to have had some Welsh miners at various times. "As late as 1871, fifteen large gold-mining projects in California were being operated by Welshmen. Of these Snowdon Hill Mine was perhaps the most successful. In time it was purchased by Jeremiah Watts, one of the leading members of the Californian Welsh settlements, who continued to operate it for some years." (Hartmann, p.78.)

Despite the somewhat alcoholic names in Sierra County, most of the Welsh miners were quite different from the rough and roistering stereotypes of gold-miners, familiar from the legends. There were several Welsh churches in these gold-mining areas, even at Brandy Wine. David Hughes mentions that there were occasional Eisteddfods held in the frontier area, between Nevada and California, three of them before the American Civil War.

Some of the Welsh made fortunes from gold, particularly January Jones who one January struck lucky (literally) at Goldfield, Nevada. It is said that, not knowing where to stake his claim, he threw his hat in the air and struck where it landed. He was a colourful character, born John Jones in Aberystwyth. He had eleven leases, employing over two hundred men. At the end of the gold-rush, says David Hughes, there were more than five hundred Welsh scattered about the Californian gold area. Some of the miners who had been unsuccessful in the search for gold had already gone home to Wales, or back to Welsh settlement areas in America, from where they had started; others had directed their mining skills to less glamorous metals in areas from the Rockies to Washington State, where there were Welsh settlements near Seattle itself, and at Spokane, Almira and Big Bend.

One well-known Welshman whose name was associated with both California and Nevada was John Percival Jones. He was born in 1829, the son of Thomas Jones, who had married Mary Pugh. They had emigrated from Wales to the United States when John Percival was an infant. They had settled in Ohio, but young Jones became intoxicated with the idea of joining the rush to California. He and several other young men sailed through the Great Lakes and the Saint Lawrence River, out into the Atlantic then down the whole East Coast of the Americas, round the Cape of Good Hope to California. There young J. P. Jones had a look round the gold-mining areas and acquired some experience. He decided however to become a farmer for a while, and also acted as sheriff of Trinity County.

In 1867, however, he left California for Nevada. Irving Stone tells the story of how this "jovial, ruddy-cheeked powerfully-built Welshman" made his presence felt in Nevada. Jones' brother-in-law, A. Hayward, held shares in Ralston's Ring, the biggest gold-mining combine in the West. Hayward recommended J. P. Jones, whom he described as "having a nose for ore", for the big job of boring deeper into the famous Crown Point Mine in Nevada. Jones was accordingly made superintendent of the mine. After a trial period of two years, Jones found nothing new, and the universally-hated Ring stopped his salary. He went on searching on his own, quietly buying up Crown Point stock at two dollars per share. Hayward and Jones decided to 'steal' the mine from the Ring, which itself had a reputation for unscrupulous dealing with unfortunate miners. Hayward and Jones went on increasing their holding of Crown Point stock, and when they had enough for control of the Company, they went back into the mine, and on the basis of J. P. Jones's research, they took out 30 million dollars worth of gold and silver.

According to Irving Stone (*Men to Match Mountains,* 1967) Jones had already been a hero to miners, for the brave part he had played in a fire underground at Yellow Jacket Mine at Comstock. "As well as being hero of the Yellow Jacket fire, he was second-time hero with the miners for having taken Crown Point from the hated Ring." (Stone, p.312.) The men wanted John Percival Jones as Senator for Nevada, and in 1873 he attained this high honour.

These Western mining States became well known to miners of all nationalities. Often the first stop on the hard journey from points East would be somewhere in Colorado; increasingly this tended to be Denver, the 'mile-high city'. In that city, hotels such as John Brown's Hotel were rising to meet the needs of miners, that is to say the more prosperous of them. At mid-century the Governor of Colorado was the Welshman, of whom more will be said later in the biographical section, namely John Evans. Not only in Denver, but in much smaller places, hotels and boarding-houses were being built such as the one started in Cripple Creek, near Colorado Springs, by a Welshman, D. C. Williams, whose first accommodation for visitors was a large tent. Denver over a century ago was an uproarious town, as can be seen from old photographs and descriptions. A near neighbour of Governor John Evans in Colorado was another Welshman, Griffith Evans "a hard-drinking

97

Welshman from Llanberis". M. Sprague (in his *Gallery of Dudes)* explains that this Welshman was the very first to start one of the 'dude-farms' that are so popular all over the United States. Obviously having some money, he bought up Estes Park, North-West of Denver, which had been given its name by its first settler. Estes Park in the Rockies is now a beautiful and popular place which I have visited myself. Griff Evans, as everybody called him, had bought it from Estes in 1867. Four years later he had ten guests, nine of them men. The one woman guest there in 1873 was joined by a very strange person, Miss Isabella Lucy Bird. She rode into Estes, astride like a man, and wearing a gown tucked into bloomers, over which she had full Turkish trousers (gathered no doubt from her travels in East Asia). She was a well-known travel-writer, aged about forty at that time.

Griffith Evans welcomed her, and charged her eight dollars a week for cabin, board and use of a pack-horse. She told friends later that she liked Griff Evans on sight, despite the smell of whisky from his bushy beard. She loved Estes Park with the vast range of mountains above it, its wandering bighorn sheep, and its spectacular dawns and sun-sets. Evans took her riding around the neighbouring hills; in return Sprague says, "she dealt with Griff's hangovers and herded his cattle at such times".

She reserved her love however for the handsome Irishman, 'Mountain Jim' Nugent. Evans did not like Nugent, whom he suspected of having designs on his daughter, Jinnie Evans. For some weeks he did not have to worry, for Nugent spent all his time with Miss Bird, who seemed to be infatuated with him. After the affair had subsided, largely due to Jim's drinking and his uncertain temperament, Miss Isabella Lucy Bird departed from Estes. In June 1874 Griff Evans shot and killed Nugent. Evans pleaded not guilty and was acquitted, his plea being one of self-defence. Whatever the truth about the facts, people there thought Evans was correct in his suspicions about Nugent's designs on Jinnie. Later Miss Bird wrote *A Lady's Life in the Rocky Mountains.*

Perhaps one of the most uproarious occasions, and certainly one of the highspots of the Governorship of John Evans, was the visit of the Grand Duke Alexis of Russia in 1871. As he was the son of the Czar of all the Russias, the United States was giving him red-carpet treatment. Tall and handsome, twenty-one years of age, speaking very good English, this first Romanoff to visit America became a very popular figure. On his visit to the Western States, he had made it known that, in Colorado, for example, he wanted to see some mines, but also wanted to do some buffalo-hunting.

The Pennsylvania Railroad, with a special train of five Pullmans, brought the young Archduke from St. Louis; with the cooperation of Buffalo Bill, a most successful buffalo-hunt had already taken place at North Platte, Kansas. Not to be out-done, Governor John Evans, a railroad magnate among other things, sent one of his Denver-Pacific locomotives to Cheyenne, to bring the Archduke to Denver. This is where 'Welsh connections' came into the picture. To arrange the promised buffalo-hunt, John Evans contacted his old friend, Colonel Floyd Jones. Unfortunately, it turned out to be a disaster, with hundreds of white hunters, including the Archduke, nearly running into a mass of Red Indians on a serious buffalo hunt. Fortunately the distinguished visitor roared with laughter, and a most hilarious party ensued (Marshall Sprague, *A Gallery of Dudes,* 1966).

That was one of the lighter moments in the official career of Governor John Evans. There were, however, many worries, hardships and dangers everywhere, in what was still very much the wild West. Never, to John Evans, had this been so apparent as eight years earlier, in 1863. Indians of the Arapaho, Cheyenne and Sioux tribes took advantage of the beginning of the Civil War to go on the war path. Cheyenne Chief Black Kettle and Arapaho Chief Left Hand started buying guns and attacking the mails. John Evans ordered them to get back onto their reservations. The chiefs replied, "We are not reduced that low yet." There was complete panic in the growing town of Denver when scalped white bodies were brought in from the outskirts. For their protection, assuming an attack on Denver itself was imminent, women and children were put into the famous United States Mint building. Raids by the Indians went on all that summer and autumn. The Indians then sued for peace, but a massacre of over five hundred of them, carried out without orders, led to furious retaliation by the Indians, and Denver was burnt to the ground. John Evans had the enormous task of rebuilding the city and arranging for much greater security for its citizens.

In the history of the South-West American States, particularly with reference to the mining that has featured so much in this chapter, one interesting and relevant aspect was the relations between Welsh and Cornish, fellow Celts in a distant land. That good Cornishman and much-read historian, A. L. Rowse, often touched on these relationships in his *The Cornish in America* (1969). In the last third of the nineteenth century, Swansea, South Wales, was a world centre for metallurgical studies. Several Cornishmen had studied there. One was Phillip Argall, born in Ireland, but of Cornish descent. Argall's father had worked in South Wales lead and coal mines. Son Phillip took a metallurgy course at Swansea in 1879, then emigrated to Leadville, Colorado (Rowse, p.337). This was not an uncommon pattern; Wales and

Cornwall were not far from each other geographically; both produced skilled miners, whom the Americans needed.

Often Cornish and Welsh went to the same mines in the United States, or competed for jobs in the same areas. Though both were Celtic in race, they each had their own way of life, and tried to keep to it in the New World, as Rowse shows. Generally the Welsh and Cornish got on well together, but not always. For example (leaving the Rocky Mountain area for the moment) Cornish and Welsh clashed at the highest levels in Mississippi, where two senators, Henry Stuart Foote, a Cornishman, and Jefferson Davis, of Welsh extraction, could not stand the sight of each other. In fact, on one occasion, they actually came to blows and had to be pulled apart, which was scarcely a model for senatorial cooperation.

Generally, however, the two Celtic groups managed quite well together, as fellow-immigrants, highly skilled workers and near enough neighbours in the old country. Amongst the factors relevant to their relationships was that of common technical problems, where they had to put their heads together for the good of the cause. Colorado, as compared with California, had peculiar difficulties over gold extraction. As shown by experts on the history of mining in the United States (T. A. Rickard, *The History of American Mining* 1932, R. W. Paul, *Californian Gold,* 1947), the reason for this greater difficulty in Colorado was the much heavier mixture of sulphides in the lower depths of Colorado mines, as compared with those of California. Californian mining experts could rejoice in a 75% saving of gold by the ordinary processes of milling and amalgamation, compared with a figure of only 50% in Colorado.

"The problem," says Rowse, "was formidable and urgent . . . it was solved by Richard Pearce, a Cornishman, who was brought over from Swansea, South Wales." (Rowse, p.323.) Rowse proudly stated that Colorado kept Pearce's memory green in the name of a mineral special to that State — namely 'pearcite', a mixture of sulphite of silver and arsenic.

Swansea turns up again in the industrial history of Colorado. An American mining expert, Professor N. P. Hill, set up a smelter at Black Hawk, Colorado, in 1868. He had much difficulty with the ores there, until he took a sample to Swansea — several tons of it, across the plains from Colorado to Missouri, then by water down the Mississippi to New Orleans, and by sea from there to Swansea. "It was there, in the famous Copper Works of Swansea, that Hill had his ores successfully treated." (*Colorado Magazine,* Volume 34, p.184.)

It was not only Colorado that used Welsh mining skill. At Jerome in Arizona, between Prescott and Flagstaff, the United

Minneapolis Welsh Church young people, 1913, attending the 23rd annual Welsh Christian Endeavor Convention of Minneapolis, Iowa and South Dakota at Minneapolis, Dec, 26, 27 and 28.

Verde Company started to extract copper in 1883. They employed a Welshman, William Thomas, who had had his training with the Vivians at Swansea (Rowse reminds us that the Vivians were of Cornish stock) to erect a furnace. Likewise at the famous silver lode at Comstock, Nevada, "Nevada promoters hunted through the available talent, in both Nevada and California, until they found veteran Welsh or Cornish smelting-men." (Rowse, p.289 — see also E. C. Lord, *Comstock Mining and Miners.)*

At the end of the nineteenth century, an influx of tin-plate workers came from South Wales to the United States. Professor David Williams shows the repercussion of American developments on Wales itself. In Britain, tin-plate manufacture had become almost a Welsh monopoly. The development of food-canning in the United States opened up wonderful new markets for Welsh tin-plate. In 1882 the Prince of Wales Dock was opened at Swansea to ship tin-plate to the U.S.A. "In 1889, of 430,000 tons of tin-plate exported, 330,000 tons went to the United States." (Williams, p.223.) The Americans, however, were not going to let this valuable industry remain in British hands. In 1890 the McKinley Act, in the United States, imposed a big import duty on foreign tin-plate, in order to encourage a native American tin-plate industry. This meant disaster for the Welsh tin-plate industry. As a result, says Professor Williams, thousands of Welsh tin-plate workers emigrated to the United States. The new Welsh tin-working immigrants mostly settled in Pennsylvania, West Virginia, Ohio and Indiana, adding greatly to the total Welsh stock in different parts of America. As in other industries, such as iron, steel, coal and slate, the Welsh provided not only skilled workers but top leadership. Welsh businessmen deliberately aimed at a monopoly of tin-plate, with F. R. Phillips forming the Welsh-American Tin Plate Company, with its plant at Philadelphia. In West Virginia, J. C. Williams organised the Phillips Sheet and Tin Plate Company, later to become the Weirton Steel Company. J. C. Williams was one of a number of Welsh millionaires in the United States.

Industrialisation in the New World had greatly increased the total of Welsh centres of population. Some new additions of population, through skilled Welsh immigrants, were near to the old traditional centres, particularly in Pennsylvania; Philadelphia would be a case in point. Cincinnati would be another example, with Paddy's Run and Gallia-Jackson close at hand. Cleveland attracted Welshmen from the older agricultural settlements, but also from South Wales. David and John Jones founded the Cleveland Rolling Mill in 1853. Likewise in Wisconsin, and in Minnesota, Welsh flocked to the cities, again both from the older American Welsh settlements and from Wales itself.

Many of the sea-captains who sailed in the Great Lakes were Welshmen from Racine (Wis.), some of whom had had experience on the Atlantic routes. In the Northern capitals, Cleveland, Cincinnati, Columbus, Minneapolis-St. Paul, Philadelphia, Chicago and Detroit, there was often union by marriage between older generations of Welsh-Americans and new contingents from Wales. Thus 'new Welsh' in Chicago met up with, and often intermarried with, 'old Welsh' from Wisconsin. The same applied thousands of miles away on the Californian coast, particularly at San Francisco, with settled Welsh immigrants greeting the Welsh newcomers, some of whom would have made money in mining in Colorado and Nevada. North Walians and South Walians probably met each other more in the New World than they had ever done in old Wales, united by language, perhaps some home-sickness, and by distance from 'yr hen wlad' (the old country).

The Americans themselves, particularly the majority of Anglo-Saxon stock, were becoming much more aware of the fact, and the problems, of foreign immigration to the United States. This will be looked at more closely in the following chapter, bringing us into the twentieth century, when the American government imposed severe restraints upon immigration. Already however, in the nineteenth century, American observers were estimating the value, or otherwise, of this increased foreign immigration. As long as America needed skilled labour, the balance tipped in favour of the (skilled) immigrants. "During the decade 1870-1880, it was generally accepted that immigrants had already made, and would continue to make, a great contribution to the economic life of the country," states Elizabeth Abbott (*Historical Aspects of the Immigration Problem,* 1926). "Nearly all the employees in American cotton, woollen and worsted mills, and in the foundries and rolling mills, were 'of recent foreign extraction'; most of the 30,000 miners in the Pennsylvanian coal districts were English, Welsh or Irish." (Ibid.) Skilled labour obeyed economic laws, and went where it was valued.

English and Welsh skilled men were not going to put up with uprooting from their native lands, the horrors of the Atlantic crossing in those days, and the many difficulties of settling in a new land in order to do only lowly work, at low pay. "Of those foreigners whose occupations have determined their location," said Francis Walker (*'Our Foreign Population', The Advance* (Chicago), Dec. 1874), "the most notable instances are the Welsh and the Scandinavians. Why should there be nearly four times as many Welsh in Pennsylvania as in New York State? Why four times as many in Ohio as in Illinois? The reason is obvious. The Welsh are famous miners and iron-workers. Their labour has not been wasted."

The advertisements, mentioned earlier, by American railroads in Welsh newspapers, seemed to have produced results. To give one example, quoted by Alan Conway (op. cit.) a letter from John Davies, writing from New Cambria, Missouri, said that he himself was working hard, and that several men working on the railroad came from Pontypridd and Llantrisant in South Wales. Hopkin Hopkins, who came from Gwauncaergurwen (known to all South Walians as G.C.G.), writing in 1880, said that he had been in Dallas and Fort Worth in Texas, and met there a man from Neath, Glamorgan, who told him of several Welsh working in that area. David Thomas had been to the famed colony of Patagonia, but was glad to leave there to settle in Oregon. Books written at the time, often quoting newspapers, frequently mention Welsh in areas far from the celebrated districts where Welsh settled in large numbers.

It is useful to look at the distribution of Welsh people throughout the United States at the beginning of the present century, including now those working in agriculture, industry, various services and other spheres of employment, including the professions. These were the grandparents or great-grandparents of many of the present Welsh-Americans; not all, because, of course, many Welsh still came to the United States to live and work between 1900 and the present date. The numbers of immigrants, however, dwindled after 1900, which was in fact the peak year for Welsh immigration into the States, with 100,000 immigrants that year. Never again did an annual total reach that figure, especially after the American authorities tightened up on immigration. In 1900, Pennsylvania contained a third of all Welsh stock in the United States, with over one hundred thousand of Welsh blood. Ohio had nearly thirty-six thousand of Welsh stock, New York State over twenty thousand. Wisconsin and Illinois had over ten thousand each in 1900, and Iowa nearly ten thousand. According to census figures at 1900, several other States had between one thousand and six thousand of Welsh stock, from Wyoming with just over a thousand to Utah with 6174 Welsh-Americans at that date.

The census included only immigrants and children of immigrants. Hartmann thinks, as mentioned elsewhere in this book, that real totals ought at least to include grandchildren. Taking the 1900 census figures as they stand, however, the States with over one thousand Welsh, in succession upwards from Wyoming to Utah, were Oregon, West Virginia, Connecticut, South Dakota, Maryland, Michigan, Idaho, Montana, Vermont, New Jersey, Nebraska, Massachusetts, Washington — Minnesota, Missouri, California, Indiana, Colorado, Kansas — then Utah.

The following States had over five hundred Welsh, but less than a thousand: Kentucky, Tennessee, Texas, Alabama, Oklahoma, Virginia, Maine, Rhode Island. All the above would add up to quite a respectable total, if you consider that the Welsh-Americans listed above would have added considerably to family numbers by now (1983). What if all the Welsh who, say, had come to live in the States between 1670 and 1870, plus their descendants, had been added to the 1900 census figures as well? There are those who consider that quality of population counts as much, if not more, than just quantity. From this angle, even allowing for the occasional 'black sheep' mentioned in this book, it could be argued, as Professor Hartmann has done, that Wales, as one of the smallest ethnic groups, had contributed as much as any other single ethnic group to the sum-total of American Civilisation.

This chapter has mainly been about Industrial America in the nineteenth century. One Welsh-American certainly belongs to the nineteenth century, and was one of the most colourful and, in some ways, useful characters of that century. He could not, however, in any way be called 'industrial', but neither does he fit into an 'agricultural' category, as did so many of the earlier Welsh settlers. The character concerned is always known, in the history of the American West, as 'Old Bill Williams'. Very seldom is there any reference in the voluminous history of the West to his Welsh extraction. Yet his biographer shows that he was as Welsh as anyone mentioned in this chapter.

In his way, he certainly contributed a great deal to developments in the South-Western mountain areas, so often mentioned in the sections on mining in this chapter — not that Old Bill was ever a miner; he was too fond of the open air. Old Bill Williams, as he was generally called, was one of the most colourful of the mountainmen, the trappers, the guides, the Indian-fighters. He was all of these and more. In his youth he had also been a preacher and a missionary to the Indians. For a short time he kept a shop in Taos, New Mexico. Altogether, he was the kind of complicated and unique person destined to become a legend in his own life-time, which was the case with Bill Williams.

Bill's father was Joseph Williams, born in North Carolina, son of John Williams, born in Denbighshire, North Wales (A. H. Favour, *The Life of Old Bill Williams,* 1962, p.23, note 2). Old Bill's Welsh ancestry went further back than that, however, and on both sides of the family. An ancestor of his was John Lewis, who had left Wales for Virginia about 1665, moved fairly quickly to South Carolina, and then in 1675 to North Carolina.

Old Bill's mother, was Sarah Musick. The Musicks had a strange family history, their ancestor being George Musick, a foundling child from a Welsh workhouse. Musick was not his real name, because nobody in the workhouse knew what that was; they simply knew he was born in Wales. He was highly intelligent and very fond of music — so they called him Musick, and gave him George for a Christian name. As a young man, he was a strong supporter of Charles I, so left Wales for America when Cromwell came to power.

Old Bill's parents, Joseph Williams and Sarah Musick were married in 1777, as A. H. Favour says, "joining together two of almost pure Welsh blood." William Williams was born in 1787 in North Carolina. In 1794, however, the family moved to Tennessee, then Kentucky, and finally into Spanish country west of the Mississippi, but not far from St. Louis. Both his parents were literate for those days, and they taught the boy to read and write, and the rudiments of arithmetic and geography; the lad also went for some time to Owen School near St. Louis. They were an interesting family; Joseph had served in the army in the 'Revolutionary War', and been wounded. Both parents were very religious, Joseph being a part-time preacher as well as a farmer. It was very much Indian country where they lived, near the Mississippi, the local tribe being the Osages. Young William played with the Indian children, learned to speak their language, how to use a bow and arrow, and, as he grew older, a gun.

As a young man, he was described as tall, over six foot, with red hair and freckles; Favour reports that he was "a ready talker, witty and quick at repartee". Like his father, he became an itinerant

Baptist preacher; his brother Lewis and two uncles were also said to have been itinerant Baptist preachers. For a time William, or as he was increasingly called, 'Bill', tried to be a missionary among the Indians in Missouri; they were friendly to him, but not easily converted. He became disheartened, told friends that God had not intended him to become a minister. One reason for his lack of success was that he was notoriously given to strong drink. He was, even when he was in early middle-age, known for his eccentricities.

When he was twenty-six, he married an Indian woman, according to a man who knew him well, C. E. Vaughan of Owensville, Missouri. He spent increasing time in the mountains to the west, and became an excellent trapper and mountain guide. He was also a first-class shot and horseman. Because of his skill with, not just Osage, but several other Indian languages, he several times acted as interpreter for the army. He spent several years back and fro from Missouri to the Rocky and other mountains, becoming increasingly expert in the lore of the mountains, recognised as one of the mountain kings.

When he was thirty-eight, he went to Santa Fé in New Mexico. He used to gamble and drink a lot in the saloons of Taos, New Mexico (where many years later, D. H. Lawrence went to live). A sample of his eccentricity was his attempt to run a small store in Taos, with money won at the gambling tables. Never was a man less temperamentally fitted to be a shopkeeper. After some weeks, he became tired of it and gave away all his bolts of cloth to Mexican and Indian women.

He went back to what he did best, tracking, trapping, and acting as guide in the high mountains. He acted as guide on at least one of Fremont's expeditions, which made frontier history, but was killed in 1848. In fact his death came just after Fremont's fourth expedition across the mountains to California; the mission had been accomplished with Old Bill Williams as scout. Wilfully, he went back to the mountains to retrieve some lost equipment. It was cruel irony that he was killed by mistake by the Ute Indians, by whom he had been much loved and respected. Sadly, and with bitter regret, they gave him a chieftain's funeral.

Chapter 9

The Welsh in Wars and Expeditions

IN PRECEDING chapters, we have seen Welshmen in early American history as sea-captains and army captains, and as members of ships' companies and regiments, or of expeditionary forces. The men who went out into 'the Wilderness' as ministers of religion or doctors, pushing the 'Frontier' ever westwards, many Welsh included, were pioneers in a very real sense, just as much as the explorers, the Indian agents or the mountain men.

Some were, however, more specifically men of action, paid to take risks and face danger, expected to give their lives if necessary. Many stories have been told of the great push towards the West, and of the wars that either speeded or hindered such progress. It is of the Welsh among the men of action, in wars and exploratory expeditions, that this chapter seeks to tell. Foremost in the tale of exploration is bound to be the great cross-continental adventure of Meriwether Lewis (son of a Welsh father) and his fellow-captain, William Clark. Included in that adventure should be the story of John Evans, Welsh minister, already mentioned, whose map of the Missouri and the Mandan villages, made a few years before the Expedition, did so much to ensure its success.

The wars that saw so many Welsh-Americans in action, twice against Britain itself, were the War of American Independence (often in the United States referred to as 'the Revolutionary War'), the fighting against the Indians, and the 1812 War between Britain and America, of which I have the impression that many people in Britain have never heard. In the Civil War in America, later in the century (sometimes called in American books 'the War between the States'), Welshmen fought on each side. Such participants will be noted in the Biographical section.

The War of American Independence, and the events leading up

107

to it, constitute a vast topic for historians, naturally most of them Americans. We are here only concerned with the Welsh share in those momentous events. This share was not inconsiderable. In the revolutionary fervour which led to the call for independence from Britain, in the actual fighting, and in the drafting of the American Constitution, a Welsh contribution can be noted.

Everyone, in the United States at least, knows of the crucial pamphlet by Thomas Paine on *Commonsense,* which advocated independence for the Americans. (Thomas Paine's house is in Lewes, Sussex (England) near a very ancient bookshop. Both the house and the bookshop are worth a visit by Americans touring Britain. I know that many Americans have already made this part of their pilgrimage to their national roots.) Professor David Williams maintains that just as influential on educated Americans, in the late eighteenth century, was Dr. Richard Price's Book on *The Nature of Civil Liberty.* Both the Thomas Paine pamphlet and the book by Richard Price were published in the same critical year, 1776. Richard Price was born near Bridgend, in Glamorgan, South Wales. "He drew," said Professor Williams, "a glowing picture of the future of America as the home of liberty, and instilled into the Americans a faith in the future destiny of their country." Oddly enough, Dr. Price never set foot in America, but his support for American Independence was recognised in an honorary doctorate from Yale University.

In the actual fighting, it has been claimed that no fewer than fourteen of the Revolutionary generals were of Welsh descent, including General Daniel Morgan and General Anthony Wayne (known to the troops as 'Mad Wayne'). There is no doubt at all about General Morgan's heritage; his parents were in fact first generation Welsh immigrants living in New Jersey. Alexander Jones, addressing the New York St. David's Welsh Society in 1855, claimed Wayne as being of Welsh stock; this was the opinion also of Professor Hartmann. There has been however a good deal of argument, between the Irish and the Welsh, about 'Mad Wayne'. Alexander Jones maintained that Wayne had Welsh blood on both his father's and his mother's side. Other historians explain that the relations between Welsh and Irish Waynes were close; he could have been Welsh-Irish, or Irish-Welsh, of whom there are many at Green Hill, Swansea, South Wales.

Morgan, as a youth, was restless and high-spirited. He left home and went to Virginia in 1753, becoming a farmer, and a captain in the local militia. Reputedly a colourful character, he played a leading role during the American War of Independence, especially in the Saratoga campaign of 1777. He, with his forces, rushed to assist the American Northern Army against the British General

Burgoyne. The latter surrendered. At a later stage, Morgan met, and beat, the British at the Battle of Cowpens (1781). Morgan died in 1802. Both D. Higginboth and N. Callahan, in their biographies of General Daniel Morgan (both 1961) put a high value on his services to the American cause.

Boorstin (op. cit.) says of the American War of Independence, "This was the war the British could not win, just as the Americans could not win in Vietnam, and for the same reasons" . . . "the American centre was everywhere and nowhere, in each man himself." (Boorstin, p.406.) Boorstin praises the unorthodox imagination of the amateur American Generals "in sharp contrast to the professional rigidity of the British command . . . The American Generals, not least General Morgan, did well — or the Americans would not have picked a General as first President, namely General George Washington." (D. J. Boorstin, *The American Colonial Experience,* op. cit., p.406.)

Dr John Morgan, who later helped to found Philadelphia Medical School, was Philadelphia-Welsh, and served in the War of American Independence as Surgeon-in-Chief of the American Army. General Cadwallader was another of the celebrated Philadelphia Welsh. Major-General Charles Lee, Second-in-Command to the Commander-in-Chief was born in Wales in 1731, according to the Dictionary of American Biography. General Morgan Lewis has already been mentioned as the son of a New York Welshman. After the war he became the first President of the New York St. David's Benevolent Society. General Andrew Lewis came from Virginian Welsh stock, as did General Richard Winn. Other Welsh-American Generals were Otho Williams, Edward Stephens, John Thomas and James Reese.

One fascinating Welsh character who fought in the war was Isaac Shelby, son of Evan Shelby, who came from Wales in 1734. Isaac joined the army, became an officer and fought in the Battle of Point Pleasant (1774) where "he distinguished himself by his skill and gallantry". As a colonel he did well in the battles of Cedar Springs, Musgrove's Mill, King's Mountain and finally, under General Morgan at Cowpens (1781). After the war he became a member of the North Carolina legislature, then he moved to Kentucky. In 1792, he was elected Governor of Kentucky. It was a bit too sedentary for him; after four years in office, he went back to fighting with General Anthony Wayne against the Indians, and in the 1812 War, an old man, he led 4000 Kentuckians against the British, and won, ironically, at the Battle of the Thames.

These were among the Welsh-American winners, but there were Welsh losers too. Some died in the Loyalist cause; some survived but left the United States for Canada or the West Indies. One lot of

Welsh, not long arrived from Wales, were the Royal Welch Fusiliers, stationed at Boston (Mass.) right at the centre of the revolutionary events. They took part in the first exchange of shots in the war. Gwynfor Evans gave a detailed account of what happened (*The Royal Welch Fusiliers at Boston in 1775,* Transactions of the Honourable Society of Cymmrodorion, 1978). In 1775, the 23rd Regiment of Foot, the Royal Welch Fusiliers, had already served for two years in America, first in New York and then in Boston. The regiment spent an uncomfortable winter there (1774) in an atmosphere of mounting tension, with preparations by the Americans clearly perceived, "testifying to the most immediate danger and determined resistance".

The regiment spent one more peaceful St. David's Day before the fateful march to Lexington. "The officers gave a splendid entertainment to all their Welsh brethren, and after the cloth was taken away, a bumper was filled to His Royal Highness the Prince of Wales, the band playing the old tune of 'the Noble Race of Shenkin'." Then a smartly-dressed drummer-boy, mounted on the regimental goat, was led round the table three times. On the 1775 occasion there was a striking omen of evil to come — the goat jumped off the table, unseating the drummer-boy, and ran away.

The Welch had been ordered to hold the bridges at Concord, along with other regiments, and by April 18th, 1775, had reached Lexington. That was where the first spark started the war which freed the United States from British rule. In the action four men of the Welch Fusiliers were killed, twenty-six wounded, six missing. Within a few days over sixteen thousand Americans were on the hills overlooking the British. There followed the Battle of Bunker Hill, followed by much more fighting for the Welch Fusiliers in New York and Philadelphia, until the sorry end of the campaign, at Yorktown. The Welch taken prisoners remained in Pennsylvania until the inevitable end of the war. What were the feelings of the many Welsh settlers in Pennsylvania for their unfortunate kinsmen?

Interesting information was obtained about combatants in the American War of Independence from examination of applications for 'revolutionary pensions'. For Tennessee alone the following men successfully, among many others with markedly English names, applied for these war pensions: Nicholas Davies, Robert Davies, Andrew Davies, Samuel Davies, Francis Hughes, his brother John Hughes, Samuel Evans, Joseph Evans and Andrew Evans, Darling Jones, Edmund Roberts, William Roberts, Joseph Rogers and William Rogers. Most had fought for Virginian regiments, but a few for North Carolina regiments, later living in Virginia. Similar lists for other States would show a similar scattering of Welsh names (Z. Armstrong, *Some Tennessee Heroes*, 1939).

The Declaration of Independence was signed by fifty-six representatives of the Colonies. Among them there were eighteen men of Welsh descent, including William Williams, Robert Morris, Lewis Morris, John Adams, Samuel Adams, William Floyd, Stephen Hopkins and Francis Lewis. The latter signatory, Francis Lewis, was actually born in Wales, in Newport in Monmouthshire (now Gwent). He was one of the delegates for New York, and the father of General Morgan Lewis.

The third President of the United States was Thomas Jefferson. He took pride in his Welsh descent. "The tradition in my father's family," he said, "was that their ancestor came to this country from Wales, from near the mountain of Snowdon." An early biographer said, "No man was ever more proud of his Welsh blood than he." Jefferson wrote, "My father's estate on the James River was called Snowdon." So, it was a man 'of Welsh blood' who, as a lawyer, drew up the Declaration of Independence, and became President, not just once but twice, at a key period in American history.

In the War of American Independence, as in the Civil War, eighty years later, families were sometimes split in their loyalties, usually a very painful experience. Even if the family were united in sentiment, as were several of the 'loyalist' families in the Revolutionary War, it was still painful to be separated from friends and neighbours. Many had to leave their homes for Canada, the West Indies or even England. Welsh-Americans sometimes found themselves in this predicament. Noble Jones, of London Welsh stock, married to Sarah Davis, lived from 1724 to 1805. He was thus middle-aged, with a grown-up family, when the American War of Independence began. Noble Jones and his family lived in what has been called 'princely estate' of Wormsloe in Georgia. Both Noble Jones and his son, Noble Wymberley Jones, were trained as physicians. The father was loyal to England, but the son became increasingly radical in his view as he grew older. By 1771, he had begun "to enjoy the honour of being hateful to tyrants" (D.A.B.). In May 1775, Noble Wimberley Jones, with others, broke open the main gunpowder store, which his father had helped to construct, and seized 600 barrels of gunpowder for the rebels. At the fall of Charleston, he was captured by the British. On release at the end of the War, he went to Philadelphia, where he began to practise medicine. He still represented Georgia in the Continental Congress, and soon returned to Georgia to live, eventually becoming the Speaker of the Georgia Assembly.

In a sense, Meriwether Lewis and William Clark link up the two sections of this chapter — wars and expeditions. They were both Army captains, and had seen their share of military duty, but they were handpicked by Jefferson for the greatest expedition in American history, because their military training and knowledge were joined to personal qualities, which fitted them for leadership in the arduous task ahead of them. The two men were both Virginians, both well known to Jefferson. His judgement, in choosing them, was faultless — very different in temperament, they complemented each other well in the expedition. Lewis was more academic, and better educated, than Clark, but was sometimes withdrawn and moody. Clark was more practical and down-to-earth, better trained in the Army practice of cartography.

The whole expedition, which opened up the American Continent, had long been a dream of Thomas Jefferson. He had a great deal to do with the practical organisation of the expedition. It would not have been possible, all specialists on the subject are agreed, without his enthusiastic support. Politically, the expedition basically altered the struggle for the control of America. The mass of detailed information the expedition produced about the terrain, climate, native people, plants, animals, resources — and difficulties — gave the Americans the knowledge they needed for the great surge towards the Pacific.

Jefferson had long known the Lewis family, the father Welsh, the mother English. Lewis's father was a gentleman farmer who had known the Meriwether family well. He married one of the Meriwether daughters. Young Lewis was given his mother's maiden name as his Christian name. Jefferson's own Welsh blood may have fostered the friendship between the Lewises and the Jeffersons. Jefferson's Monticello estate was in Albemarle County in the shadow of the Blue Ridge mountains. Nearby was the Lewis home at Locust Hill, a plantation of more than a thousand acres. When Lewis joined the Army, he served under General Daniel Morgan, famous in the American War of Independence and himself, as we have seen, of Welsh descent. Lewis made progress in the Army and was a captain by the age of twenty-six. When offered joint-leadership of the expedition, he accepted it, and went to live with President Jefferson and family. There he stayed for two years as presidential secretary, preparing for the expedition, with every help from Jefferson.

All Americans know about the Louisiana Purchase; lying to the East of the Rocky Mountains, the acquisition of this proved an irresistible challenge. Full enjoyment of it would have been impossible were it not for the Lewis and Clark Expedition. Starting from Ohio, and pushing north-west, then west, Lewis and Clark and their party, including several military, went ahead through territory then mainly unknown to white men, mainly following the Missouri River valley. They crossed the Rockies, after many delays and difficulties which can only be appreciated by reading their journal. It was an epic journey, the story of which has been told many times, by them, and in 1814 by Nicholas Biddle.

The Lewis and Clark Trail Heritage Foundation today safeguards much of the territory traversed by Lewis and Clark. The scope of their operations can be seen in the names of the States which formed the congressional Commission of 1964, which led to the Heritage Foundation. They comprise Illinois, Missouri, Kansas, Iowa, Nebraska, North and South Dakota, Montana, Idaho, Oregon and Washington. Many place-names in the United States were tributes to the English-American and the Welsh-American who worked together so well (Roy Appleman, *U.S. National Parks. The Heritage Trail*, 1963). They include town-names, counties, streets, highways, parks, recreational areas, lakes, reservoirs and bridges, rivers, colleges and other institutions. There is a monument to Meriwether Lewis near Cut Bank, Montana, but his grave is in Meriwether Lewis Park, Tennessee, not far from where his Welsh ancestors had lived. It will also be remembered that the only man who lost his life on the expedition was a Welsh-American, Sergeant Floyd.

John Evans has been mentioned elsewhere. He had gone to America with the firm purpose of looking for traces of Madoc and the Welsh Indians. His sojourn with the Mandan Indians gave very little encouragement to him in his main purpose, but exploring around the great Missouri river area, he accumulated much knowledge of that area, accompanied by maps, all of which came into the hands of Thomas Jefferson. "It is strange," says Professor David Williams, "that the upper reaches of the Missouri were first explored by a Welsh preacher looking for Welsh Indians" (D. Williams, *Wales and America*, 1946). What he had accomplished, however, proved most valuable to the Welsh-American President, and to the Welsh-American Captain Lewis and his companion. In the course of research, particularly where the American West is concerned, one notes the large number of Welsh names among army officers. Some can be traced back to long-settled Welsh families from Virginia, Kentucky and other States; notes on these have been included elsewhere in this book. Much that we in Britain know about the American West, apart from specialists here in American Studies, is derived from novels and films. In American films about the nineteenth century, the American cavalry feature strongly, and probably rightly. Yet an account of American Army activities, with less emphasis on the cavalry, seemed to give a more complete picture (W. H. Goetzman, *Army Exploration in the*

113

American West, 1979). The American Corps of Topographical Engineers, as they were called last century, seemed to have contributed a great deal to American progress Westwards. Many of the topographical engineers had been to Westpoint Military Academy, including George W. Hughes. He led a party making a survey from Texas into Mexico in the critical year 1846. His suggestions for the defence of South Texas, including San Antonio, were followed to the letter (ibid. p.150).

Another Welsh name that appears, in the story of the Topographical Engineers, is that of Captain William G. Williams, later killed in battle at Monterey. He it was who first instructed that great Western explorer, pioneer through the Western mountains, J. C. Fremont. During the period 1836-1837 in Cherokee country covering Georgia, Tennessee and North Carolina, Williams carefully taught Fremont the elements of his craft, as Jefferson had taught Meriwether Lewis thirty years earlier.

Senator John B. Floyd of Virginia had strong views about having Oregon opened up for settlers. When he became Secretary of War and Head of the Bureau for Western Explorations, at mid-century, he was in a good position to use his influence to promote exploration and development into Colorado, and northwards and westwards of that State. The matter was becoming urgent because of pressure from all sides to build railroads going West. The question was — by what route? Fierce arguments went on from supporters of the various alternative routes, particularly between the advocates of the northern and the southern routes. This led to a series of reports, including those of Captain Humphreys of the Topographical Engineers, and later by Secretary Jefferson Davis, who succeeded Senator Floyd.

A special expedition, with railroads in mind, was made by Isaac Stevens, naturally with concern for the Northern Route, as he was Governor of the new Washington Territory, soon to become Washington State. Goetzmann says of him, "He had been a brilliant young Lieutenant in the Army Engineer Corps with incredible energy, a smart, active ubiquitous little man who wears a red shirt, and helps pull on the rope when we get stuck in the mud." (Ibid. p.279.) The Report by Stevens was described as a very thorough, comprehensive and scholarly one.

While all consideration was being given to taking railroads through the mountains, the other side of them, in California, Captain R. S. Williamson was carrying out 'railway exploration' down as far as San Diego. It is safe to say that the United States Topographical Engineers had a great deal to do with the extension of the railroads coast to coast, and hence with the spread of American civilisation Westwards. It is interesting to note the Welsh names involved, some of them e.g. Jefferson Davis definitely of Welsh extraction, and others having names associated with old Welsh-American families like the Hughes family, rich and established enough to send their sons to West Point. The Humphreys family may not have been in America quite as long as some of the Lloyds and Hughes, but the Captain Humphreys mentioned above could look back to a respectable record of family service to the United States. His grandfather, Joshua Humphreys, came of Welsh Quaker stock, his ancestor having come from Merionethshire in North Wales, by name Daniel Humphreys. Joshua Humphreys (1751-1838) was a naval architect and ship-builder. He had married Mary Davids of Philadelphia; they had eleven children. At the date of American Independence, the American Navy was at a low ebb. Several ships had been lost in the war, and badly needed replacements. Most of these were designed and built by Joshua Humphreys, who could have put in quite a claim to be a founder of the United States Navy.

Captain Andrew Atkinson Humphreys (1810-1883) is described in the *American Dictionary of Biography* as "engineer, scientist, soldier". Born in Philadelphia, he seems to have inherited the engineering skill from his grandfather, Joshua. He went to the United States Military Academy, became a lieutenant in 1831, a civil engineer with the Corps of Topographical Engineers. By 1848 he was a captain in the Corps. He made a name for himself with a survey he did of the Mississippi Estuary. This led to his being entrusted with the all-important railroad survey for the Southern area, from the Mississippi to the Pacific; his survey gave a choice of five routes in the South. In 1861 he became a major, fought in the Civil War in the battles of Fredericksburg and Gettysburg, ending his career as Brigadier-General (1866) and subsequently Chief of the Corps of Army Engineers.

Chapter 10

The Welsh in the Southern States

WELSH immigration to the United States was not limited to certain popular areas in Pennsylvania, New York State, Ohio, Minnesota and other States in the north. This can be clearly seen by looking at the history of American States far from the more famous Welsh centres of population, starting with the Welsh place-names on the map. Tennessee is a good example. The Watauga settlement was founded in 1768 by James Robertson, of Scottish-Irish stock. In his party, however, was Evan Shelby, a Welshman who had come from Maryland. His sons, Isaac and John received a letter from him. His Welsh was probably better than his English, for the letter reads: "Dr. Children, This is to litt you know we are all saffe after a Jurney of Three Weeks. Collonel Gaits was amenshuning to to me if I cood git him proper Lockations for a large Quantity of Land". Shelby was to have a third of any such land (T. P. Abernethy, *From Frontier to Plantation in Tennessee,* 1931).

There was the usual 'trouble' with the Indians about this land. Shelby's 'arrangements' with the Army obviously worked well. In 1774, Colonel Andrew Lewis sent out an army contingent from Virginia to quell the Indians; Evan Shelby raised a company from his estate to cooperate with Lewis. By 1779 Shelby had colonel rank in the local militia. The Shelby family were to play a big part in American history; the above incident gives some idea of how they, and others, became established.

The Virginian Colonel Lewis just mentioned was active in the exploration of the famous Cumberland Gap; his 'Loyal Land Company' had existed since 1750. Several men from Tennessee were involved in the exploration; it is significant that adjacent to the Cumberland Gap was Powell Valley. The Pugh family were equally prominent in Tennessee. The Sheriff of Washington

116

County, Tennessee, was Jonathan Pugh. There was a so-called 'Regulator' called Joseph Pugh, and another Pugh was an official in Orange County.

The Jones family was also in Tennessee in its early days. William Jones had been a prominent North Carolina politician, a friend of Thomas Jefferson. Abernethy described him as 'the aristocratic leader of the Radicals' and 'a wealthy planter of the Roanoke region' (famous for its early settlement by Raleigh). By 1786, 'Willie Jones', as he was often called, had managed to get himself appointed as Tennessee delegate to the Philadelphia Conference on the Articles of the Convention. A member of the Lewis family, William B. Lewis of Nashville, also played a part in Tennessee politics in the early nineteenth century. So did John Williams, a State Senator from East Tennessee. Lewis was a close friend of the famous Andrew Jackson; Williams, on the other hand, attacked Jackson in Senate over his land dealings, with which much of Southern politics was concerned. There were therefore several Welsh names current in Tennessee politics, Irish and Scottish too — it was by no means an Anglo-Saxon monopoly.

For a time one branch of the Elstons lived in Tennessee. As with the Shelby family, the 'English' surname disguised a very Welsh reality, for the Elstons of the Southern States were as Welsh as the Shelbys. The Elstons, three brothers, came from Cardigan in West Wales in the eighteenth century. They came first to New York, then split up, one brother staying in New York while the other Elstons headed south. Some of the Elstons of Smith County, Tennessee, according to Zella Armstrong, moved north to Missouri, where their descendants are said to be still living. Other Elstons in the south continued to play their part in local history (Z. Armstrong, op. cit. 1918). The best-known episode concerning the Welsh in Tennessee is the venture by the Reverend Samuel Roberts to Brynffynon in East Tennessee. Some reference to this has already been made, but more needs to be said about that remarkable man, and about the reasons for the failure of the enterprise. Samuel Roberts was a Congregational minister of great influence in North Wales in the early nineteenth century. Shepperson described him as "a leader of public opinion, a man of cultivated literary tastes, and an authority on agriculture" (Shepperson, op. cit. 1957). The latter was a necessary quality for what was intended as very much a rural settlement. He was an outspoken enemy of slavery, which made Tennessee possibly an odd choice for settlement for him and his party, especially when his cousin, Governor Bebb of Ohio, was well-known for his anti-slavery views. S. R., as he was often called, was widely known by the Welsh in America as the publisher of *Y Cronical,* the leading Welsh political journal.

Evan Jones, a Welsh-American land surveyor, helped S. R. to buy 100,000 acres of land in the East Tennessee counties of Scott, Anderson, Cumberland, Campbell and Morgan. In 1856 the first detachment of about seventy Welsh, mainly young men, left Wales and travelled the long journey to Brynffynon. Failure appeared inevitable, right from the time they arrived there. "Many who originally promised to purchase land, and to emigrate, changed their minds; the estates were isolated; the soil lacked fertility; dissension soon became apparent among the settlers — and the vendor did not have a clear title to the land." (Shepperson, p.36.) The whole scheme disintegrated. Disillusioned settlers scattered, mainly to the Northern States, but some to Kentucky or other parts of Tennessee.

Virginia. From Louis B. Wright's research, it is clear that there were Welsh among the wealthier planters in Virginia, in addition to the Lewises, of whom some mention has already been made, because of the fame of Meriwether Lewis (L. B. Wright, *The First Gentlemen of Virginia,* 1940). Wright refers to Captain Samuel Matthews, of whom it was said, "He hath a fine house, and married the daughter of Sir Thomas Hinton; he is worthy of much honour," (quoted by Wright). A letter from the Governor and Council of Virginia in 1648 described him as "this courageous, energetic and capable man who has the best estate yet known in Virginia". This same letter referred to his home as Matthews Manor. Strangely enough, an archeological dig in 1964 came across some artifacts from the old manor, including several sword-hilts, gun-parts and other objects. Ivor Noel Hume, Director of Archeology at Colonial Williamsburg, described the site as an extremely rich one, in an archeological sense, down the James River in Warwick County. The reference to Matthews in the 1648 letters shows that a little earlier trouble with the Captain had been forgiven; thirteen years earlier, Matthews, as I. N. Hume comments, had been the ringleader of the first revolt against the colony's administration (*Martin's Hundred,* 1982, p.25). Major David Gwin was also a leader in Virginia society; it was to him that Robert Beverley wrote in 1703, complaining of Robert Quarry's sarcastic remarks about Virginian gentlemen (Wright, op. cit. p.293).

T. T. Wertenbaker attacked the traditional view of Virginia as the home of lordly planters of great wealth, owning thousands of acres on which to grow cotton and sugar. There were some such, but he lists the hundreds of small planters owning a good deal less than a thousand acres, some with few, even no slaves at all, compared with the hundreds on each of the limited number of big estates. In the course of developing this thesis, Wertenbaker examines the Virginia Rent-Rolls of 1704-1705 (T. T. Wertenbaker, *The Planters of Colonial Virginia,* 1922). The striking thing is, not only the large number of planters with much less each than a thousand acres, some of them indeed tenant-farmers, but also the numerous Welsh names among these less wealthy planters. Taking just two Virginian counties from those that Wertenbaker examines, namely Henrico County and the County of Prince George, fairly representative counties, we find, in Henrico, Thomas Jefferson and Hugh Jones (who wrote *The Present State of Virginia)* among the bigger planters, but also, among the smaller ones, Charles Evans, James Gower, Philip Jones, William Lewis, Edward Matthews, Thomas Owen, Robert Powell, William Watkins and Joseph Watkins.

In Prince George County Rent-Rolls are the names of Thomas Daniel, William Davis, Christopher Davis, Robert Ellis, John Ellis, Mary Evans, Peter Evans, Charles Howell, Jonathan Howell, William Jones senior, William Jones junior, and a score more of Welsh names including six Vaughans, Captain James Wynn, Captain Thomas Wynn, James Williams and George Williams. It would seem that, not only do the Rent-Rolls give strong support to Wertenbaker's central argument, but also to Professor Hartmann's assertion that Southern landholders were not purely of English stock.

Virginia saw some stirring times and some interesting characters in the eighteenth century. One resolute Welsh character at the start of eighteenth-century Virginia was Colonel Cadwalader Jones. He had been a noted Indian fighter during the last part of the previous century, combining this with vigorous trading in the few peaceful interludes, venturing into North Carolina. Like his fellow Welshman, Price Hughes (see later), who was active in Louisiana at the same period, Colonel Cadwalader Jones had imaginative schemes for westward expansion. He wrote an essay in 1699 entitled *Louisiana and Virginia Improved.* He proposed a company of gentlemen adventurers to find a pass to the West through the mountains, in order to develop trade from Virginia to the Great Lakes to the North (W. W. Crane, *Southern Frontier,* 1928). This very ambitious plan came to nothing at the time, but played a part in arousing the ambitions of later adventurers.

Some adventurers, Welsh included, were an asset to the progress of the American nation; some were not. In the latter category was Welshman and pirate, John James. In the biographical section of this book will be found reference to another Welsh-American pirate, John Williams. In his ship *Providence* (an odd, not to say cheeky name in the circumstance) John James fought off the British warship *H.M.S. Essex* in 1699, and captured the merchant-ship *Maryland Merchant* (R. L. Morton, *Colonial Virginia,* 1960, p.373). Captain Burgess of the merchant-ship later described his encounter with the pirate. "He was a swaggering Welshman named John James, who claimed to be Captain Kidd. He was courteous, saying that he wished no prejudice to the English nation." Burgess stated that the *Providence* had on board £3 million in gold and silver. Zella Armstrong (op. cit.) included in her account of notable Southern families, not only the Welsh Elstons, but the Welsh Gaines. At the risk of repetition, this shows the error of looking only at the more obvious Welsh names in studying the history of the Welsh-Americans. This applies in looking at family-names, or place-names. The Gaines were as Welsh as any of the Joneses, and dated as far back in history. In fact Zella Armstrong, who had consulted the genealogists zealously, maintained that the Gaines family, originally of Brecon, in mid-Wales, came in unbroken line from Brychan, King of Wales in the fifth century (died A.D. 450). Brychan was said to have been the ancestor of Cadwalader, Howel the Good, David ap Gwillam and Llewellyn the Great.

In fact the family-name of the Gaines, in the Middle Ages, had been Llewellyn. At the Battle of Agincourt, David ap Llewellyn had saved the life of Henry V, one of our more heroic monarchs. Later in the battle David was killed, but not before he had been knighted in the field by King Henry. The latter, noting David's bad squint, knighted his saviour as Sir David Gam, which then signified a squint. The family nevertheless proudly adopted the name 'Gam', which became Gaine, then Gaines, in the course of history. The famous Welsh family of the Herberts, states Zella Armstrong, were a branch of the Gaines family. The Herberts were members of Sir Walter Raleigh's Virginia Company in the sixteenth century, at the height of the Elizabethan era. The Gaines family of Virginia, however, descended from Sir John Gaines (1559-1606) of Brecon, mid-Wales. Six members of the Gaines family had settled in Virginia before 1650. One of these was Thomas, son of Sir John. Thomas in turn was father of Daniel, Robert, Thomas and James. Daniel was an ancestor of James Madison, who became President of the United States.

A Welshman, another Jones, played a minor part in the early history of South Carolina. At the end of the seventeenth century and the beginning of the eighteenth century, the interests of Britain and France were opposed in the Southern States of America, as they were in Canada. Nairne, in charge of the political-military situation in South Carolina, wanted the French off the scene there, just as much as Price Hughes did in Louisiana. Like Hughes, Nairne conspired with the Indians (to become a regular practice of the British in the War of American Independence and the 1812 War between Britain and U.S.A.). In 1705, South Carolina signed a treaty with the Creek Indians. This was a remarkable document, a copy of which is in the British Museum in London. By the treaty, British and Creeks would combine against French forces and traders wherever their joint interests were threatened. The Creeks pledged loyalty to the current British monarch, Queen Anne.

Captain John Jones and Captain John Musgrove were Nairne's Lieutenants in this peace agreement. Captain John Jones acted as interpreter in the arrangement of the treaty, so he must have been in the area long enough to learn the Creek language. "My design," said Nairne, "was to fall down among the French with a fleet of eighty canoes and five hundred Indians" (Crane, op. cit. p.81). The whole plan fell through when Nairne was massacred by Indians. Captain John Jones survived and went on playing an important role in relations with the Indians, trying to carry out Nairne's policy.

As South Carolina was that rare phenomenon, a successful Welsh group settlement in the South (see chapter on Religion and Welsh Immigration), a bit more about it will not come amiss. One of the best short accounts of it is by Robert Meriwether, Professor of History at the University of South Carolina *(The Expansion of South Carolina,* 1948). In August 1736 the Lieutenant-Governor and Council of South Carolina read, and granted, a petition from David Lewis, Samuel Wild and Daniel James. They were representatives of a colony of Welsh Baptists living in Newcastle City, then part of Pennsylvania. They were given rights to a tract of 10,000 acres of land, including Queensboro, and land above it along the Pee Dee River for eight miles "a reservation for immigrants with which no township could compare in area of fertile and convenient land" (Meriwether, p.91). Records of the Welsh Tract Baptist Church, which soon started there, show that they arrived, and started settling, in 1737.

Every head of family was given six bushels of corn and a bushel of salt. Most of the Welsh there came from Pennsylvania. Professor Meriwether goes into some detail about the dimensions and geography of the Welsh Tract and the area called Welsh Neck. During seven years from 1738, nearly a hundred plots were taken up, on an average of about five hundred acres each. Under the leadership of the James family, the settlement soon grew to 2300 members. The settlement, said Meriwether, did not suffer much from Indian attacks, but did suffer considerably from horse-thieves, an intolerable nuisance in rough country. Captain William James, one of the leading members of the leading Welsh family, called out the militia to deal with them. "The Welsh immigrants constituted a religious group as compact and vigorous as that which settled Williamsburg . . . by 1759 the Welsh Tract was far the most populous part of the middle country, and, next to Williamsburg, the most prosperous.''

North Carolina never had as many Welsh as South Carolina, but there is still much interest in the early history of the State, particularly from 1729-1775. Studying the history of Welsh dispersal in North Carolina proved to be a lesson in geography. Physically the State goes in steps, the lowest being the Atlantic sea-coast; the next step is the Piedmont Plateau running roughly North-South. West of the Piedmont Plateau come the high mountains. Welsh pioneers learned their geography the hard way. Some Welsh came north from South Carolina, some came up the Upper Cape Fear Valley from the sea-coast, some came south from Pennsylvania, and some came from Wales itself. Those from Philadelphia came south along the 'Great Philadelphia Wagon Road' through the big valley of Virginia, crossing the James River. All this pioneering occurred mainly from 1730 onwards. Morgan Edwards, however, the early Baptist historian, said that there had been some Welsh Baptists in North Carolina as early as 1695; certainly it is known that the first schoolmaster in the State was Charles Griffiths in 1705.

James Davis was a Welsh printer who printed the official documents and Public Acts for the North Carolina authorities in the early part of the eighteenth century; he also started the first newspaper there, the *North Carolina Gazette.* Well-known in the State was Gooden Bowen — not a Welshman, however, but a negro, a free black 'slave-holder' of black slaves (Lefler & Newsom, *North Carolina History,* 1963, p.398).

In most of the Southern States the majority of wealthier planters were of English stock, with whom the minority of Welsh stock shared a common way of life, and sometimes intermarried; there is little trace in the South of the 'Welsh way of life' that was found in several of the Northern States. Among the minority of rich Welsh planters were the Lloyds of Maryland, with their big home at Wye House on the Eastern Shore of Maryland. Mississippi had the Bowens, who had left Massachusetts, where they had been one of the leading families (L. K. Matthews, *The Expansion of New England,* 1962, p.126). Hugh Davis had his plantation of Beaver Bend in Alabama. He was one of the planters who was praised by Clement Eaton for humane treatment of slaves (Clement Eaton, *The Growth of Southern Civilisation,* 1966). Davis grew cotton on less than half of his plantation of over 5000 acres, growing food crops on the rest in order to feed his workers well. Among the Georgia planters was Button Gwinnett (1735-1777) who signed the

American Declaration of Independence. Gwinnett's father was a Welsh clergyman. Gwinnett junior became a Justice of the Peace in Georgia, a member of the Georgia Assembly and its Speaker. He helped to draft the Georgia constitution; he seemed all set for a brilliant and most serviceable career, when he was killed in a duel. The Georgia planters continually recruited (white) labour from Britain as shown by Coulter and Saye (*Early Settlers of Georgia*, 1949). They quote the list drawn up by the Earl of Egmont, the original President of the Georgia Corporation (1742). In that list, among the many English immigrants, are the names of Daniel and John Evans and John Hughes (servants), Joseph Hughes, cider merchant, Thomas Jones, constable, Noble Jones, carpenter, Richard Hughes, blacksmith. At an early stage in Georgia history, Saint David's was a prominent name on the map. During the Trustee period of Georgia, the Act of 1758 divided Georgia into eight parishes, of which St. David's was one. Later St. David's became incorporated into Glynn County, called, however, after the eminent Irish counsellor of that name (A. B. Saye, *New Viewpoints in Georgia History,* 1947).

The early days of Georgia were troublesome times, with so-called 'malcontents' at loggerheads with the authorities. Little did they know that in twenty years' time, with the American Revolution, there would be a complete change of 'authorities'. One of the leading peacemakers in Georgia in 1757 was the Governor, Henry Ellis, reputed to be of Welsh stock. On the other hand, in this 'Trustee period', the main malcontent was Thomas Stephens, the 'wayward' son of President William Stephens. The case being referred back to England, the House of Commons found the charges against Stephens 'false, scandalous and malicious'. At that time in Georgia the Judge of Admiralty was James Edward Powell and the Treasurer was Noble Jones, descendant of the Noble Jones from Wales mentioned earlier; the Clerk of the Court was Charles Pryce.

The name Noble Jones crops up again in Noble Wymberley Jones, one of the foremost radicals of Georgia, who had been elected Speaker of the Assembly in 1772. Jones and three other prominent citizens issued a notice in the *Georgia Gazette,* 14th July 1774, against the 'Intolerable Acts'. Another of the rebel leaders in Georgia was John Glen, and John Wynne Jones was one of three delegates to the Constitutional Congress in Philadelphia. After the American Revolution, the Constitutional Committee for Georgia included Josiah Lewis, Henry Jones and Button Gwinnett, the latter soon to die in the duel with Scotsman, Lachlan McIntosh.

Louisiana. Although Price Hughes, referred to in the historical literature of the time simply as 'a Welsh Gentleman', had over

3000 acres of land, this set no boundary to his ambition. He had set his heart upon a new province in the lower Mississippi valley. Crane says, "His assassination in Louisiana, in 1715, brought unmerited oblivion on his name and his enterprises. For surely Price Hughes was an authentic prophet of Anglo-American westward expansion." (V. W. Crane, op. cit. p.99.) The 'Anglo' in the quotation above was not quite what Price Hughes had in mind. Professor Crane recognised this, for he continues, "Thither he was determined to lead the great numbers of Welshmen who, he believed, would come over at his bidding." Hughes wrote to a friend, John Jones, back in Wales, "tell them that I will let them starve for timorous drones," that is, "if they do not come when called."

Hughes intrigued among the Indian tribes, hoping and promising to free them once and for all from French influence. "This summer," he wrote, "I have been a considerable way to the Westward upon the branches of the Mesisipi (sic), where I saw a country as different from Carolina as the best parts of our country (Wales) are from the fens of Lincolnshire." (Ibid. p.100.) He was so certain that his countrymen would come that he appointed Bristol as their port of departure from England; he also selected leaders for the party. For funds, additional to his own, he depended upon Queen Anne. "I hope," he told the Queen in a letter, "that the secureing so fine and spacious a countrey to the Crown will clearly outbalance so small a charge." He even had a name for that 'countrey', not the most euphonious — Annarea.

The growth of 'Southern Civilisation' owed much to the ideal of the English country gentleman. "Henry Stanley, the future explorer of Africa (where took place the celebrated meeting with Livingstone) encountered this powerful social force while clerking in a country store in Arkansas . . . Stanley, who had spent his childhood in a workhouse in Wales, and had been cuffed about as a sailor on a merchant ship, succumbed to the pervasive mores of his Southern community." (Clement Eaton, op. cit. p.2. See also Dorothy Stanley (editor), *The Autobiography of Sir Henry Morton Stanley,* 1909.)

This is not the place to go into the relationship between this noble ideal and the fact of slavery in the South. Great variations occurred in the actual practice of slavery, "the Peculiar Institution", as Kenneth Stampp called it in his book of that title (1956). Yet it is fair to note that Jefferson Davis and his brother Joseph, Welsh by descent, were admitted to be model planters in their care of their slaves. No doubt there were Welsh among the less humane planters also. It seems from most accounts that the worst conditions for slaves occurred where there was absentee landlordism, of which there was a great deal. One of these absentee planters was George

Noble Jones, who spent most of his time travelling in Europe. He left the care of his estates, El Destino and Chemonie, to overseers. John Evans was the overseer at the latter estate. Evans considered himself moderate in the use of flogging with slaves, compared to some masters and overseers (U. B. Phillips & J. D. Glunt, *Florida Plantation Records,* 1927, W. T. Jordan, *Hugh Davis and his Alabama Plantation,* 1948). The question of whether flogging should be allowed at all was at least discussed; what was seldom discussed was whether slavery should exist at all.

Kentucky remembered its Welsh in the name of some of its counties. Thus Floyd County was named after Colonel John Floyd, born in Virginia, as were many of the pioneers of Kentucky. Floyd was a surveyor, a very useful accomplishment in opening up new territory. He was also experienced in military matters and in legislation, overall a most useful asset to Kentucky as a developing State. He was described as intellectual and handsome (L. Collins, *History of Kentucky,* 1850). At one exciting point in his career, he accompanied Daniel Boone in the rescue of his daughter. His life ended early however, for he was killed by Indians in 1783. His son, Clark Floyd, commanded an infantry regiment at the Battle of Tippecanoe (1811). Another son of Colonel John Floyd later became Governor of Virginia. More will be said about the Floyds in later short biographies.

Daviess County, Kentucky, was named after Colonel Joseph Daviess, who died at the Battle of Tippecanoe. It will be noticed that a big town in Daviess County is called Owenboro. There is, however, in Kentucky, also an Owen County, named after Colonel Abraham Owen, born 1769. Like Colonel John Floyd, he was born in Virginia, and migrated to Kentucky. Colonel Owen became a member of the Kentucky Senate, after he was wounded in the American War of Independence. Like Colonel Daviess, he also was killed at the Battle of Tippecanoe, which clearly played a large, and sad, part in early Kentucky history. Colonel Owen left a son who, according to Lewis Collins, writing in 1850, was at that date "a distinguished citizen of Texas".

The link between Virginia and Kentucky, and its significance for Welsh-American history, can be clearly seen by looking at some of the local Jones family. The original wealthy Jones in the Southern States was Captain Roger Jones, born 1625, a young Cavalier in the army of Charles II. He came to Virginia in company with Lord Culpeper in 1680. The Joneses originally came from Monmouthshire (now Gwent), as did the mother of Roger Jones' son, Thomas. It is recorded that Thomas Jones came to London from Virginia in 1706. While there he visited Leeds Castle in Kent, the beautiful home of the Culpepers.

Judge L. H. Jones, who wrote the history of the Jones family in the South, states that this Thomas Jones was the ancestor of the many Army and Navy Jones families to be found in Kentucky and Washington D.C. (L. H. Jones, *Captain Roger Jones of London and Virginia*, 1891). The London Welsh Joneses were wealthy from lands in South Wales, and, for those who crossed the Atlantic, their wealth bought them large plantations and high social position in Southern society. Colonel Thomas Jones was the father of Catesby Jones, a name later to be well-known in Californian naval circles. One of the Virginian Jones family, Skelton Jones, was, like Button Gwinnett, addicted to duelling — and like Button Gwinnett, he died in a duel.

The Kentucky branch of the Southern Jones family was derived, according to Judge L. H. Jones, from Thomas ap Thomas Jones, who was born in Virginia in 1784, but moved to Kentucky in 1810. His family seat in Virginia, before the move, was Bathurst. Sally Jones, a daughter of the family, married James Davis of Frederick City, Virginia. Their son was Colonel Jekyll Lucius Davis, a graduate of West Point. He was related to Jefferson Davis, Southern leader at the time of the Civil War, and himself, as already mentioned, of Welsh extraction. Colonel J. L. Davis fought in the Civil War at the battles of Brandy Station, Yorktown and Gettysburg. He died in 1871. A casualty of the Civil War itself was another member of the family, Llewellyn Catesby Davis. Other members of the family were Bathurst Mervyn Davis who lived in Texas, and Frank Tudor Davis, a Baptist minister in Virginia. Modern historians, as we have seen, tend to minimise the importance of the 'Patricians' in these Southern States. The Southern Jones and Davis families however seem to have been as patrician as Samuel Mathews who, as was shown earlier, was a rich man when he came to Virginia in 1649, calling his house and plantation 'Denbigh', the house being served by twenty-three servants; Denbigh was described at the time as a self-sufficient village (J. M. Smith, *Seventeenth Century America*, 1959).

Oklahoma had its share of Welsh-named persons, as it had its share of Welsh place-names, the counties of Hughes and Stephens, for instance. Looking back at the early history of the State, we hear of parties of Cherokee Indians, who had suffered during the Civil War, being brought up-river to settle in Oklahoma, seventy from North Carolina and eighty-seven from Tennessee. They came up the Arkansas River by the steam-boat *American*. The man who had the task, by no means easy, to settle them in Oklahoma was John B. Jones, Indian Agent (Grant Foreman, *History of Oklahoma*, 1942, p.151). At roughly the same period in the State, surveyor A. H. Jones had a guard of Creek and Seminole Indians as he went about his duties in wild country. Still, however, being under threat from the fierce Comanches, greatly superior in numbers, he appealed to the Army. They gave him extra protection under the leadership of Lieutenant James Powell.

Coming to more peaceful times in Oklahoma, that is, nearer our own times, the Governor of the State in 1901 was William M. Jenkins; the United States Senator for Oklahoma from 1908-1925 was Robert L. Owen; the Governor of the State from 1915-1919 was Robert L. Williams, in what Foreman called "an outstanding administration".

In looking at Welsh names in the history of the various American States, Southern or otherwise, one must always remember that even the Joneses are not always of Welsh extraction. Yet, taking the Jones family in the South, its members can be seen to belong to a stream of Welsh-American Joneses traceable back to Wales, or at least to London Welsh. In a further consideration of another branch of the Jones family, in the Biographical chapter, it will be seen that the same applies to the Jones family of New York, or more specifically, Long Island. Likewise with other 'Welsh' names (or even the 'non-Welsh' names of the Shelby and other families) occurring frequently in American history e.g. in the Civil War — on both sides; examination of the official American Genealogies, discussed in the concluding chapter, often shows similar continuing chains leading back to earlier Welsh ancestors.

Chapter 11

Some Short Welsh-American Biographies

INTRODUCTION. Paul Angle was doing research for his book *Illinois Prairie State* (1968). He happened to stay at Evans Hotel, Vandalia. The owner, in fact Mr Evans, explained that he had built the hotel in 1924, along with a hardware store and a real estate business; he was in consequence one of the richest men in Vandalia. In 1961 he presented the town with a new library. Being complimented on his enterprise and public spirit, he declared "We are Welsh by descent", as if that explained everything.

It was interesting that Mr Evans, very much the practical businessman, was conscious of his Welsh descent, and put so much emphasis upon it. This was quite common with many Welsh-Americans of first, second and third generations, even among those tracing their Welsh connections further back still, usually grouped together as of 'Welsh stock'. Many stressed their continuing Welshness by giving their children Welsh Christian names to go with Welsh surnames. Thus a Griffith Jones encountered in 1972 could have been first or second generation Welsh-American, or could have traced his ancestry back much further (actually in this case my informant stated that his great-grandfather came from Merthyr Tydfil in 1852). Sometimes, as with Evan Shelby in the eighteenth century, to most Welshmen the surname would not sound Welsh, but the Christian name would be a hint to follow up. Not always — some Welsh names became popular with Americans as Christian names, particularly perhaps Lloyd and Floyd.

There are so many Welsh-Americans who gained fame locally or even nationally over the centuries that it would be impossible to include them all in this section. Many have already been mentioned in earlier chapters of this book. Professor Hartmann in his valuable survey of Welsh-Americans used a four-fold classification — immigrants; children of immigrants; grandchildren of immigrants, and 'Welsh stock'. This section will simply try to illustrate the wide variety of fields in which, over the centuries, men, and women, of Welsh ancestry contributed to the growth of the American nation. This will have already been made clear to a large extent in preceding pages, but the selection of additional brief case-histories quoted here may fill out the total picture, particularly in more recent days.

Early on in American history, a precedent had already been established, in the Easton family from Wales for example, for Welsh in the United States to carry on from generation to generation a tradition of public service. Nicholas Easton (1593-1675), a Quaker, came from Wales in 1635, his occupation originally having been that of a tanner. He established himself so well in Rhode Island that he became its Governor. His son, John Easton (1625-1705) carried on the tradition, and was Governor of Rhode Island from 1690-1695. The Eastons were landholders on an extensive scale; several of them had scholarly and historical interests. Thus John Easton wrote *A History of King Phillip's Indian War.*

So far in this work there have been frequent references to the Welsh in agriculture, industry, religion, education, music and other fields of American life, not neglecting the military and naval. One of the spheres about which not much has been said is the important one of law and government. That is why the Eastons were quoted early in this section. The maintenance of law and order, coupled with fair and efficient administration of public services, is essential in modern states. A glance through the many excellent volumes of the Dictionary of American Biography will reveal many Welsh names in central and local government, in the separate States, and at Washington D.C. itself. The spheres of law and order are perhaps not as glamorous as other fields of life, compared with, for instance, the heroic figures of American history and legend. Administration is concerned with public service, but it is also concerned with power. Several of the best known administrators in American history, some of them Welsh by origin, were both powerful and colourful characters. Often they had led exciting lives in their youth, in the wilderness, at the frontier, in the mountains, serving in the army. In many cases they had helped to introduce law and order in wild territories, often among wild men. One fact that strikes one forcibly was the variety and rich life experience of many who became, for example, State Governors or Senators. This applied to the Welsh as it did to the English, Irish, Scots and others among American community leaders.

Take, for instance the Morris family of New York, as well known there as the Lloyds in Pennsylvania. Father of the family in

New York was Richard Morris. He had come to New York from Barbados, and it is said that he had originally been of London Welsh extraction. He had fought in Cromwell's army in mid-seventeenth century, and fled from England at the accession of Charles II in 1660. More famous was his son Lewis, who also had a son called Lewis. The rise of the Morris family in New York coincided with the rise of the New York Assembly. By the end of the seventeenth century and the beginning of the eighteenth century, Lewis Morris "had built up a party which came to dominate the Assembly between 1708 and 1739". Lewis Morris senior was "a remarkable figure who maintained party leadership despite his brusque manners, incurable tardiness and frequent drunkenness". (D. M. Ellis, *A History of New York State,* 1957.)

Lewis Morris distributed patronage with great skill, and attracted to himself able young men, notably Cadwallader Colden — of Scottish extraction. The Morris party appealed to the middle class of small traders, artisans and Hudson Valley farmers, plus many Dutch and Quakers. Gradually he and his son came to be recognised as the party of reform. The wealthier merchants of New York and Albany disliked the Morris programme, and supported instead Adolphus Philipse, a big landholder. Morris published details of his reform programme in the *New York Weekly Journal,* read by all his supporters.

His son, Lewis Morris junior, became Chief Justice of New York in the 1730's. He made decisions that angered Cosby, the Governor of New York. Cosby had Morris dismissed, but this drastic action boomeranged against Cosby. In the elections of 1733, both the Morrises, father and son, won sweeping victories. The Morris family established itself safely throughout the rest of the century, Lewis Morris junior being on the Provincial Congress of the Revolutionary era (1775) along with another of Welsh lineage, Francis Lewis. Other members of the Morris family, Robert, the 'financier of the Revolution' and Gouvernor Morris, have been mentioned earlier in this book. Robert, an expert in public finance, also managed quite well for himself; he was a land speculator on a big scale, and in 1788 bought one million acres of land.

Francis Lewis has been mentioned above. He was one of the Welshmen who signed the American Declaration of Independence. His son, Morgan Lewis, was a native of New York City and a Colonel during the War of American Independence, later becoming a General. After the War, he engaged in legal studies and soon became a Judge. In 1804 he became Governor of New York State. Having helped to make some American history, he took up historical studies in later years, and became President of the New York Historial Society.

Already there must surely be support for earlier claims that Welsh-Americans became involved in both public service and positions of power, after earlier days of struggle and adventure. Another example would be the **Dr John Evans,** mentioned earlier, who qualified as a physician last century, became celebrated as a founder of universities, but equally well-known as a railway magnate in the pioneer days of the railroad companies, founding the Denver-New Orleans Line. In 1862 he entered the field of public administration as Governor of Colorado; he was well-known, and honoured, in Illinois, Wyoming and Indiana (where he founded a mental hospital). "He was a personal friend and strong supporter of Abraham Lincoln, a man destined to exhibit his firm character and sterling worth in the building of Colorado." (A. Hafen, *History of Colorado,* 1933.) The new town of Evans (Colorado) was named after him. Many years later, in 1917, his grandson, also called John Evans, was appointed Provost Marshal, raising troops for America in World War I.

Jefferson Davis (1808-1889) has been described as soldier, statesman and author. He was born in Kentucky, his father Samuel Davis being of Welsh stock, his mother Scottish-Irish. Jefferson Davis was the leader of the South in the American Civil War. He had already become a military hero when he commanded the Mississippi Rifles in the Mexican War; at the Battle of Monterey he had shown great bravery, and been wounded in action. In the Civil War he occupied the position for four years as President of the Southern Federate States. His second wife, Varina Howell, was a member of the Virginian aristocracy. She later wrote his biography. He also was a writer, with his *Rise and Fall of the Confederate Government* (1881). It is interesting to note that Jefferson Davis's grandfather Evan Davis, had commanded a troop of horse in the War of American Independence. Having looked briefly at one Davis of Welsh lineage who occupied a leading role in government (even if on the losing side) let us look at a few more of the same surname; the distinction we sometimes make today between Davis and Davies, the latter being now more likely to be seen as a Welsh surname, was not a distinction that prevailed in either Britain or America a century ago.

James John Davis (1873-1947) was born in Tredegar, South Wales. He went as a child with his parents to Pennsylvania. He started in the steel industry there at eleven years of age. From that early start, he worked his way up the ladder to such a point of eminence that in 1921 he was appointed Secretary of Labour by President Hardy. As an immigrant himself, he helped in that post to draft legislation on immigrants; he also drafted labour

131

legislation for better wages. He became a United States Senator in 1930, and backed Roosevelt's New Deal and social security measures.

Joseph Davies (1877-1958) was famous as United States Ambassador to Moscow in the very critical pre-War Stalinist era. He was born in Wisconsin, both parents being immigrants from Wales, his father from South Wales and his mother from Anglesey, North Wales. He studied law as a young man, and was called to the Wisconsin Bar in 1901. He became very much a specialist in company law, being appointed Commissioner of Corporations in 1912; this led to other important public appointments. During World War II, after his historic period as Ambassador to Moscow, he carried out important missions for Presidents Roosevelt and Truman. Joseph Davies later wrote *Mission to Moscow,* which became a best seller, and was also made into a film, with the same title. In 1938, before the National Eisteddfod at Cardiff, he had given an impassioned address on 'Liberty and Democracy'.

It would be very odd if there were no Joneses in this preliminary look at Welsh-Americans in the sphere of law and order. There has in fact been one such example earlier in this work — John Percival Jones, who became Senator for Nevada, specialising in mining legislation, a subject in which he was expert. Going back more than a century before J. P. Jones, **Gabriel Jones** (1724-1806) is described in the *Dictionary of American Biography* as "pioneer lawyer of the valley of Virginia". The key word here is 'pioneer', which this Jones definitely was. He was born at Williamsburg, Virginia, his father Welsh, John Jones, his mother English. Gabriel was in fact educated in London, but returned to Virginia as 'apprentice lawyer'. It is well known in the States that he 'discovered' George Washington and sponsored his entry into public life (1758). "Gabriel Jones is represented as having done yeoman service among the frontiersmen on behalf of the youthful political aspirant" *(D.A.B.).* He was held in so much esteem and respect among his neighbours and colleagues that they kept on electing him to represent them in public affairs — somewhat, it is said, against his own inclinations, which were to get on with his own job as lawyer. He was the pioneer of a long line of frontier circuit-riding lawyers; he was to them as Daniel Boone was to the hunters and trail-blazers. His eccentricities were celebrated, but set a model for frontier characteristics and idiosyncracies. "The outbursts of the peppery old gentleman became classics."

George Wallace Jones (1804-1896) was born just as Gabriel Jones was reaching the last two years of a long life; it can be seen that G. W. Jones was to have an even longer life. It has been said of him that he was a striking figure in the early years of Wisconsin and

Iowa. Actually he was born in Indiana, son of John Rice Jones, a well-known Welsh immigrant. George graduated from a Kentucky university, and thus became friends with many Southerners, including Jefferson Davis; the Welsh connection would have helped in this. His warm feelings towards the South survived the Civil War. On leaving university he returned north, however, and, rather oddly became a store-keeper and miner for several years. He must have learned something about soldiering, for in the Black Hawk Indian War, he served as aide to General Dodge. He then became a delegate to Congress from the then Michigan Territory. He obviously impressed the leading figures in the northern States, for in 1840, still a comparatively young man, he was appointed Surveyor-General for both Wisconsin and Iowa. In 1848 he became the first United States Senator from the latter State; he served in this capacity for twelve years. He was very successful in securing legislation for public improvements. He was equally successful when the railroad boom started in mid-century, ensuring that a main railroad came through Iowa, and securing the necessary land-grants to make it possible.

John Glancy Jones (1811-1878) was descended from David Jones who in 1721 emigrated from Merioneth to the Welsh Tract in Delaware County, Pennsylvania. J. G. Jones, fittingly enough, was born in Caernarvon Township, Pennsylvania, but went to Ohio to study for the Episcopalian Church. He gave this up to study law, and for this purpose returned to Pennsylvania. Law led him, as it so often does, into politics, as a Democrat; he became a Congressman, representing Pennsylvania.

It can be seen, even from this small selection of the Joneses in law and administration — and there were several others — that they played a considerable part in the development of the separate States. Their roles, i.e. the Welsh-American Joneses as a whole, will be illustrated from fields other than law and administration later in this section.

Charles Evans Hughes would come high in any list of foremost Welsh-Americans in law or administration. He was born in 1862, his father, David Charles Hughes, a Welsh Baptist minister who had emigrated from Wales earlier in the century. Charles Evans Hughes went to Brown University and then on to Columbia Law School, New York. He became a lecturer in law at Cornell University for three years up to 1893. He ascended the ladder of public service until 1907, when he became Governor of New York. He soon found himself involved in a prolonged battle to bring efficiency to New York government, starting with an epic dispute with the powerful Otto Kelsey. His biographer, R. F. Wesser, said of him, "Governor Charles Evans Hughes emerges as one of those exceptional public servants who functioned as an agent for the reform of political, economic and social disorders. His independent spirit, his unquestioned integrity and his indomitable will placed him well above the average politician of his day.'' (p.346.) It is amazing that after such a strenuous career, he then accepted the post of Chief Justice of the United States, having already been a member of the United States Supreme Court (1912), and Secretary of State (1921) under President Harding. It has been said of him that, when made Chief Justice of the United States in 1930, one of his main aims was to expand the concept of constitutional liberties.

Still in the sphere of law and administration, following a celebrated Hughes, we find other Welsh-Americans, a Price, a Howell, another Davis and a Gwin. The latter name, obviously corrupted from Gwyn, emerges frequently. First the Price; **Eli Kirk Price** (1797-1884) was a lawyer and a noted law reformer. He was born in Pennsylvania, son of a Welsh couple. Price's father was a descendant of Philip Price, a Welsh Quaker who had been a personal friend of William Penn. Philip Price and family had settled at Haverford, Montgomery County, Pennsylvania. Eli Kirk Price prospered as a lawyer, and served in the Pennsylvania Senate for some years. He helped to pass an Act which laid the foundations of Philadelphia's prosperity as a city. A main concern to Price was the law of real property, which he did much to reform. His work was embodied in the so-called Price's Act on real property. Not as dramatic a career as some surveyed in this chapter, but part of the essentials for a civilised society.

Richard Howell (1754-1802) had a more dramatic career before becoming a State Governor. He was the son of Ebenezer Howell, who had come from Wales to Delaware early in the eighteenth century. Richard Howell had been a patriotic figure in the American War of Independence. As a young man he had studied law and started a career as a lawyer; at the same time he became a Captain in the New Jersey militia. During the War, he took part in several actions before becoming an army intelligence agent, in which capacity he rendered valuable service to the insurgents. In 1793 he became Governor of New Jersey, but in his forty-eighth year died in office. He left a family; his granddaughter married Jefferson Davis.

David Davis (1815-1886), son of Dr David Davis of known Welsh ancestry, went to Yale University Law School. From there he went to Bloomington, Illinois, to practise law. Becoming well-known and popular, he became a member of the State Constitutional Convention (1847), and a well-experienced Judge. Abraham Lincoln appeared as an advocate before him. In fact he became a close friend of Lincoln. Before the latter became

President of the United States, he sometimes, as an advocate himself, took David Davis' Court for him when Davis was otherwise engaged. David Davis was the acknowledged leader of Lincoln's supporters in the Republic Convention of 1860. His biographer said of him, "To Judge Davis more than anyone is the American people indebted for the nomination of Abraham Lincoln." In February 1861, he accompanied Lincoln to Washington "his great bulk and white hat being as conspicuous as the rugged frame of the President." David Davis became a member of the Supreme Court of the U.S.A., and later a Senator.

William Mckendree Gwin (1805-1885) became a very famous figure in California. He was the son of James and Mary Gwin. When Gwin became a Senator, he recalled his Welsh father's rough journey through the mountains from South Carolina to Tennessee. Senator Gwin mentioned that his father had been a well-known Indian-fighter who became a close friend of the great Andrew Jackson. In 1803 he settled for a more sedate life as a Methodist minister. His son, William M. Gwin, was born in Tennessee and educated there, taking degrees in medicine and law. He moved to Clinton, Mississippi, where he practised medicine until 1833. In that year he was made United States Marshal for Mississippi. He became a Congressman in 1840, but soon moved to New Orleans, where, for some reason, he built a customs-house. He stayed there until 1848, when, at the beginning of the Gold Rush, he decided that California was the place for him. California was seeking full recognition as a separate State of the U.S.A. after its freedom from Mexican domination. The big bulky Gwin, it is said, entered the political arena there with gusto. He and Fremont, the famous explorer of the West, were chosen as the new State's first Senators.

Gwin represented San Francisco. With a strange similarity to the Welsh Governor of Colorado, and like Governor John Evans a qualified physician, Gwin concerned himself vigorously with the future of the railroads. As Senator he was equally concerned about the efficiency of the mail service. This was the summit of his importance. The end of his career was tragic. When the Civil War broke out, he was taken prisoner by the North; on his release he went to France, and from there came to Mexico. On re-entry into U.S.A. he was arrested again. He lived on for twenty years, but his important public life was finished. We have already seen that Senator Gwin was the powerful son of an interesting father. This illustrates the fact that the family was the key-note of many Welsh-American life-stories. Study in detail of Americans from Wales shows that the family-factor was of much, probably major, importance in several different ways. To start with, there was the close-knit nature of the family in the homeland, often strengthened

135

and sanctified by the religious background. This was usually transported to the United States as a set of interrelated social institutions affecting most of the major aspects of daily life from birth to death. Traditions of family support lived on in the often hazardous conditions of the New World.

That essential support was extended further by inter-marriage, where families were linked together, very markedly in the days before easier divorce, in constant relationships of mutual interest and assistance. Amongst the richer Welsh-Americans this led to a network of family alliance and family wealth and influence. From earlier chapters there are the examples of the Lloyds and the Morrises, which could be matched wherever Welsh communities were found.

Scrutiny of the family factor sometimes has the additional merit of leading to closer study of parts of the United States where no large Welsh settlements occurred; in these cases the family circles were more isolated from group support, and depended more on individual family alliances in times of trouble, or, for that matter, of social mobility from class to class, as families became established in new environments. Such was the case in New Hampshire with the Vaughans and the Cutts. The latter surname is yet another reminder that not all Welsh-Americans had names such as Jones, Owen or Rees instantly recognisable as Welsh.

Some old Welsh names did occur very early in New Hampshire. The elected 'governor' of Strawberry Bank, New Hampshire, before it became Portsmouth, was Francis Williams. Portsmouth soon saw the emergence of the Vaughan family. William Vaughan had come from Wales as a protegé of Sir Joshua Child, a London merchant. Vaughan soon became a leading citizen of Portsmouth, engaged in the flourishing fish and timber trades. He was on the New Hampshire Council, one of its eight members (David Van Deventer, *New Hampshire 1623-1741,* 1976, p.239). His son George Vaughan, working in the same trades as his father, later became Lieutenant-Governor of the State (1715-1717). In addition to the fish trade and the timber trade, George Vaughan and his father (who died in 1719) had been speculating in land in Maine for several years. George in turn had a son who carried on the family traditions, and added to the family fortunes.

The other well-known Welsh family in that area was that of the Cutts. Richard Cutt had been a member of the English House of Commons for a Welsh constituency before his emigration to America, in the early seventeenth century. The Cutts established themselves in the fish trade in the Isles of Shoals, New Hampshire. Richard and his son John, moved into Portsmouth as it developed. Eager to expand in territory and wealth, they obtained from the

Portsmouth authorities land grants and a grant for a saw-mill, vital in the lumber business. By the 1670's Richard and son John were wealthy 'mariner-merchants', as Van Deventer called them. Other male members of the Cutt family, Robert and Richard, took part in the family businesses.

Four daughters in the Cutts family circle married into other rich and prominent families in New Hampshire — the Vaughans, the Waldrons, the Penhallows, the Daniels and the Hiltons. In 1679 John Cutt was appointed President of the new Royal Colony of New Hampshire; he and his father had already held important city offices in Portsmouth. The Cutts had also expanded into shipbuilding; they also owned hundreds of acres of land. Wealth and social prominence, according to local complaints, had made the Vaughans somewhat 'uppish'. George Vaughan and his son, William, had been to Harvard, and George had become an officer in the local militia. William Vaughan expressed the opinion that it was 'indecent' for members of the Council to have to sign the royal oath of allegiance along with 'the Rabble' or among the 'tag, rag, and bobtail' (Van Deventer, p.216). There was a very marked social class system in the new colony, with 'gentlemanly designations' most important as marks of rank. The highest of these was 'Esquire' — by common consent awarded to Colonel George Vaughan.

Another Welsh immigrant arriving in New Hampshire with some capital was Thomas Daniel; he soon became a wealthy dealer in timber and ships' masts. Like the Cutts he soon also became a shipbuilder and owner. He also had a liquor licence, as indeed did the Cutts and the Vaughans. This was useful, as well as profitable, since much of the fishermen's wages was paid in rum. Other Welsh names occurring among leading New Hampshire families were those of Nathaniel Rogers and Colonel James Davis. Intermarriage between leading families strengthened them all, as when one of the Daniel family married into the Cutts family.

A hundred years later it was still obvious that these families were well established. On 13th December 1774, Paul Revere finished his celebrated ride by delivering his important despatches at the house of Samuel Cutts, leading merchant of Portsmouth. When a Committee of Safety was set up in 1776, Samuel Cutts was a member of it (R. F. Upton, *Revolutionary New Hampshire, 1936,* p.22). Also in New Hampshire was Lieutenant Elijah Williams, said to be of Welsh stock. He however was on the Loyalist side. After the War, he had the courage to return to New Hampshire, but was promptly expelled.

To return to the Jones family in America. One of the most remarkable of that name was 'the Jones family of Long Island' the title of a book recording the family history, written by Helen F. Jones, one of the descendants, in 1907. Helen Jones stated that this family came from Wales, but had early intermarried with Irish. "Not only is the name indicative of Welsh race, but the traits and characteristics of the Welsh race are very pronounced in all its leading members", she declared. The first one to reach New York from Wales was Major Thomas Jones. He held the position in 1704 as High Sheriff of Long Island; in 1710 he was also made a Justice of the Peace. His eldest son, David, became a Judge of Queen's County in 1734. In turn, his son Thomas was Recorder of the City of New York and then Judge of the Supreme Court. At the Revolution, Thomas was loyal to the Crown, and had to leave America. In England he wrote a book *New York during the Revolutionary War.* Apparently, Thomas having been ejected, no blame was attached to the rest of the family, for at the end of the century, Thomas's cousin Samuel became Recorder of New York, and in turn his son, also Samuel Jones, became Chancellor of the State of New York. Many other members of this remarkable Jones family were Judges at one Court or another. "For nearly two hundred years, from 1700 to 1892, the Bar and Bench of the City and State of New York have been represented by some member of the family." (p.16.) At the end of the nineteenth century Major Thomas Jones left seven children; among all the Judges, he was not, however, the only one of the Jones family to hold military rank like the first of the Long Island Joneses, for there were others, including Colonel Delancy Floyd-Jones who served with distinction in the nineteenth century Mexican and Civil Wars.

This Jones family could have been discussed earlier under the heading of law and administration; rarely in history could one family, in any country, have produced so many Judges? Yet it seemed better to postpone the Long Island Joneses a little to illustrate the important point about continuity and cohesion within families, and in our brief, particularly Welsh families.

The name 'Jones' is as common in the United States as in Britain. Not all the Joneses in America were of Welsh extraction, a point that has been admitted earlier. Even those of definitely Welsh blood covered an enormous range of activities and would, on their own, give a wide and vivid sample of American life.

John Jones (1729-1791) was a surgeon and writer on surgery in the early days of American medicine. He came from Welsh Quaker stock, a stock that produced many physicians over the years. He studied medicine in Europe, and, from his wide experience there, gained much of value when he played a big part in founding New York Hospital. He was the author of the first surgical textbook in the American colonies.

138

David Jones (1736-1820) was a clergyman described in one biography as a "farmer, minister, author and scholar". He was born in Delaware, the son of an immigrant from Wales. His mother was the daughter of Roger Evans who came from Wales to Philadelphia. David Jones wrote a famous pamphlet, based on a sermon of his during the time of the American Revolution. The title given the pamphlet was *Defensive War in a Just Cause Sinless.* It was highly influential in strengthening American resolve. During the war itself, he became a chaplain to a Pennsylvanian regiment.

Jacob Jones (1768-1850) whose father was a farmer of Welsh stock, eventually became a naval officer. The word 'eventually' is meaningful, for he had first qualified as a physician, which profession he gave up to become Clerk of Delaware Supreme Court. Only at the age of thirty-one did he enter the Navy, as a midshipman, which was unusually old for that junior rank. He quickly became a Lieutenant, but had the misfortune to be captured by Arabs off Tripoli in 1803, and was held prisoner for twenty months. On release he went back into the Navy and became a Commander. In the 1812 War with Britain he commanded the *Wasp,* and came off best against British attackers.

Calvin Jones (1775-1846) was a doctor, in direct descent from Thomas ap Jones, a Welsh emigrant to Weymouth (Massachusetts) in its early days. Calvin's father was Ebenezer Jones, a soldier in the Revolutionary Army about the time of Calvin's birth. Young Dr Calvin Jones practised in Massachusetts for a few years then, still only twenty, moved to North Carolina. He immediately plunged into all aspects of social, medical and political life there. He founded the North Carolina Medical Society, and also became an officer in the local militia; by 1812 he was a Major-General in the latter body. For some years he was a Congressman for North Carolina. Still not having enough scope for his abundant energy, he founded a newspaper, *The Star.*

David Rumph Jones (1825-1908) was one of the wealthier of those of Welsh stock. His ancestors had come from Wales in 1635, to settle in Massachusetts. He went to West Point, and became a professional soldier, taking part in the Mexican War in 1847. He became a Major, then a Brigadier-General. In the latter capacity he fought for the North in the Civil War, and led a brigade at the Battle of Ball Run.

Thomas ap Catesby Jones (1790-1858) was mainly of Welsh descent. He was descended from Roger Jones who emigrated to Virginia in 1680. Thomas joined the Navy in 1805, and became a Lieutenant by 1812, just in time to fight the British in the brief war which occupies so much space in American history-books, but so little in British ones. He was wounded in battle in 1814 but gave a good account of himself, the British losing more men than the Americans in the particular action. He rose in rank over the years, and in 1842 was in high command in the Pacific. He distinguished himself by prematurely invading California, which was still a Mexican territory. He thought the British fleet in the Pacific was about to take California, so got in first on behalf of his country. His men landed at Monterey, but soon had to withdraw, on orders from Washington. Apologies were tendered to Mexico, peace was sealed — for the moment — by a pleasant dinner-party that the Mexicans at Monterey gave to the American officers, Ap Catesby Jones included; the Mexicans, it is said, sent the bill for the dinner to the American government the next day. Ap Catesby Jones was not all that wrong. The Mexicans *were* losing their hold on California; the British *were* interested. America moved formally into California a few years later. Ap Catesby Jones was not at the time reprimanded or reduced in rank, although there was some trouble between him and the American top naval authorities some years later. His nephew, Catesby ap Roger Jones (note the retention of the 'ap' in the family) was also a naval officer and actually served under his uncle for a time. During the Civil War young Catesby ap Roger Jones fought as a Captain in the Virginian Navy, so the old family links with Virginia were renewed.

George Heber Jones (1867-1919) became a missionary. Brought up in Utica, New York State, a favourite place for Welsh immigrants, he was said to be a mixture of Welsh, Irish and English, with the Welsh predominant. He became a missionary in Korea. He did valuable work there for his denomination and became an expert on several aspects of Korean life. In 1905 he became a university lecturer on the subject, also writing extensively on Korean affairs.

George Jones (1811-1891) was the son of John and Barbara Davis Jones, immigrants direct from Wales. He went in for journalism and became a newspaper publisher, starting in Vermont where he was born. He acquired much experience in newspaper publishing, which was really his true bent rather than journalism as such. In fact he is reputed to have done very little writing himself; rather he devoted himself to the managerial aspects of newspaper work. This special ability must have been the driving motivation which led George Jones, with his partner, H. J. Raymond, to start that great American newspaper, the *New York Times*. It was said of him that one of his few interests, apart from his newspaper and his family, was "his Welsh Baptist love of song".

Charles Colcock Jones (1831-1893) was the great grandson of a Welshman, John Jones, who came to Georgia from South Carolina. There was clearly wealth in the family because young

140

Charles went to Harvard, after a period at Princeton; at Harvard he read law. His real interest however was in history, particularly the history of his own State, Georgia, on which he became an authority. He was not just a studious academic however, for he was Mayor of Savannah for a time, and was a Colonel of artillery for the South in the Civil War.

Amanda Theodosia Jones (1835-1914). This lady had Welsh blood on her father's side, and said a good bit about her Welsh connections in her *A Psychic Autobiography* (1911). On her mother's side she had English, Scots, Irish, French, Huguenot and Dutch blood. Her interests were also decidedly mixed, ranging from spiritualism to fruit preservation, and the provision of homes for poor girls. She wrote on all these and many other topics, and, on the fruit-preservation, had claims to be known as an inventor. It is said of her that she was in fact a very business-like journalist and editor of newspapers and journals.

Benjamin Franklin Jones over-lapped in time, but not in interests with the lady. His family had come from Wales in 1682, and settled near Philadelphia. Benjamin was brought up there, but with the coming of the Industrial Revolution moved to Pittsburgh, becoming celebrated for his iron works and blast furnaces.

John Peter Jones (1847-1916) was born at Wrexham, Denbighshire, North Wales. He worked in the Welsh coal mines at the age of twelve. In 1866, when he was nineteen, he crossed the Atlantic to work in the mines in Pennsylvania. Later he moved to Ohio, again to work in the mines, but occasionally preaching in Welsh to the Welsh miners there. After some time he became a full-time Congregational minister, but spent several years as a missionary in India.

Herschel Vespasian Jones (1861-1922) was a journalist and man of letters. He came of mixed Welsh, Scots and English stock. Despite the mixture, it is certain that H. V. Jones' father, William Jones, was descended from Massachusetts Welsh immigrants of 1663. Jones was a reporter on the *Minneapolis Journal,* but later founded several specialised financial newspapers. Though successful in his profession, he was even better known as a book-collector. He accumulated a large and choice library, which went intact to his estate.

Hugh Bolton Jones (1848-1927) brought from the nineteenth to the twentieth century a contribution to American art, highly valued then and now. He studied art in Baltimore, and then France and Spain, during the last century, specialising himself in landscape painting. He won several awards, including medals at Paris in 1889 and 1900, and many in the United States when he returned home. His paintings hang in the Metropolitan Museum, New York, and many other American and European galleries.

Evan William Jones (1852-1908) was a mechanical engineer and inventor; Oliver Evans was by no means the only Welsh-American inventor. Evan Jones came from Monmouth (now Gwent), South Wales. His father, an iron-worker, brought the family from Wales in 1854, and settled, appropriately, at Ironton, Ohio. Young Jones entered the mills as an apprentice. After a time working at Pittsburgh he next moved to Portland, Oregon; there he became the manager of the Union Iron Works. He married Margaret Helen Abrams, also of Welsh descent.

Jenkin Lloyd Jones (1843-1918). His parents came direct from Wales and encouraged him always to keep up Welsh connections. He studied to become a clergyman, but much against his will and his principles, he was caught up in the Civil War, and fought in the battles of Corinth, Vichsburg, Chattanooga and Missionary Ridge. Only then was he free to take up the career, or vocation, he so much wanted; he became an Unitarian minister. He entered into his calling with much enthusiasm, and started many successful societies in connection with his church, some of them having considerable Welsh membership.

Samuel Milton Jones (1846-1904). Never was a Welsh-American more popular in his American home-town. He had been born in Beddgelert, Caernarvonshire, North Wales. His parents emigrated to up-state New York when he was only three years old. He started work at ten years of age, trying several jobs until he found his true metier in the oil-fields of Pennsylvania. He soon had a small oil-field of his own in that State, but moved to Ohio where the opportunities in the oil industry were greater. By 1885 he was well-established in the Ohio oil-business. He was the inventor of several improvements in the process of oil-extraction. He started his own company to make oil-well machinery at Toledo, Ohio. In 1897 he became Mayor of Toledo. He had earned the nickname of 'Golden Rule Jones' for his care for his employees — much in advance of such provision in those days. He ran his oil-wells and factory on Christian and humanitarian principles, with health insurance, eight-hour day, forty-eight hour week, vacation with pay. He tried to make Toledo a model city, with eight-hour day also for city employees, municipal playgrounds, kindergartens and golf-links. At his death, he was very much mourned and missed throughout the area.

After this limited but fairly representative selection of Joneses, now a selection of Thomases, starting with one from the earlier days of Welsh migration.

Isaiah Thomas (1749-1831) became a very well-known printer and publisher. He was a descendant of Evan Thomas who had emigrated from Wales to Massachusetts in 1640. By the age of seventeen, Isaiah was already considered an excellent printer. He read widely, wrote fluent English with a marked bent for satire, and occasionally some verses if needed to fill up columns. He was described at the time as tall and handsome, always smartly dressed. He was very popular in Massachusetts and made many friends, some of them influential. He worked for some time for the *Charlestown* (South Carolina) *Gazette,* where he gained newspaper experience to add to his printing experience. He started his own paper, the *Massachusetts Spy,* which was famous for supporting the liberties of the people. In this paper there was plenty of scope for his satirical vein. The government of the day often tried to suppress particularly outspoken editions of the 'Spy'. At the beginning of the American War of Independence, he joined Paul Revere's group, and aided the cause by writing and printing pamphlets and broadsheets for the patriots. After the war he turned to the publishing of books. He became the leading American publisher of his day, employing over one hundred and fifty people, and using seven different presses at various places. He also published several different magazines, including a popular one called *Thomas's New England Almanack.* His work was noted for "the beauty of his typography, and the popularity and importance of the books he published" *(Dictionary of American Biography).* Among works he published were scores of educational books, an important *American Dictionary,* a *Greek Grammar,* and the famous *Blackstone's Commentaries* on the law. Hundreds of books that he published were children's books. Becoming very wealthy, he became semi-retired, but spent his 'retirement' in studying, over a wide range of scholarship, and the writing of an excellent *History of Printing in America.* In 1812 he founded the American Antiquarian Society. He was, additionally, a member of every learned society in the United States. A most interesting and cultured man, his personal friends included Benjamin Franklin, George Washington, the celebrated Adamses and Thomas Jefferson.

David Thomas (1794-1882) came from my home-town, Neath, born there at Cadoxton, just outside Neath. He worked at Neath Abbey Iron Works, near to the ancient abbey ruins. He became an expert in blast furnaces and pumping engines, and became manager of a South Wales iron works more advanced in techniques than that at Neath Abbey. In 1839 he emigrated from Swansea to Allentown, Pennsylvania. He prospered there as iron works manager. He became the first President of the American Institute of Mining Engineers. His three sons all followed their father into iron and steel manufacture.

Francis Thomas (1799-1896) was descended from Hugh Thomas, who came from Wales to Pennsylvania about 1702. Francis Thomas studied law, and became one of the leading lawyers in Maryland. Elected to Congress, he served there during the period 1831-1841. He became a personal friend of Andrew Jackson, who was President of the United States during that decade. Francis must have had a little of the reputed wild Welsh blood within him, for he became involved in a duel with another Welsh-American, William Price, and survived a scandalous divorce to become Governor of Maryland.

Frederick William Thomas (1806-1866) was one of those Welsh-Americans whose life was interesting for some surprising changes of career. He appears to have been a man of dynamic energy and very wide interests. He, like Isaiah Thomas, was descended from the Evan Thomas who came from Wales to Massachusetts in 1640. He started as a journalist, and tried his hand at printing and publishing. He gave these up however for the law, and in 1828 became a lawyer at Baltimore; he kept however some of his former interest in the newspaper world by becoming editor of the paper *Democratic Intelligence*. For a time he was also Professor of Literature at the University of Alabama. He next studied for the ministry and became a Methodist minister in Cincinnati. He wrote several novels, and through his literary interests became a close friend of Edgar Allan Poe.

George Henry Thomas was of Welsh descent on his father's side, French Huguenot on his mother's side. Born in Virginia in 1816, he soon showed interest in a military career, and went to the United States Military Academy in 1836. He took to the military life, became an efficient soldier, rising to the rank of Lieutenant after gallantry in action in the Indian Wars. He served for a Southern regiment in the Mexican War of the 1840's. He served also in Texas, and was wounded in the face by an Indian arrow. Despite his Southern birth and military experience, he opted later to transfer to a Northern regiment, and fought for the North in the Civil War with the rank of Colonel. He fought valiantly at Mill Springs in 1862, and became a Major-General for his share in the capture of Corinth. In 1863 he had much to do with the victory of the North at the battle of Chattanooga in an important holding operation; for this he was ever after known as 'the Rock of Chattanooga'. He died in 1870.

Amos Russell Thomas (1826-1893) was another descendant of the Evan Thomas who came from Wales to Massachusetts in 1640. He had a very different career from George Henry Thomas, except that for a brief period he saw service for the North in the Civil War. He was born in New York and studied medicine at Syracuse and

Pennsylvania Medical University. During the Civil War he served as an army surgeon. After the war, he returned to Pennsylvania as Professor of Anatomy at Philadelphia Medical College. He occupied this post for many years, and wrote many books on anatomy and general medical matters. Amos R. Thomas was not the only Welsh-American Thomas in medicine as a specialist during the last century. Philip Thomas left Wales in 1651. His descendant, **Richard Henry Thomas** (1854-1904), like his ancestor, was a Quaker. He was in fact a minister of that faith, combining his work as minister with being Professor of Diseases of Throat and Chest at Baltimore Medical College. Like so many Quakers, he had of course qualified in medicine as a young man. This versatile Welsh-American was also a man of letters, writing much good poetry and many sets of essays.

   Thomas Clifford Thomas (1839-1909) was a grandson of John Thomas, who had emigrated from Wales to America in 1802. Thomas C. Thomas went to work in a Philadelphia bank as a young man. His ability recognised, he soon was invited to become a junior member of the company. He prospered with the firm and rose to senior position, becoming rich. He was famous in Philadelphia for his generosity to many charities. His charitable impulse was based on strong religious belief, which led him also to become Superintendent of Sunday Schools. He used his plentiful energy and wealth additionally to finance and organise several different missions.

   Of the Morgans, though the Welsh tend to think of them as all Welsh, some were in fact Irish or Scottish. Only those definitely known to be of Welsh extraction will occur in this brief sample of Welsh-Americans. Thus **George Morgan** (1743-1810) was the son of Evan Morgan, who came from Wales to Philadelphia at the beginning of the eighteenth century. George was born in that city. As a young man he became apprenticed to a merchant firm. In due course he became one of its principals. He was sent from Philadelphia to Illinois to look after the firm's fur interests when the fur trade was very profitable; the firm also supplied Indian goods to the Crown, and provisions to military posts in Illinois. George Morgan came to be an important man in that State at this early stage in its growth; he was appointed a Judge (or in reality what we would call a magistrate). During the American Revolution, he served in a double capacity as Indian Agent for the United States, and officer in charge of supplies for the Army Western District, with the rank of Colonel. After the war he became a gentleman farmer at Prospect, New Jersey, far away from 'the Frontier'. He took up scientific research and writing as a hobby, and had several articles published in learned journals. In his later years (1796) he moved to another farm, at Washington, Pennsylvania.

Charles Morgan (1793-1878) was descended from James Morgan, reputed to be Welsh, who emigrated to Boston in 1636, and then settled in Connecticut. Charles Morgan's father was a Colonel in the Army. At the age of fourteen Charles went to New York, which became his permanent home, though in fact for business reasons he saw a great deal of the South. To start with, however, he had his own small shop in New York City, by the docks, selling provisions to ships. He started importing fruit from the South; this led to the ownership of a small fleet of sailing ships trading with the West Indies. He began to acquire interests in early steam-ships. Soon he had ships running from Galveston, Texas, to New Orleans and return. His shipping line, small to start with, began to run to many more places in the South. With a partner he established the Texas-New Orleans Mail Line, the Mexican Ocean Mail Line and Southern Mail Steamship Company. They did most of their business in the Gulf of Mexico. Charles Morgan later expanded into owning the Morgan Iron Works, making naval machinery. Despite this side-line, he was known mainly as a ship-owner; in fact he was called "the biggest ship-owner in the United States". A few years before his death, he started buying railroads e.g. the Texas and Louisiana Railroad and the Houston and Central Texas Railroad.

Edwin Baker Morgan (1806-1881) was descended from the James Morgan who emigrated from Wales to Massachusetts in 1636. Edwin's father was a merchant, but Edwin specialised more than his father, and built a large business in agricultural machinery, boat-building and express companies. With reference to the latter, he became one of the founders of the United States Express Company in 1854. He had political interests also, and at mid-century became a Congressman for the Republican party; he was strongly anti-slavery and used his wealth to equip troops for the North in the Civil War. He was awarded the honorary title of Colonel for this. In later years he became very much interested in education and became a trustee of Wells College, Aurora, New York, where he had been born and brought up; he was also a trustee of Cornell University. This is a reminder that many Welsh-Americans who became wealthy put their money and experience into educational projects.

Edwin Denison Morgan (1811-1883) was a descendant of the same James Morgan as was E. B. Morgan; that is, the two Morgans were cousins, and both were New Yorkers. Edwin made a fortune in wholesale grocery, became interested in politics and was elected to Hartford City Council. This led to considerable advancement in

146

the sphere of politics and power, as he became Governor of New York and United States Senator. To New Yorkers he is chiefly remembered for the big part he played in initiating Central Park.

George Washington Morgan (1820-1893) was descended from the George Morgan discussed above. At sixteen years of age G. W. Morgan joined the Army, in a company raised and led by his brother, Thomas Jefferson Morgan. George fought in the war which ensured independence for Texas, becoming a Captain. After his spell in the army, he studied law, and became a prosecuting attorney. He apparently tired of this and went back into the army, this time with the rank of Colonel, with the Ohio Volunteers. He was still only twenty-six. He had further promotion in the army, eventually to the rank of Brigadier-General, in which rank he served under Sherman. At one time between 1856 and 1861 he did consular duties abroad; later he entered politics.

Bruce Price (1845-1903). From a Morgan to a Price, and from a soldier to an architect. Bruce Price was descended on his father's side from Peter Rees Price, an early Welsh settler in Maryland; he had a second Welsh line of descent, this time a very long one. For he was also descended from William Williams, claimed to be in direct descent from Owen Glendower (as spelt by the English) the famous Welsh prince of the middle ages. In fact in quite a few of the genealogies of Welsh-Americans such claims, dating back to the Middle Ages, can be found. Bruce Price's father was a Judge, but young Bruce had no interest in the law. Instead he studied architecture, for which he showed an obvious talent. He built many of the Victorian (it is interesting to note that the American writers freely use the term 'Victorian' and indeed 'Edwardian' with American reference) churches and chapels of the last century, several of which still exist. One was the Methodist Church of the Welsh settlement which had grown into Wilkes-Barre, Pennsylvania. In 1877, Bruce Price moved to New York, where he specialised in building hotels, at that important period in the history of the city. Price also built the noted 'Welch dormitory' at Yale University, and several colleges and railway stations in Canada. It is interesting to note the old alternative spelling of 'Welsh' at the Yale dormitory.

Several of the earlier Welsh immigrants to the United States were called Jenks or Jenkins. **Joseph Jenks** (1602-1683) was one of the earliest inventors in America of any nationality. He had descended from an old Welsh family, one of the first to emigrate to the New World. Jenks was by trade an iron-worker — two centuries ahead of the many Welsh iron and steel men who later came from Wales to Pennsylvania and other industrial States. Jenks produced many small inventions, the most celebrated of which was the first fire-engine in the United States, which made its appearance on the streets of Boston.

Micah Jenkins (1835-1864) was born in South Carolina of an ancient Welsh family which claimed descent from Llewellyn, the last Prince of Wales in medieval times. Joseph Jenkins had emigrated from Wales to South Carolina in 1670. He became a planter at Edisto Island in that State. His descendant, Micah Jenkins, like so many of his ancestors, was likewise a planter — until the American Civil War started. He became a Colonel of a South Carolina regiment, a body of picked men who came to be called 'Jenkins' Palmetto Sharpshooters'. Jenkins was promoted to the rank of General, but was mortally wounded in 1864.

Howard Malcolm Jenkins (1842-1902) had a very different background and life-story from Micah Jenkins. Howard was born at Gwynedd, Pennsylvania, where his ancestors had been among the earliest Welsh settlers. He became a journalist, an editor and a specialist writer on local history. He had been educated at the Friends' school in Gwynedd. In time he became the editor of a Delaware newspaper, and held other important posts in the newspaper world. He maintained throughout his life his enthusiasm for Pennsylvania's history, on which he wrote numerous books and articles.

Most of the Evans family who came from Wales to the United States were sober, serious, hard-working citizens who contributed much to the developing United States. We have already had some examples in the first part of this chapter. **John Evans** (1703-1731) unfortunately was not an ornament to the Evans clan. His father, Thomas Evans, was a Welsh sailor, an exceptional man who was a friend of William Penn. Because of the latter connection, young John Evans, as mentioned earlier, was appointed Deputy Governor of Pennsylvania. William Penn's son was also in Pennsylvania, and no doubt their Welsh blood brought them together. The story has already been told of the wild life they led, much of it in taverns, shocking the Quaker colonists. The Pennsylvanian Assembly complained to Penn, and John Evans was sent back to Denbigh.

George Alfred Evans, many years later (1850-1925), was more the kind of man of whom the Welsh Quakers would have approved. His father, Norris Evans, was born in Wales and emigrated to America. George Evans became a doctor, and a pioneer in the cure of pulmonary tuberculosis. He practised at San Antonio, Texas, in its wildest days. His biographer said of him, "his life as a doctor was full of excitement through the proximity of hostile Indians and bad white men".

Edward Payson Evans (1831-1917) was a scholar and a man of letters. His parents, Evan and Mary, were immigrants from North

Wales, Evan Evans being a Presbyterian minister. Edward became a lecturer, then a professor at the University of Michigan. He left Michigan however to live in Europe, at Munich. The wander-lust must have struck him again, for he departed from Germany to become Professor of Sanskrit at Lahore, India.

James Wiltberger Evans (1823-1897) must have been one of the more unusual of the Welsh-Americans of the nineteenth century. He could have been described as dentist, author, diplomat and philanthropist, the first and the last of these more validly than the other two, though Evans made claims for them. He was descended from a family of Welsh Quakers who had emigrated to Philadelphia in 1682. He was undoubtedly a very skilful dentist, indeed a pioneer in some branches of dentistry. From being a successful dentist in Pennsylvania, he rose to being, in Paris, the dentist to Napoleon III, and other European royal families. It was said of him that as his success grew, his conceit became boundless. He fancied himself as a diplomat, and, in his influential relationship to royal persons, was able to function as such to a limited extent, not always wisely. Likewise he attempted authorship, again with limited success. Despite his conceit, he was kind and charitable by nature. For example, he spent large sums of his considerable fortune on ambulances for the Crimean War and the Franco-Prussian War. The rest of his fortune went at his death to the Dental School of Pennsylvania University.

William Cooper Howells was born in the village of Hay in Breconshire, mid-Wales, in 1807. His father, Joseph, had been born in the same house where William was born; Joseph had married Anne Thomas of Pontypool, South Wales. The family were Quakers and emigrated to a Quaker centre in the States; that was in 1808. William Howells recalled unpleasant days for him in 1812, when Britain and America were at war; he could not forget the hostility he met from the American children at that time. Young Howells hit back. "My combativeness got the better of my Quakerism," he said later. There was one odd little incident in the Howells's family history. Long before Joseph Howells thought of emigrating to the States, *his* father had already been there. The latter had been a watch-maker in Wales, who surprisingly gave up watch-making to make Welsh flannel. "To sell his flannel, he travelled to Philadelphia, where he was introduced to George Washington. The latter advised him to buy land in Virginia." The ancestor of the Howells did in fact do that, but nevertheless returned to Wales and the red flannel. When Joseph Howells came to the States in 1808, he came first to New York, then Virginia, where he lived out his life.

William Dean Howells (1837-1920) famous in the United States for his writing, was the son of William Cooper Howells. The quotation above was taken from W. D. Howells' biography of his father, *William Cooper Howells; Recollections of Life in Ohio* (1895). William Dean Howells was well known in the States as novelist, editor and critic. He first became known as the editor of the *Atlantic Monthly,* a leading literary magazine in America. As editor, he published the work of Mark Twain and Henry James, among other eminent writers. From 1882 he turned more to the writing of fiction, and wrote several novels, including *Modern Instance* which was one of the first to establish him as a leading novelist. As well as his many articles and essays, the latter mainly in the field of literary criticism, he took a keen interest in many aspects of social welfare policy e.g. he helped to found the National Association for the Advancement of Colored People.

William Dean Howells and his father, William Cooper Howells, or even Joseph Howells, were by no means the first of the Howell or Howells in America. **Thomas Howells** had actually gone over on the same ship as William Penn (the *Welcome*) in 1677. According to J. G. Leach, he was an important and wealthy man in Wales, with his own coat-of-arms (Leach, *Genealogical and Biographical Memorials of Families,* 1898).

William Howell of Castlebright in Wales went over twenty years later, settling in Pennsylvania. According to Leach, he was an immediate ancestor of Major Richard Howell, officer in the American Revolutionary Army, and later, Governor of New Jersey. Another Howells in the Revolutionary War was Lewis Howells, who was an Army surgeon, and father of Rear Admiral Howells.

An interesting later member of the Welsh-American Howells family was **Thomas Jefferson Howell** (1842-1912) who claimed to be descended from Howel, king of South Wales in the early Middle Ages. Coming a bit more up-to-date, T. J. Howell's great-great-grandfather was Job Howell who was born in Wales in 1650. As a young man, Job emigrated to Pennsylvania. Many years later Thomas Jefferson Howell made the long journey with his father, who was a physician, from the American mid-West to Oregon, in the North-West of the United States. The journey, in 1850, was by ox-cart. As a boy, T. J. Howell had little schooling, but learned a lot from his doctor father, particularly in science subjects. Despite big gaps in his basic education, Thomas Jefferson Howell became one of America's top botanists, discovering several new species of plant. Strangely enough, another Welsh-American botanist **Lewis Ralph Jones** (1864-1945) with a more orthodox education, became a specialist in agricultural biology, becoming Professor of Botany at Wisconsin University.

Generally the genealogical background of eminent Americans has had to be traced by expert genealogists, looking back into family histories. It is not often that a detailed account of the family was made at the time, or if made, survived for later readers. This however was not the case with the **Hughes family**, studied in their home-surroundings of Pennsylvania and New Jersey in the 1690's by another Welshman, Gabriel Thomas. His study was first printed in 1698 and was re-printed in 1903. He started by tracing the Hughes family in America back to various Welsh princes of medieval Wales. The preface to the 1903 edition gave some examples of prominent Hughes in Britain at a later date in history. Thus, Sir Richard Hughes was Commissioner of Portsmouth Dockyard at the time of a visit by King George III in 1773. Thomas Hughes, author of *Tom Brown's Schooldays,* was another member of the Hughes family in Britain.

Several members of the Hughes had, however, emigrated to the United States at the end of the seventeenth century. One of their descendants was James Hughes, who was a member of George Washington's bodyguard. These Hughes from Wales had settled in Massachusetts and Connecticut. Another of their descendants was Joseph Hewes (sic) who was one of the signers of the Declaration of Independence, and, also, another descendant from them was George Robert Twelve Hughes whose name stands at the head of the 1773 Boston Tea-Party list.

Gabriel Thomas, writing in the 1690's, had looked at some of the Welsh Hughes who had, even at that date, departed for the United States. He maintained that the very first Hughes to reach America was Richard Hughes in 1640. He also mentions Arthur Hughes at Salem in 1676, James Hughes of Gloucester (Mass.) and Henry Freeman Hughes, who added the 'Freeman' to his former name, plain Henry Hughes, when he jumped his Royal Navy ship at Boston in 1748. He was born in Wales, and had a brother, Bodwell Hughes, who joined him in New England. Then the brothers went separate ways; Henry Freeman Hughes moved to Connecticut, where many members of his family settled over the years at East Haven, whereas Bodwell Hughes moved West to Ohio.

David Edward Hughes (1831-1900) was another Welsh-American inventor. He was born in London of Welsh stock, son of David Hughes. When he was seven, his parents emigrated to Virginia. David Edward Hughes was educated in Kentucky, and became a teacher of music and philosophy. He became interested in current inventions in the field of telegraphy and tried his hand at them, very successfully, but going on making a living by giving private music lessons. The Commercial Printing Telegraph Company became interested in his inventions, and bought one of them, obviously in the telegraphy line, for 100,000 dollars. This was in 1856, and within a few years many European countries bought the Hughes printing telegraph system. Part of his work brought him recognition as the inventor of the microphone. Towards the end of his life, he received the Gold Medal of the Royal Society in London, and in fact spent the last years of his life in London.

The **Bowen family** is well known in Wales; some of their members emigrated to Massachusetts in the middle of the eighteenth century, according to *Savage's Genealogy,* led by Valentine Bowen, said to be the first Bowen in America. He was a farmer, who settled at Cheshire (Mass.) with his wife, four sons and two daughters. One of the early Bowens was Lieutenant Henry Bowen, one of the settlers of Woodstock, Connecticut; he had come from Wales with his father Griffith Bowen. The Bowens kept the country store and tavern at Woodstock. It was in Woodstock that **Henry Chandler Bowen** (1813-1896) was born. After education at Woodstock, he spent four years in his father's store, then went to New York to work in a grander store, specialising in silk. In 1838, he started his own business in the firm of Bowen and McNamee. He prospered in this, and also became well-known in Congregational church circles. In 1868 he founded a Congregational journal with strong anti-slave principles. He also helped to organise the Congregational Union, from which developed the Congregational Church Building Society. He was a generous benefactor to the Woodstock Academy and Woodstock Agricultural Society; he also presented the township with a public park.

Reuben Lewis is best known as the brother of Meriwether Lewis of the famous expedition. After the Expedition, William Clark and Reuben Lewis were made directors of the Missouri Fur Company of St. Louis. Meriwether meanwhile had been made Governor of Upper Louisiana Territory. The Company used the connection to obtain a profitable contract for equipping local army units. It also paid Meriwether Lewis seven thousand dollars to delay licences to trade for other companies, until the Missouri Fur Company had made a good start. Today this might be considered corrupt, but in frontier days it seemed only commonsense, and a fair reward for service to the nation. Reuben and William Clark made the most of it. One of the Company's agents who was not so lucky was another Welshman, Robert Jones, who in 1822 was slaughtered by Indians.

As with the Evanses in America, the **Williamses** also had a black sheep among the worthy vast majority of the clan. The Williams family in America had done as much for their new country, as the Williamses back home had done for Wales. **John Williams** of New York however in 1682 captured a small ship from the Spaniards of

Cuba, and turned pirate. In his ketch, *Ruth,* he robbed various ports and other places in Virginia, and even attempted to kidnap Lord Baltimore at Maryland, with a view to ransom. Failing in this, he went eastwards of Long Island, and there captured several more vessels. So, to the Welsh highwayman mentioned in an earlier chapter, must be added a Welsh pirate, not with pride, but in an attempt to keep an honest balance.

In talking about Welsh families in the United States, the surname 'Floyd' does not come to mind as easily as most of the usual Welsh surnames. Yet it is a name that keeps recurring in American history. Members of the family are reported to have left Wales in the seventeenth century, and settled in Long Island where they prospered as landholders and large-scale farmers. **William Floyd** (1734-1821) was one of their descendants, who had however the misfortune to see their estates, held for over a century, ruined during the American War of Independence. Floyd moved Westwards to another part of New York State. He is famous howevever as one of the signers of the Declaration of Independence, and became a Senator. During Senator Floyd's lifetime, another Floyd, Sergeant Charles Floyd, was one of the party in Lewis and Clark's expedition; Sergeant Floyd was the only man to die on that arduous journey; there is a memorial to him at Sioux City, Iowa.

General John Floyd fought in the War between Britain and the United States (1812) and was in action at the Battle of New Orleans in that war. General Floyd was a member of the family of landholders of that name mentioned by Abernethy (*The South in the New Nation, 1789-1819,* 1961, p.283). The same applies to **Davis Floyd** who was operating in land-buying in Indiana. He was acting as an agent for the notorious Aaron Burr. At the end of the eighteenth century, President Thomas Jefferson had been warned about these activities by Federal District Attorney, Joseph H. Davies, who assured Jefferson that Burr was using Davis Floyd to buy up huge tracts of land, contrary to the public interest. Another Floyd by contrast, Congressman John Floyd in 1825 was behaving in a more social and responsible manner in trying to persuade Washington D.C. to give federal aid to immigrants, including some Welsh, into the newly opened territories of Oregon.

The task of tracing back to their Welsh ancestors people with a Welsh name is far from an easy one; in some cases the task is made a little less formidable when they can be traced back in the first · place to one of the famous Welsh settlements such as those of Pennsylvania and Minnesota, or Utica, New York State. Such was the case with the early nineteenth century inventor, Oliver Evans, mentioned earlier. Similarly with another eminent Evans,

Lawrence Boyd Evans, writer and lawyer (1870-1928) whose grandparents came from Wales to Pennsylvania in 1828, the grandfather being the Reverend Evan Evans. Lawrence Boyd Evans went to Harvard Law School and became Professor of Law at Tufts College in 1900. Similarly, even earlier last century, **Thomas Evans** (1798-1868), a Quaker minister and editor of the *Friends Library,* came from the well-known Gwynedd group of Welsh settlers in Pennsylvania, being a third generation descendant of an Evans family at that settlement.

The same applies to the **Cadwalader** family of Philadelphia. When the Welsh Quakers moved from Wales to Pennsylvania in the 1680's, they occupied, as shown earlier, the Welsh Tract or Barony, which comprised 50,000 acres in what Nathaniel Burt calls the 'Main Line' in Philadelphia. "The Cadwaladers," he states, "have an impeccable reputation among Philadelphians. They belong to the Welsh Tract that still provides the central enduring core of Philadelphian aristocracy" (Burt, *The Perennial Philadelphians,* 1964, p.58). Right from the start of the city, the Cadwaladers made alliances by marriage with all the other leading Welsh Quaker families, and later with other well-to-do families. "Many of Philadelphia's oldest and best family names, Roberts, Pugh, Price, Evans, Lewis, Lloyd and others came from the settlers in this area." (Ibid. p.58.)

Sometimes the task of tracing back Welsh connections is facilitated by the study of local place-names. Thus **Colonel Abraham Owen,** of the Kentucky Owens, who was a veteran of earlier so-called 'protective' wars against the Indians, was remembered by grateful citizens in the name of Owensboro City, Daviess County, Kentucky. Another early Welsh-American hero so honoured was **Zackwill Morgan** of West Virginia. Zackwill's father, William ap Morgan, had helped to develop the original settlement. This failed, owing to a series of Indian raids. Zackwill founded it again in 1766 with Morgantown as its name. This practice had been the source of several Welsh names on the map of the United States. Thus Morristown, the seat of Morris County, New Jersey, was named after Lewis Morris, discussed earlier. Another Morristown in Tennessee was named after Gideon Morris, who settled there in 1787.

It is remarkable how often sons of Welsh-American farmers, or merchants, became doctors in the United States. Sometimes they stayed in that profession, helping to develop it, sometimes however turning to other fields of endeavour and public service. The latter case could be illustrated, of course, by John Evans in the nineteenth century in Colorado, as already described. **John Morgan** (1735-1789) belonged to the first category. Born of

Philadelphia Welsh stock, son of a rich merchant, he did much to further medicine in Pennsylvania. He had studied, and qualified, in medicine, in Edinburgh, Paris and London. (No wonder that his biography, by W. J. Bell, was entitled *Continental Doctor.*) For several years he was an army surgeon. Returning to civilian practice of his profession, he did much to found the Medical School at Philadelphia College, as it was then. As Professor of Medicine at America's first medical school, he insisted on more division of labour between physician, surgeon and pharmacist. This took a long time to put into practice, but it gradually developed, and helped to open up new fields of medical research. Prominent in the latter was the work of Dr. Thomas Cadwalader on lead-poisoning (which, incidentally, was published by Benjamin Franklin).

Collections of American biographies, up to the present date, name other Morgans who made a name in the world of medicine, such as Elizabeth Morgan, plastic surgeon, who was born in Washington in 1947, daughter of William James Morgan. The biographies also reveal however that the Morgans among Welsh-Americans have done well in other fields this century, like Graham James Morgan, manufacturer, son of Caradoc James Morgan, born 1917; or Roy Edward Morgan, born Nanticoke, Pennsylvania 1908, son of Morgan J. Morgan and Margaret Edwards Morgan, becoming a well-known broadcasting executive and critic. He married Mary Parry.

To turn now from the Morgan family to the equally gifted Davieses, **Samuel Davies** (1723-1761) has already been mentioned in the chapter on Religion and Welsh Emigration to the United States, but his importance in Welsh-American history justifies a little more on him. Like his Welsh parents, David and Martha Davies, he was a Presbyterian, but a very tolerant one, defending the civil rights and liberties of all nonconformists. This was recognised by his biographer, who said of him, looking primarily at Davies's role in the foundation of the University of Princeton, "He was the animating soul of the whole dissenting interest in Virginia and North Carolina." (V. L. Collins, *Princeton,* 1914, p.59.) As well as his close connection with Princeton University, Samuel Davies was a close friend of the celebrated Jonathan Edwards, recognised as America's leading intellectual at that time. It was fitting that, when Jonathan Edwards became the first head of Princeton, he should be succeeded by Davies as second President of Princeton.

For centuries, Welsh with the surname Davis or Davies left Wales for the New World, making a name in many spheres of American life. Thus, from Samuel Davies in the fields of religion and scholarship, we can turn to **Arthur Bowen Davies** (1862-1928) who became one of America's finest artists. His father, David Thomas Davies, was a Welsh emigrant to Utica, New York; by trade a tailor, he also became choirmaster to a Welsh chapel in Utica. Arthur Bowen Davies was fortunate in having the help of an older Welsh artist, Dwight Williams, who encouraged him in his art study. Hence A. B. Davies pursued his art education at Chicago and New York. He married a Welsh lady doctor, Virginia Meriwether Davies. They farmed at Congers, New York, also selling Davies's paintings in the big city. Experts say that a prolonged study-period in Italy and Paris much influenced his later work.

An interesting project in Welsh-American history would be a comparison between the careers, and influence in the United States, of two very famous Welshmen, Robert Owen in the nineteenth century, and John Llewellyn Lewis in the latter nineteenth and early twentieth centuries; such a comparison would throw much light on some of the essential components of Welsh character over the years.

Robert Owen (1771-1858) has already been mentioned in this book, but only with reference to his son, who became an American citizen. Robert Owen was probably as well known in America as in Britain; born in 1771 in Newtown, Montgomeryshire, North Wales, he had become a wealthy industrialist in Britain before trying to put into practice his Utopian ideas. In Britain today he is probably better remembered as the founder of the Cooperative movement. In his middle age he went to New Harmony (Indiana) to attempt his idealistic community experiment. There had in fact already been a peaceful religious community at New Harmony, whose land Owen bought up. The experiment did not prosper and Robert Owen returned to Wales. Robert Owen, however, had made a deep impression on many thinking Americans, despite the failure at New Harmony. His book *The New Moral World* was widely read and much discussed in the United States, and remained the inspiration for other Utopian experiments there. When in the States, he met and impressed many eminent thinkers, including the American President, John Quincy Adams.

John Llewellyn Lewis (1880-1969) could not have had a more different career and life-style, and yet had his own brand of idealism, for which he was always ready to fight. He had started in the mines in Ohio, son of Welsh immigrants, worked at mining in various other parts of the States, meanwhile gaining more and more respect and influence amongst miners in his struggle for the human rights of his fellow-miners. By 1920, he was the President of the United Mineworkers. After many struggles with the coal bosses, he spread his wings into other spheres of American labour, and created the Committee for Industrial Organisations in 1937. This expanded in strength rapidly under Lewis's vigorous leadership. The history of American labour in this century' has had, as one of its main themes, the competition between the C.I.O. and the rival labour organisation, the American Federation of Labor. Although this competition often generated much heat, much of it on Lewis's side, his main struggle was still with 'the bosses'. He had dramatic, successful and highly newsworthy confrontations with the mighty General Motors, the United States Steel Companies and other industrial giants. Before he ended his working life, there came agreement with the A.F.L. .

One thing one learns in the search for 'Welsh-Americans' is that it is not wise to assume that someone with a 'Welsh' name is necessarily Welsh, or even of remote 'Welsh stock'. The warning came early in reference to John Paul Jones, Scottish-American. More warnings came concerning black men in North America who had left the South, still with the adopted names of Southern slave-owners, some of them Welsh. More surprising to me, though possibly not to native-born Americans, was that several American-Indians, from various tribes, had adopted non-Indian names, some of them 'Welsh'. This happened in quite early American history, sometimes on the adoption of the Christian faith. Thus, in early nineteenth century United States such names could be found, as, for example, in Texas where there was the well-known and highly intelligent Robert M. Jones; he was a member of the Choctaw Indian tribe, and had been at the Choctaw Academy in Kentucky. He was associated in business with the traders, Berthelet, Heald and Company before the Civil War. He was rich, and owned many black slaves, with whom he cultivated several extensive tracts of land (Grant Foreman, *Advancing the Frontier; 1830-1860,* 1933). At the same period, in Oklahoma, one Baptist mission was conducted by John Lewis (Creek Indian) and another by John Davies, also Creek.

A page or so back we were looking at John Llewellyn Lewis, whose life bridged the nineteenth and twentieth centuries. This was the case with many well-known Welsh Americans, as with, of course, all other ethnic-group members. We have already had examples in this chapter, additional to John Llewellyn Lewis; several of them were, like Lewis, sons of Welsh immigrants, often miners or steelworkers who sought success in other fields, as Welsh miners have often done in the home country. Ben Ames Williams, novelist, and Frank Lloyd Wright, architect, were both grand-children of Welsh immigrants, both dying in the 1950's. Others, of Welsh stock some generations back, who died during this century were David Llewellyn Griffiths, the film director, Sinclair Lewis,

157

satirical novelist, Idwal Jones, another Welsh-American novelist. Leading Welsh-Americans in the fields of natural history, botany and agriculture who died this century were respectively David Charles Davies, David Pryce Davies and David Griffiths; all three were immigrants themselves, born in Wales. So was Thomas Jesse Jones, leading sociologist, author of *The Negro in America.*

John Charles Williams and Silas James Lewis were Welsh immigrants who became Presidents of Steel Companies; so was Hywel Davies, born at Brecon. The list continues. New Welsh-Americans become famous, or at least successful in their own fields, as older ones die. As such lists are, of course, compiled from the American equivalents of our 'Who's Who', one hears nothing of the failures, the unhappy and the despairing, who must have existed amongst Welsh immigrants, as among those of every ethnic origin. Such lists also generally confine themselves to those who have taken American nationality, like Ray Milland, the film actor from Neath, South Wales, reputed to be originally a Jones, taking the name of the steelworks where his father worked. With the coming of the jet plane, many artists (using the term to cover all the arts) especially those who become media personalities, belong to a kind of trans-Atlantic culture. From stage, screen and 'teenage pop culture', as well as from literature, music and the arts generally, many of these 'household names' have their origin in Wales. Some of the best known are Emlyn Williams, Richard Burton and Sir Geraint Evans.

In the ranks of those who do take American nationality, following the long line of Welsh immigration to the United States, the amazing diversity of interest and ability that has been demonstrated in these pages still manifests itself. Briefly to illustrate this 'continuity of diversity' among new Welsh-Americans, we note Floyd John Lewis, born 1916, pioneer in heart surgery; David Lewis, born 1941, philosopher of science and language; John Hughson Jones, awarded an honorary O.B.E. in 1963 by Queen Elizabeth for his services to Anglo-American cultural relationships; Elwyn V. Jenkins, son of Welsh immigrants, Ohio Judge and civic leader, born 1917; Gwilym Alexander Price, born 1895, President of the great Westinghouse Electrical Company.

And so the list goes on, some famous, some rich, some born in Wales, some born in the States of Welsh parents, many giving their children the old Welsh Christian names. We take note, for instance, of John Morgan Bevan, born in Pennsylvania. A university graduate, he married Elizabeth Jones. They have a son, John Morgan Bevan, and a daughter Megan Anne. Then there is Charles Hugh Bevan, born in Alabama in 1923. He became an

158

electronics engineer and served in the Navy. He married Nina Gwen Stevens; their sons were called David Hugh and Charles Hugh. Another Bowen is David Reese Bowen, born in Mississippi in 1932. His father had exactly the same name, quite a common phenomenon in the old Welsh family circles; David Reece Bowen junior was educated at Harvard and Oxford, and became a Congressman.

To continue the theme of Welsh Christian names being handed down, it is noted that David George Davies, a lawyer, was born in the old Welsh settlement of Waukesha, Wisconsin, in 1928; he was the son of David Evan Davies. The combination of names would be very familiar in Swansea or the valleys of South or North Wales. John Victor Evans was born in Idaho in 1925, and became Governor of that State; his father was born David Lloyd Evans, his mother Margaret Thomas. Ivor Hughes was born in Porth, Rhondda, South Wales; he became a tobacco executive in Kentucky. Just one last name to illustrate the theme of this paragraph. John Hughes was born in Neath, South Wales. His father was Evan John Hughes, his mother was, before marriage, Dilys Williams. John Hughes had experience in administration and journalism; in 1970 he was Pulitzer prize-winner. What may seem the rather jumbled format of this chapter is due to a deliberate attempt to demonstrate this continued stream of Welsh, crossing the Atlantic to add new Gwyns, Bryns and Glyns, new Bronwens and Megans to the old Welsh stock in the United States.

Chapter 12

Conclusion

IN PRECEDING chapters a few brief references have been made to 'the Welsh way of life' and to eisteddfods as part of it. More seems necessary, in these concluding remarks, on this central theme, especially in order to try and unravel how much of the well-established nineteenth-century pattern has lingered on into the United States of this twentieth century.

The Eisteddfod, as an important Welsh social institution, is said to have originated in the days of Howel Dda (Howell the Good) in the tenth century A.D. The first of which there is knowledge in medieval times is said to have been that at Carmarthen in 1450 A.D.; an eisteddfod was held at Caerwys in Flintshire, North Wales, in the presence of Elizabeth, the Tudor Queen. There followed, for nearly two centuries, a prolonged lapse in Welsh cultural life, alleged to have been due to the 'anglicisation' of the Welsh gentry. Other aspects of that culture may have endured, but it was not till the end of the eighteenth century that the Eisteddfod revived as a great Welsh institution. After Thomas Jones of Llangollen, North Wales, had held successful eisteddfods a⁺ Llangollen and Corwen, the whole idea of this festival of music and the arts was taken up enthusiastically by the London Welsh Society, the Gweneddigion.

The eisteddfods of the 1780's and the 1790's, initiated by Thomas Jones, led to many local eisteddfods in the first half of the nineteenth century, culminating in the first National Eisteddfod, held at Llangollen in 1858. It did not take long before a close association developed between the Eisteddfod and the Gorsedd of the Bards. The first Gorsedd was in fact organised by Edward Williams, a stonemason of genius, who assumed the bardic name of Iolo Morganwg. Wyn Griffith said of him, "His fertile brain invented an institution which he called 'Gorsedd Beirdd Ynys Prydain' (Session of the Bards of the Isle of Britain).'' (W. Griffith, *The Welsh*, (Pelican), 1950.) It was held in the open air, for the first time in history, on Primrose Hill in London (1791). If it seems strange to the reader that such a very Welsh institution should first see the light of day in London, and not Wales, the place of the Honourable Society of Cymmrodorion in Welsh culture should be appreciated. This learned society, closely associated with the Gweneddigion, the Welsh Society of London, led the way in the revival of Welsh literary and musical life at the beginning of last century; founded as early as 1751, it still flourishes and holds an important place in the cultural life of Wales.

If preceding paragraphs seem far removed from the tale of the Welsh in the United States, this is not at all the case. It is quite remarkable how quickly the revival of Welsh cultural life spread to the New World. Eisteddfods were introduced to the United States in the 1830's and have ever since been an influential source of close relations between Welsh and Welsh-Americans. Every year at the National Eisteddfod of Wales, whether it is in the North or the South, there is a special welcome for 'Welshmen in Exile', including emigrants, or their descendants, who have returned to attend the festival. Grouped by countries, the Americans forming the biggest group, they march into the vast Eisteddfod tent to the singing of the nostalgic old hymn, 'Unwaith Eto Yng Nghymru Annwyl' (Once again in dear Wales) and are greeted with warm enthusiasm.

It has been claimed that the first eisteddfod in America was in New York in 1838. As one would expect, having read about the Welsh in Pennsylvania, two of the earliest Welsh-American eisteddfods were held in that State, at Carbondale and Pittston in the 1850's. Eisteddfods were held at Utica, New York State (1858), Scranton, becoming with industrialisation, as we have seen, a favourite for Welsh immigrants (1859) and, rather surprisingly, among the Californian gold-miners on July 4th 1860.

From then on to the end of the century, eisteddfods played as big a part in typical Welsh-American life as the chapels; in fact there was a good deal of overlap between the two, with chapel choirs often winning the choral competitions. Naturally, eisteddfods were particularly popular in the Pennsylvanian coal communities, likewise in Ohio, Wisconsin, Minnesota and Iowa, and among the Mormon Welsh in Utah. Scranton led the way in organising an all-American Eisteddfod in 1867, to be copied by Chicago, Atlantic City, New Jersey, Seattle and even Alaska-Yukon (1909).

Just as the Gorsedd had become allied to the Eisteddfod in Wales, so in the United States; compared with the rapid alliance

CWRS CYMRAEG MINNESOTA
OFFERS YOU

Welsh-language instruction by teachers from Wales
A concert by the world-famous Rhos Male Choir
An evening cruise on a Mississippi paddleboat
PLUS... singing, folk-dancing, forum on Wales today
Welsh films, seminar on Welsh history, noson lawen

ALL THIS, AND MUCH MORE, FOR ONLY:

$275 for adults, $225 for full-time students, and $165 for children 12 & under
(Fees include tuition, room and board for seven days, and all events)

To register, mail $50 deposit (payable to Cwrs Cymraeg Minnesota) to:
MARY MERGENTHAL,
2393, BOURNE AVENUE,
ST. PAUL, MN 55108.
DO NOT DELAY – COURSE PLACES ARE FILLING UP

HAMLINE UNIVERSITY, ST. PAUL
JULY 31 - AUGUST 7, 1983

Co-sponsored by
Cymdeithas Madog
and the
St. David's Society
of Minnesota

A contemporary newspaper notice

between the two institutions among the Welsh of Wales and
London, the link-up took much longer to achieve in the United
States. The first American Gorsedd was formed in 1913 at the
Pittsburgh National Eisteddfod. Although Gorsedd meetings did
occur elsewhere e.g. San Francisco, it was in fact Pittsburgh that
had most to do with the Gorsedd in the United States. One example
from Pittsburgh is given by Professor Hartmann, of an eisteddfod
organised in that city to honour a very aged Welsh-American
doctor, affectionately known as 'Bonesetter Reese'. In 1940, a
similar honour was paid to Senator James D. Davis, first
generation Welsh immigrant and formerly American Secretary of
Labor. The American Gorsedd welcomed Lloyd George when he
visited America in 1923.

The Gymanfa Ganu has already been discussed in this work in
connection with the part religion played in the life of nineteenth
century Welsh, in cities or in countryside. The institution
flourished even more from the 1920's, leading to the National

Gymanfa Ganu Association of the United States and Canada, based at Youngstown, Ohio. The association grew out of the efforts of the Welsh Society of that city, and this is the place to point out that such Welsh Societies were common throughout the States at the beginning of this century, sometimes, as in Youngstown, called St. David's societies, or, more rarely, Cambrian societies. Music, so cherished and encouraged by eisteddfods, was often extended even more by the various Welsh societies, with the introduction of Glee Clubs and Choral Unions, such as that of Scranton. The Male Voice Choir, so popular in Wales, had its counterparts in the States; for example, at Cleveland.

As well as social and musical functions, many of the Welsh societies had charitable functions; some of these, to new immigrants in particular, have been mentioned in earlier chapters. As Philadelphia was often the first big city that the Welsh immigrant would head for in the old days, its Welsh Society became as famous for its benevolent functions as for its lively social functions. The latter, of course, reached the highest point on St. David's Day, as was equally true of many of the eisteddfods. "So that no destitute Welsh person would have to die in a pauper's grave, the Society had its own cemetery provision. Some of Philadelphia's most illustrious citizens belonged to the Welsh Society." (Hartmann, p.46.) Professor Hartmann himself wrote the introduction to the *History of the Welsh Society of Philadelphia, 1729-1979*. New York's St. David's Society was originally called the Ancient Britons' Society. The New York Society had the custom of awarding an annual medal for the most meritorious achievement by a Welsh person in any sphere of life; like Philadelphia, it had its cemetery plots, but also hospital beds for Welsh in need. Chicago, Cincinnati and other large cities had some such provision supplied by their Welsh societies, as they did in California (See David Hughes, *Welsh People of California,* 1923).

The lively Welsh social, religious, and cultural life of last century, extending into the first part of this century, was reported and stimulated by Welsh newspapers and journals such as *Baner America,* the *Druid,* and *Y Drych;* these were in addition to the denominational journals which were often the most read of available periodicals. Many an aspiring Welsh-American journalist had his first training in writing short pieces, poems and other items for the 'chapel paper'.

While it is important to realise that much of the total social life of the Welsh communities centred around the chapels, as it would in any Welsh valley community of the time, this does not necessarily mean that all chapel-goers were strictly teetotal. Several inns in Welsh communities had names such as 'Cambrian' and 'Caernarvon Castle' (Berthoff). Professor Berthoff reports that "the Pennsylvanian coal towns had dozens of 'saloons Cymreig' "; he mentions one famous tavern, the 'Owain Glyndwr', famous for the harp-playing that could be enjoyed there.

The Welsh in the nineteenth century, though true to their own language and institutions, were generally free from the prejudice, even hostility, sometimes directed by native-born Americans against immigrants. Most Welsh could at least speak some English, and, if they were not so good at it, worked hard to improve it. Professor Berthoff maintains also that they were amongst the readiest of the incoming ethnic groups to seek American nationality. "No national group," he states in his *British Immigrants in Industrial America,* "had a higher proportion of fully naturalised Americans" (p.132). This was confirmed by contemporary articles in journals such as *Y Drych.* J. D. Spencer at the end of last century noted how much quicker the Welsh were than some ethnic groups to adopt American ways (*'Young Welshmen Abroad', Wales, Vol. IV,* 1897). The Welsh sometimes noticed prejudice against the English in the States. Welshmen mistaken for English "when accosted, were likely to startle the Americans by most heartily seconding the indictment of England." (Berthoff, p.138.)

Understandably, the Welsh-Americans, however Americanised they became, still enthusiastically welcomed visits by Welsh from the homeland. "In 1890, the visit of a party of Welsh ironmasters stirred Pittsburgh working men from Swansea, Morriston and Llanelly to troop down to meet them with patriotic greetings." (Ibid.)

It is undoubtedly true that many of the former manifestations of the 'Welsh way of life' discussed in this chapter and elsewhere with reference to the United States of America, have disappeared, or at least been considerably modified. Much of this could be, as in Wales itself, attributed to gradual weakening of the hold of the Welsh language. This in the old days was the cement that held the whole culture-pattern together. Consequently, with its disappearance, or much less frequent use, the older Welsh communities in the States lost some of their distinctive 'Welshness'. Yet, in the States, some Welsh-based societies and institutions have actually come to life during this century, such as the Gymanfa Ganu Associations, the famous Poultney Welsh Male Chorus (1939) and national and local Welsh Women's Clubs in some parts of America. Thus Professor Ronald D. Dennis of Brigham Young University, Utah, currently researching into the history of the Welsh Mormons, has kindly furnished me with particulars of some recent Welsh-American activitie˙ in the Western States. These do, in fact, include a class that he himself takes in 'beginning Welsh' (1983). The University of California at Berkeley has a 'Celtic Colloquium', which includes a class in medieval Welsh, with selected readings from Geoffrey of Monmouth's *History of the Kings of Britain,* the ninth-century poetry of Llywarch Hen and the fourteenth century poetry of Dafydd ap Gwilym.

The Berkeley Celtic Colloquium (referring to one of their newsletters) invites lecturers to address them who are experts on aspects of Celtic Britain. Thus, in March 1982, Dr. Susan Pearce, Curator of Antiquities to Exeter Museum, lectured on 'The Christian Church in Roman Britain'. At Berkeley, also in March 1982, Megan Jones-Davison lectured with the title 'Conversations about Wales'. Plans were made for students and 'associated students' to 'tour Wales, and spend three days at the world-famous Eisteddfod (singing competitions and ceremonies)'. At Cornell University, Ithaca, New York, a Summer School programme recently included a lecture entitled 'An introduction to Celtic Culture and Civilisation' by Professor Bedwyr Lewis Jones of the University College of Bangor, North Wales, and two sessions of an 'Introduction to Modern Welsh'. Eleri Wynne Jones assisted Professor Jones, as did an Irish specialist on Irish Studies, to cover the general Celtic theme of the Introductory lecture. The social side of summer-school items mentioned above was not neglected; this gives an excellent, and congenial, opportunity to discuss all aspects of formal lectures and seminars.

A notice in the Berkeley, California, newsletter read: '**Prynhawn Llawen.** The Welsh-American Society of Northern California will celebrate St. David's Day with a pot luck, raffle and program of song and readings. The Prynhawn Llawen will be held on February 27th at 3 p.m. at the Community Church in North Berkeley. You are asked to bring food, one dollar per person, and a hymn-book'. It is clear that the same kind of event occurred at Los Angeles about the same date; the venue was named as 'The Alameda, L.A.'. That other ethnic groups were not altogether ignored was proved, on the same page of the newsletter, by an invitation to 'reserve a place now at the traditional Chinese Banquet at the Fourth Annual Celtic Conference in Los Angeles' (1983).

A good picture of the current general range of Welsh-American activities and interests can be obtained from any issue of the Welsh-American newspaper *Ninnau* (We also) published in New Jersey. Thus, taking an appropriate date, March 1st 1983 a brief survey of contents is most revealing. It should interest not only Welsh in Wales and elsewhere in Britain, the Welsh-Americans and Welsh-Canadians for whom it is intended, but anyone who has friends or relatives of Welsh stock in America. Prominent in *Ninnau* is the monthly calendar of 'Welsh' events in Canada and the United States. The above-mentioned issue has, on its front page, a passage written in 1346, and translated from the Welsh, on the death of Saint David. On the same page is an appreciation of Judge G. Mennen Williams, of Welsh extraction, former Governor of Michigan from 1948, and now Chief Justice of the Michigan Supreme Court. It is interesting to note that the grandfather of Chief Justice Williams came to the States from Pembrokeshire, West Wales, via Canada. Judge Williams was an Intelligence Officer in American aircraft-carriers in World War II, and, in 1955, received the prized medallion of the Welsh Society of Philadelphia as 'Distinguished Welsh-American of 1954'. The same front page also has an article by Professor Hartmann on the Welsh of Wilkes-Barre.

Ninnau follows with, on the next page, short news-items about other Welsh celebrities in the States and Canada, letters from readers and obituaries, both the latter, of course, with Welsh or Welsh-Americans in mind. An early section of the paper gives accounts of 'Wales Today', and is followed by reports of Welsh-American and Welsh-Canadian social, musical and literary occasions for the preceding month, and those to come in the near future.

Included in each issue is a Welsh language section, and a Welsh Crossword puzzle. Prominent in this St. David's Day issue is a full-page advertisement for the 1983 Welsh National Eisteddfod, and another advertisement, for an United States concert tour by a Thousand Voice Welsh Male Choir, visiting Pittsburgh, Baltimore, Philadelphia and New York. Amongst other events noted in the issue is a Welsh Festival of Song (Gymanfa Ganu) at Grand Rapids, Michigan, the beginning of a course on Welsh History at the University of Minnesota, the celebration of St. David's Day by the Welsh Society of Central New Jersey, the National Gymanfa to be held at Wilkes-Barre in September 1983 and another Welsh choir giving concerts in New York, Wichita, Kansas, Indianopolis and Pittsburgh.

Book reviews include one on *The Welsh in Wisconsin* by Phillips G. Davies of the Wisconsin State Historical Society, and a book by David James (University of Wales) on *A Social History of St. David's, Wales*. Prominent on the main advertisement page, next to the one on the Welsh National Eisteddfod, is a full-page one for the Welsh Festival of Castles, 1983.

One of the main articles in this March 1983 issue of *Ninnau* is on 'The Welsh of Blue Earth County, Minnesota'. A short account is given of the success of New Jersey in the competitions of the Welsh

Pony Society of America. The drama review in the issue describes a new musical play based on Dylan Thomas's poem *A child's Christmas in Wales;* the play is being performed at the Ohio Theatre, Cleveland. American readers of *Ninnau* are invited to the Ontario Welsh Festival, just across the border, which is sponsored by the Ontario Gymanfa Ganu Association.

While looking closely at the Saint David's Day number of *Ninnau*, it must be pointed out that subsequent numbers (for July and October 1983) keep up the same high standard, the former having a special supplement on the American National Gymanfa Ganu. Subscriptions to *Ninnau* can be made at Ninnau Publications, 11 Post Terrace, Basking Ridge, New Jersey 07920, U.S.A. at £4 per annum — overseas Air delivery at triple price. The May, 1983, number of *Y Drych* (published at De Pere, Wisconsin) has wonderful old Welsh-American photographs from last century, also a review of Ellen Evan's *Chicago at fifteen* (in 1903).

One very interesting feature in this St. David's number of *Ninnau* is the genealogical article, which seems to be a regular item in the paper. It links up usefully with the many genealogies of American families, many of them Welsh, in the genealogical lists maintained by the United States Library of Congress. The task of tracing families back through the ages has been made easier by the efforts made by individual families in the United States. Just to take a sample at random from the Library of Congress lists, let us look at genealogies prepared by members of the Evans families in America.

Taking just a few illustrative items from the many in the Library of Congress lists, we have:

5751　Evans. *Descendants of David Evans of Charlestown (Mass.)* by S. A. Evans, 1893.

5752　Evans. *History of Nathaniel Evans of Cat Fish Creek, Virginia, and his descendants* by James Daniel Evans, 1905.

5754　Evans. *Sketch of the Evans family of Monongalia County, West Virginia* by Vergil Lewis, 1911.

5757　*Genealogy of Evans, Nivin and allied families* by Septimus Nivin, Philadelphia, 1930.

Earlier collections of such genealogies were numbered as above; later ones, classified as 'Complements' are unnumbered, but equally valuable. Thus,

Evans *Descendants of John Evans. 1790-1871.* 1875.

Evans *family of Harrisburg, Pennsylvania,* by Sam Evans, 1895.

Evans *Genealogy of William Evans family of Neath, Pennsylvania,* 1912.

Evans *Robert Evans family, Virginia and Georgia,* by Cleo Evans, 1966.

Evans *Across the Years with the Evans Family,* by Hazel Evans, 1972.

Incidentally, the Pelican Book of Surnames considers it possible that the surname 'Evans' had some connection with the Roman-British name Eugenius, meaning 'well-born'.

As can be seen from the two items immediately above, American families are still looking for their ancestors. Some of the genealogies give explicit details of first entry to the United States, sometimes giving place of departure in Wales. Often they give clues to the link-up of families by marriage, but sometimes also by friendship and/or business connections.

Historical and biographical sections of this book have drawn attention to family connections across the Atlantic, generally among the more famous families. Many of these are dealt with in biographical dictionaries; they are interesting and important — in a disordered world they give continuity, and promise of continuity, as surely as shared institutions such as those of freedom and free speech. The same applies to historical connections of ordinary families, not likely to be in the main reference-books. This is where many of the items in the Library of Congress lists become particularly useful.

Many of these trans-Atlantic connections result from the various group and individual immigrations from Wales to the United States, in cases where contacts one way, or both ways, have been kept up for at least a few generations. One instance reported was where a married couple, now in their seventies, have visited a son working in the States every four years since he emigrated there thirty years ago; he comes to see them in Wales in the intervening years. In other cases, where the 'folks back home' have become too old or ill to travel far, the visits have become one way only i.e. West to East.

Sometimes there have been more sporadic factors, such as the influx to the United States (and, of course, Canada) of so-called 'G.I. brides' after both World Wars; many of these were Welsh. There may still be living, in various parts of the United States, a few such G.I. brides of the First World War period and the early nineteen-twenties, now probably great-grandmothers of American children. The latter may sometimes hear the old lady speak of her childhood in Caernarvon or Swansea. Similarly there were hundreds of Welsh girls married to Americans during and after World War II. Many of them keep in touch with the old country in one way or another, and so family links still endure.

A very important factor in facilitating this link has been more widespread, and comparatively cheap, jet air-travel, particularly over the last five years. Many of the big airlines have their own

Reunion Clubs, sometimes offering discount fares or other inducements such as free life-insurance, to bring together families separated by the oceans of the world. Thus British Airways have such clubs looking after Britons venturing many thousands of miles to Australia or New Zealand, and to Canada or the United States. Often the skilled and caring services of such Reunion Clubs take mothers and fathers, brothers and sisters, to see relatives, very often grandchildren, in Toronto and Pennsylvania, Vancouver and Seattle. The fortunate clients of Reunion Club jumbo-jets can do in half a day what took many weary and dangerous months of travel in the old days, many emigrants, for instance, never reaching their goals, often dying in the Atlantic. Welsh families, like many others, have used such services to keep up family ties.

An additional link between Britain and America is that of intercultural exchanges. To take 'intercultural' in its narrowest sense, this normally means exchange in the sphere of scholarship and the arts. Wales has taken part in this beneficial exchange as enthusiastically as other areas of the British Isles. To start with scholarship, because of a shared English language, there has traditionally been, for centuries, an exchange of learned men, and more recently, learned women, between Britain and America. Even at the undergraduate stage, where lifelong interests, and often friendships, frequently start, this can be seen. At Oxford we welcomed the American Rhodes scholars; one I met there was Welsh-American. I had the pleasure of taking him home to a Wales he had never before seen, and showing him round the Gower Peninsula, near Swansea. After a few lessons in pronunciation, he read to my old grandmother from the old Welsh family bible; she knew little English, and his efforts were much appreciated — and understood. So successful were they in fact that the next evening numerous neighbours and friends called in to hear the Welsh-American rendering of the Scriptures.

Many of our young men and women in this century have learned from, and enjoyed, their sojourns at American universities, often taking up American Studies as a major university, and often lifelong, specialism. Some of these have been Welsh, and have retained a strong interest in Welsh-American activities and relationships. With university staffs of both countries, again there has been much interchange, not only between Oxford and Cambridge on the one hand, Harvard and Yale on the other, but between universities large and small, Ivy League and State Universities on the American side, ancient, red-brick and plate-glass, as we sometimes, rather wryly, distinguish our own, on this side of the Atlantic.

Of particular relevance to this book, of course, is the highly specialised field of Celtic Studies, mentioned earlier. Obviously the University of Wales, with its constituent colleges of Bangor, Aberystwyth, Cardiff and Swansea, has played a large part in this sphere of scholarship.

To turn from the groves of academe to the theatre, to the concert-hall, to poetry and other branches of literature, the Anglo-American exchange has been enormous and fruitful. This is an instance where the better phrase might be 'British-American', for translations have made more than just the English contributions to cultural life available to the Americans, while the Welsh have long appreciated American contributions. It is well beyond the scope of this book, and of its author, to try to describe the vast scale of this exchange. One can only say that, as far as Wales and the United States are concerned, the regular exchange of Welsh Choirs for American choirs, such as the famous Mormon choir, has for many years been common practice. Nor is this confined to choral music. On many occasions our B.B.C. Welsh National Orchestra has, like other British orchestras, played the compositions of Charles Ives, Barber, Bernstein and Aaron Copland, while American orchestras have included in their repertoires music by Peter Maxwell Davies, William Mathias and Hoddinott. American opera-lovers are familiar with the singing of Sir Geraint Evans and other Welsh opera singers.

When it comes to literature, including drama, there is the difficulty that much of the Welsh literary heritage, and much fine modern Welsh literature also, is in the Welsh language. Not many Welsh-Americans these days can understand the old native tongue of their ancestors. There are however, as already pointed out, excellent translations; in any case, much Welsh verse, fiction and drama, for example, Dylan Thomas's *Under Milk Wood* were written in English, while thoroughly Welsh in subject-matter, tone and spirit. Dylan Thomas's travels in the United States were well-publicised at the time, thirty years ago now, and so was his miserable death. His poems, however, and perhaps particularly *Under Milk Wood* will be treasured as much by Welsh-Americans as by his many admirers in his homeland. Perhaps the best epitaph on him are the last two lines of his poem *Fern Hill:* "Time held me green and dying, Though I sang in my chains like the sea."

Another Welsh poet, not as famous as Dylan Thomas, but quite well-known in the United States and Britain in the 1920's, was W. H. Davies. He knew the United States better than most Americans. He travelled the States train-jumping, or as they used to call it, 'riding the rails' along all the main tracks, writing about the railroads as he traversed them. His arduous and dangerous travels ended in tragedy, with the loss of a leg. His life-story,

Autobiography of a Super-Tramp became a minor classic. Americans today would find it lucidly written, giving a vivid picture of America in the 1920's. His poetry, though perhaps not of the very highest quality, is good enough to be included in several anthologies, especially those concerned with Wales and its many poets, such as Collins' *A Book of Wales*.

Earlier remarks about Welsh poetry included in Courses of Celtic Studies in America may be recalled. Such courses, which many Welsh-Americans and no doubt many others, have attended often include selections from Welsh poetry over the whole range, from Taliesin in the sixth century onwards; not only poetry but Welsh prose also, in other words the total range of Welsh literature from Aneirin, Dafydd ap Gwilym, Prince Hywel ab Owain Gwynedd to Henry Vaughan, Ann of Swansea, Idris Davies, R. Williams Parry, Prosser Rhys and many others, in Welsh and in English including the famous prose works from the Mabinogion, the Black Book of Carmarthen, Giraldus Cambrensis onwards.

It could be said that such reading is for the more intellectual among both Welsh and Welsh-Americans, and it may well be so. It would not have done, however, to have left out any reference to the loftier studies common to those of Welsh stock, whether at home in Britain or overseas. That would not have given the whole picture. Nor, however, would it give the total Welsh and Welsh-American scene if less literary aspects of life were ignored. There already have been references to newspapers and also the media generally; particularly with the dominance of television over all the other media, as far as many people are concerned, it is important to know what knowledge of other nationalities is presented by the media. Older people in Wales will remember the coverage of the Depression by the newspapers, the radio, the news-reels at the cinemas. Over here, we saw the facts of the Depression in the United States, and Americans, Welsh-Americans included, saw what it was like in the Welsh valleys at that time. Thinking and concerned people in both countries read and heard about attempts to escape from the Depression and create a better life for all. We in Britain, through the media knew about Roosevelt's New Deal, and Americans knew about Beveridge and Aneurin Bevan, our progress towards social insurance and a National Health Service. All British take it granted that the so-called 'special relationship' between British and Americans means that we need to know as much as possible about each other — and our problems.

The Welsh in America have through the media, as well as by more studious reading, been able to obtain a general picture of how things are going in Wales, economically as well as in other matters. Today however, much more so than fifty years ago, pictures

171

presented by the media can be supplemented by personal observation, thanks to air-travel. American versions of films such as *How Green was My Valley* left with American viewers, not only memories of social conditions in Wales, but also some idea of the beauty as well as the sufferings of Wales. Nowadays many more Americans can see for themselves, through tourist excursions, the beauty of the Welsh mountains, sea-coasts and castles. Many of the more prosperous Welsh have also seen something, by mass travel, of the scenic beauty and grandeur only previously seen on the screen, in many different areas of the United States.

America has rightly been known as the 'melting-pot', a name first used by William Penn. It has absorbed into itself the peoples of many European and other countries, creating a new trans-Atlantic culture which from its earliest days strove to leave behind the injustice or poverty of the old world in the freedom of the new world. While the hope was always high, the cost was often great to the immigrants who survived the terrors of the sea voyage. They next had to endure the dangers and difficulties of early days in alien territories. The Welsh-Americans of today who, like the people of other ethnic groups, seek their roots in the old country may find much to remind them of their forebears as they read. The poet, W. H. Davies, might have been writing for them in his *Days that have been:*

Can I forget the sweet days that have been,
The villages so green I have been in;
Llantarnam, Magor, Malpas and Llanwern
Liswery, old Caerleon, and Alteryn.

He was recalling, in his travels in America, the scenes of his youth in Monmouthshire, now called Gwent. To his relatives and friends in Cymru he addressed the words of another poem, *Sweet Stay at Home:*

Sweet Stay-at-Home, sweet Well-content,
Thou knowest not of strange continent;
Thou hast not felt thy bosom keep
A gentle motion with the deep.
Thou hast not seen black fingers pick
White cotton when the bloom is thick
Nor heard black throats in harmony.

Probably the majority of Welsh Americans of Welsh descent alive today have no personal knowledge of the land from which their forefathers came. But an abiding affection for Wales, and their own rich cultural heritage, still brings many of them together in the St. David's or Cambrian Societies, the Cymmrodorion and Gymanfa Ganu Associations, and the Welsh Choirs and Clubs which continue to flourish from one end of the United States to the other. Those who have had the opportunity to cross the Atlantic eastwards, to seek their family roots in Wales, will have their own memories of the people and places closest to themselves. Those who have not yet had that opportunity will find, if they too try to trace those roots of their origin, the warmest of welcomes awaiting them in the ancient land of their fathers.

Thank **GOD I'm WELSH**

BUMPER STICKERS

WELSH HERITAGE WEEK

Wales

Welsh and American flags in several sizes available

North America's
FIRST Welsh
Newspaper

Y Drych
"The Mirror"

1851

ANSWERING THE NEED FOR A STRONGER
LINK BETWEEN THE MANY WELSH
COMMUNITIES IN NORTH AMERICA

NINNAU

THE NORTH AMERICAN WELSH NEWSPAPER

Each issue of NINNAU* brings you

activities in

BOOKLIST

E. Abbott, *Historical Aspects of Immigration Problems*, 1926.

T. P. Abernethy, *Tennessee from Frontier Days*, 1967.

C. M. Andrews, *The Colonial Period of American History*, 1934.

R. Appleman, *The Lewis and Clark Trail* (U.S. National Parks), 1963.

Z. Armstrong, *Notable Southern Families*, 1918.

G. Ashe, *Quest for America*, 1971.

G. & D. Bathe, *The Life of Oliver Evans*, 1935.

H. Bebb, *The Bebb Genealogy*, 1944.

W. J. Bell, *Dr. John Morgan: Continental Doctor*, 1965.

R. T. Berthoff, *British Immigrants in Industrial America*, 1953.

P. Blake, *Frank Lloyd Wright*, 1963.

D. J. Boorstin, *The American Colonial Experience*, 1966.

C. M. Browning, *Welsh Settlers of Pennsylvania*, 1913.

S. J. & E. Buck, *Western Pennsylvania*, 1939.

R. C. Buley, *The Old North West*, 1951.

N. Burt, *The Perennial Philadelphian*, 1964.

K. B. Carter, *The Welsh in Utah*, 1949.

B. W. Chidlaw, *The Story of my Life*, 1890.

A. Conway, *The Welsh in America*, 1961.

W. F. Craven, *The Legend of the Founding Fathers*, 1956.

W. P. Cumming, R. A. Skelton & D. B. Quinn, *The Discovery of North America*, 1971.

Cymmrodorion, The Honourable Society of,
Dictionary of Welsh Biography, 1959.
Transactions 1978, *The Royal Welch Fusiliers in Boston*.

H. D. Davies, *Oshkosh, Wisconsin*, 1947.

W. H. Davies, *Autobiography of a Super-Tramp*, 1926.

P. G. Davies, *The Welsh in Wisconsin*, 1982.

W. T. Davis, *Bradford's History of Plymouth Plantation*, 1936.

R. Deacon, *Madoc and the Discovery of America*, 1967.

A. H. Dodd, *The Character of Early Welsh Emigration to the United States*, 1953.

D. M. Ellis, *New York: State and City*, 1979.

H. Evans, *Across the Years with the Evans Family*, 1972.

A. H. Favour, *Old Bill Williams*, 1962.

E. G. Gambier, *The Evans Family*, 1907.

L. H. Gipson, *The Life of Lewis Evans*, 1939.

T. A. Glenn, *The Welsh Founders of Pennsylvania*, 1915.

W. H. Goetzman, *Army Exploration in the American West. 1803-1863*, 1979.

J. T. Griffith, *Morgan John Rhees*, 1910.

J. T. Griffith, *Baptists of Pennsylvania and Wales*, 1913.

W. Griffith, *The Welsh*, 1950.

E. G. Hartmann, *The Movement to Americanize the Immigrant*, 1948.

E. G. Hartmann, *Americans from Wales*, 1967.

E. G. Hartmann, *American Immigration*, 1979.

W. D. Howells, *Recollections of Life in Ohio*, 1895.

D. Hughes, *Welsh People of California*, 1923.

T. E. Hughes, D. Edwards & H. Roberts, *The Welsh in Minnesota*, 1895.

H. M. Jenkins, *Gwynedd, Pennsylvania*, 1884.

R. T. Jenkins & H. T. Ramage, *History of The Honourable Society of Cymmrodorion*, 1951.

D. Jones, *Welsh Congregationalists in U.S.A.*, 1934.

Maldwyn Jones, *American Immigration*, 1960.

Maldwyn Jones, *Destination America*, 1976.

H. F. Jones, *The Jones Family of New York* (Long Island), 1907.

L. H. Jones, *Captain Roger Jones of London and Virginia*, 1891.

W. T. Jordan, *Hugh Davis: his Alabama Plantation*, 1948.

A. Koch & W. Peden, *The Life of Thomas Jefferson*, 1944.

A. Lloyd, *Quaker Social History*, 1950.

R. N. Lokken, *David Lloyd: Colonial Law-maker*, 1959.

S. E. Morison, *European Discovery of America*, 1971.

R. B. Morris, *Encyclopaedia of American History*, 1953.

R. L. Morton, *Colonial Virginia*, 1960.

C. Myers, *Early Pennsylvania*, 1912.

E. Oviatt, *The Beginnings of Yale University*, 1916.

R. D. Owen, *Threading my Way* (by son of Robert Owen), 1874, reprinted 1967.

M. E. Pugh & J. D. Roberts, *The Welsh in Racine*, 1948.

M. J. Pusey, *Charles Evans Hughes*, 1951.

T. M. Rees, *The Quakers in Wales, and their Emigration to North America*, 1925.

A. L. Rowse, *The Expansion of Elizabethan England* (chapter 2 — Wales), 1955.

W. S. Shepperson, *British Emigration to North America*, 1957.

W. S. Shepperson, *Samuel Roberts*, 1961.

I. Smucker, *History of the Welsh in Ohio*, 1869.

P. A. M. Taylor, *Expectations Westwards: the British Mormons*, 1965.

G. Thomas, *The Hughes Family in America*, 1698, reprinted 1903.

R. D. Thomas, *History of the Welsh in America*, 1872.

W. B. Trask, *Descendants of the Joneses of Roxbury (Mass.)*, 1878.

Paul Wallace, *Pennsylvania*, 1962.

B. Whitlock, *The Life of Samuel Jones*, 1925.

David Williams, *Wales and America*, 1946.

David Williams, *John Evans and the Legend of Madoc*, 1963.

David Williams, *A History of Modern Wales*, 1977.

D. J. Williams, *The Welsh of Columbus, Ohio*, 1913.

D. J. Williams, *A Hundred Years of Welsh Calvinistic Methodism*, 1937.

Gwyn Williams, *Madoc: the Making of a Myth*, 1980.

Gwyn Williams, *The Search for Beulah Land*, 1980.

R. Williams, *A History of Llanbrynmair*, 1889.

Otis O. Wright, *A History of Swansea (Massachusetts)*, 1917.

INDEX OF TOPICS

INDEX OF PLACES (see also Chapter 2)
(Native Welsh names are in italic)

179